BAKE OFF

Crème de la Crème

Martin Chiffers and
Emma Marsden

HODDER &
STOUGHTON

This book is published to accompany the television series entitled *Bake Off Crème de la Crème* first broadcast on BBC TWO in 2016

Executive Producers: Anna Beattie, Richard Bowron and Richard McKerrow
Series Producer: Tara Jang
Series Director: Emma Reynolds
Food Producer: Vic Proctor
Home Economists: Sam Head and Becca Watson
Production Manager: Claire Jackson
Commercial Director: Rupert Frisby
Commissioning Editor: Clare Patterson

First published in Great Britain in 2016 by Hodder & Stoughton
An Hachette UK company

1

Editorial Director: Nicky Ross
Project Editors: Sarah Hammond, Caroline MacArthur and Patricia Burgess
Designer: Nathan Burton
Photographers: Liz and Max Haarala Hamilton
Food Stylists: Emma Marsden and Martin Chiffers
Assistant Food Stylists: Angela Nilsen, Sam Dixon and Dara Sutin
Props Stylist: Alexander Breeze
Production Manager: Claudette Morris
Art Editor: Kate Brunt
Art Director: Alasdair Oliver

Typeset in Baskerville, Bambino and Bodoni

Printed and bound in Germany by Mohn Media, GmbH, Gütersloh

Hodder & Stoughton policy is to use papers that are natural, renewable and recyclable products and made from wood grown in sustainable
forests. The logging and manufacturing processes are expected to conform to the environmental regulations of the country of origin.

Hodder & Stoughton Ltd, Carmelite House, 50 Victoria Embankment, London EC4Y 0DZ

www.hodder.co.uk

CONTENTS

ABOUT THE SERIES

◆ ◆ ◆

The *Great British Bake Off* has been delighting audiences with the exploits of home bakers since 2010, so Love Productions and the BBC decided it was time to give professional pastry chefs an opportunity to showcase their amazing skills.

Bake Off: Crème de la Crème invited fifteen teams of top professional pastry chefs to Welbeck Abbey in Nottinghamshire to take part in the first-ever professional pastry team competition in the UK. The teams, each with three professional chefs, came from famous hotels, Michelin-starred restaurants and high-end patisseries. And they came from some unexpected places too, such as the development kitchen of a leading supermarket, the Armed Forces and the exclusive private dining rooms of the City of London.

In five heats and two semi-finals the teams faced two big challenges designed to test a range of sophisticated pastry skills. 'The Miniatures' test required them to make high-volume, fine patisserie with a strong emphasis on uniformity, while 'The Showpiece' asked them to reinvent popular desserts and present them as elaborate and eye-catching centrepieces.

The series tells the story of how these fifteen teams got on and which three made it to the final, where one really big challenge stood between them and the *Bake Off: Crème de la Crème* title.

This book, featuring some of the best recipes featured in the series, shows ambitious home cooks how to make patisserie and desserts to professional standards. Good luck home chefs! Your time starts now…

INTRODUCTION

◆ ◆ ◆

A few steps from the frenzy of a main restaurant kitchen lies the patisserie kitchen. In contrast to the urgency of producing exquisite plates 'right now', here is an ordered, methodical arena, where forward planning is key. It's a world of wonder and fun, where a handful of ingredients is stirred together with extraordinary artistry and transformed into an edible piece of art.

Like the BBC series, this book takes you behind the scenes of the patisserie kitchen to show you a wealth of magnificent creations. Here we share the tips and tricks of the pastry chef's trade. We also show you how the ingredients, skills and chemistry of the recipes work to create this high-end patisserie so that you too can make them at home.

Many years of experience, dedication and passion are required to learn the art of professional patisserie. Pastry chefs understand the technical and scientific relationship between different ingredients, harnessing all their creativity to design, craft and produce stunning patisserie.

For budding pastry chefs, we've broken down the skills to their simplest elements so that you can achieve these delights at home, and hopefully go on to create your own. Whether making a croissant for breakfast or an eye-catching petit gâteau for afternoon tea, it's important to add your own personal touch.

Be patient. You have to wait for the right time to complete certain stages or it can drastically affect the finished product. When you're waiting for bread to prove, for example, it's ready when the dough springs back to the touch, not before – bake it too early and the loaf will be dense.

Have a steady hand and a calm attitude when it comes to the finer details. Piping buttercream or attaching small garnishes and delicate pieces requires a delicate approach to achieve perfection.

There's an element of mathematics involved too. Sometimes you'll be working out ratios to scale up ingredients for a big order. At other times you might not need so many, but a quick recalculation will help you do this.

All the recipes in this book have been adapted from those used in professional kitchens. We've made the quantities more convenient for the home cook and used ingredients that are easy to get hold of. All the equipment you'll need is listed alongside each recipe, and we've included lots of tips to help you along the way.

Patisserie is all about the big reveal, the 'ta-dah' moment when you present your masterpiece to family and friends. Every satisfied mouthful and gasp of amazement reflects the time and care it's taken to produce.

We hope you have as much enjoyment making – and eating – these recipes as we have had producing this book.

MARTIN CHIFFERS & EMMA MARSDEN

Martin Chiffers is a renowned patisserie chef and chocolatier, and the expert consultant on the BBC series that this book accompanies. He has written most of the recipes, and helped ensure exacting patisserie standards in the photographs.

Emma Marsden is a food writer, stylist and former cookery editor of *Good Housekeeping* magazine. She worked closely with Martin on the recipes and oversaw the photography in this book.

ADVICE FROM THE JUDGES

◆ ◆ ◆

BENOIT BLIN
Master of Culinary Arts, Chef Patissier at Belmond
Le Manoir aux'Quat Saisons and Chairman of the
UK Pastry Club

I grew up in Normandy in France, surrounded by a strong food culture. There were two bakeries and the owners each had sons around my age. From a very young age I would play among the flour bags in the bakery kitchens while the loaves were laid out, rising, proving and baking. Of course, my mother would also cook. My father owned a shop and his generous spirit meant that we regularly had twenty people around the table for lunch, as my mother provided not only for the family, but for his employees too.

Those early days were inspiring – from the age of eight, all I wanted to do was work as a baker or in patisserie. At 14 I began a baking apprenticeship.

Two years later I enrolled on a patisserie apprenticeship.

I soon learnt that patisserie is the art of dessert in all its glory. At every stage there is skill, science and a requirement to understand how different ingredients work together. It is creating a dessert that's special and truly beautiful. It is not only about the flavour of the finished dessert; it's so important to consider which textures are going to complete it.

My tip for making a really good piece of patisserie is first to ensure it is something that you want to make, eat and share with your friends. And for that reason you need to try it first on your own. Before starting, read the recipe carefully and make sure all the ingredients are to hand. Changing even one of them can alter the outcome. For instance, pastry is a combination of ingredients working together at different temperatures and timings. If you change one of those, you will end up with a different result.

My second tip is to buy the best ingredients you can afford. If it's fruit, make sure it's in season so the flavour will be the very best. If it's from the store cupboard, such as chocolate, try it first to check it's good. Finally, look for produce that has been grown and sourced as fairly and naturally as possible. To be a great patisserie chef you need to strive for excellence, not only in what you are creating but also in working with the team around you. Patisserie doesn't have to be complicated. My favourite tarte tatin is an excellent example as it calls for just a handful of simple ingredients, but it needs to be well executed and taste of the ingredients from which it is made. If a flavour distracts from the finished piece, the patisserie chef has lost direction and hasn't delivered what was initially intended.

My final advice, if you're training to be a patisserie chef, is: do not stand still. Give total dedication to your development and training. Enter competitions to push yourself further and achieve recognition among peers and colleagues, then continue to inspire and take pleasure in teaching others as you continue through your career.

CHERISH FINDEN

Executive Pastry Chef at the Langham Hotel, London; Macallan Lifetime Achievement Award 2015 from the World Gourmet Summit

Preparing food for others has been a passion of mine for as long as I can remember. Compliments from my mother and siblings inspired my love of food from an early age. I was born and brought up in Singapore, where children are taught to help around the house. When I was young my father became ill and my mum had to go out to work, so I learnt from about the age of eight how to feed and look after my family. I had a bike that I'd ride to the market, and an allowance to buy the food for dinner. I would plan and create my 'menus' — in reality the family meals — so I knew what to get. Dinner was simple, but everyone loved it.

Volunteering in a pastry shop, where I had to decorate around 80 cakes a day with whipped cream, reinforced the passion I felt towards cooking and helped me realise I should train to be a chef. It was during the course that I found I most enjoyed baking and patisserie, so I made them my focus. Back then I was very competitive and I would enter competitions every year, the pinnacle being when I represented Singapore at the Culinary Olympics, where I helped the team win gold for pastry. It's important to do that to push yourself further.

Patisserie to me is an edible art. I enjoy it so much that I never think of what I do as a job — it feels like a really enjoyable hobby. I eat, sleep and dream it and often wake in the middle of the night with a crazy idea and have to write it down, as I know I will be able to use it in some way.

The subject is fascinating. It's not strictly about baking or cooking; it's about taking lots of different elements and considering the science behind them. You need to understand the how and the why. For instance, why is strong flour better than plain flour for certain viennoiserie? And why should I use one type of chocolate rather than another?

If you're making patisserie for the first time, start simple. The recipe shouldn't have too many ingredients in it and should taste as its title suggests. If there are too many ingredients, the flavours will merge into one another and it'll end up being a disaster. Planning and research are key to ensuring you achieve exactly what you set out to do. Try to be a trendsetter and create new combinations. For me, art is often my inspiration.

My top tip for anyone making a patisserie recipe is to arm yourself with a set of microscales. An extra gram here and there for key ingredients, such as raising agents and gelatine, can make a significant difference, so take care to measure everything correctly.

CLAIRE CLARK, MBE
Patisserie Consultant and MOGB (Meilleur Ouvrier de la Grande Bretagne)

The dreams you have as a child don't always turn out the way you intend. I wanted to be a classical musician, inspired by my mother, a semi-professional cellist. When I didn't make the grade, she persuaded me to choose an alternative career as a chef. I had baked with her from a very early age on an old, coal-fuelled Aga. She made everything from scratch, so I learnt the basics – biscuits and cakes – from watching what she did.

After catering college, I started work as a grill commis chef, but soon switched to pastry as I enjoyed the science behind it. When I'm encouraging others to make patisserie, my first tip is to follow the recipe to the letter – don't deviate in any way. It's important to read it through from start to finish before you begin, and if there are several components within it, as there often are, plan ahead, break it down and spread the preparation over two days. It's much easier to make the foundations on one day, let them cool, firm or relax, then assemble the whole dessert the following day.

Many items of patisserie have a base consisting of sugar, flour, butter and eggs, so buy the best you can afford and you'll have a first-rate foundation. The main flavour of the recipe is also highly important. For example, if making a chocolate cake or dessert, make sure the chocolate is good quality as it will be the overriding flavour in the finished dish. Similarly, always choose seasonal (ideally local) fruits as the flavour will be fresher and more intense.

To make good patisserie at home, you need to be just as organised as someone running a professional pastry kitchen. Get into the habit of being disciplined and methodical – whether that's ensuring all the ingredients are stored correctly, or cleaning the work surfaces before you start a recipe and wiping them well afterwards too. Many patisserie techniques require precision, timing and attention. Bread will not stop proving because you need to focus elsewhere, and chocolate will not stop crystallising because you aren't ready to complete the process.

My favourite part of being a pastry chef is working with chocolate. Once tempered correctly, it can be sculpted, shaped, moulded and transformed into just about anything you want it to be. The complexity of its compound structure is unrivalled, and it takes years to really understand it. I love making moulded chocolates and petits fours – those miniature creations, which need to be executed with finesse and precision, always make my heart sing.

MEET THE TEAMS

Kumiko's Team

Julien's Team

Christophe's Team

Tomas's Team

James's Team

Karl's Team

Neil M's Team

Sebastien's Team

Reece's Team

Neil R's Team

Stephen's Team

Felicien's Team

Sajeela's Team

Liam's Team

Mark's Team

INGREDIENTS

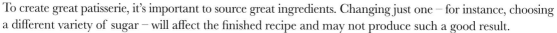

To create great patisserie, it's important to source great ingredients. Changing just one – for instance, choosing a different variety of sugar – will affect the finished recipe and may not produce such a good result.

It is essential that the patisserie chef's kitchen is organised so that they can easily gather their *mise en place* (ingredients and utensils) for each recipe. This is just as relevant when you're cooking at home. Ingredients should be kept at cool room temperature, stored carefully in labelled, airtight containers to maintain freshness.

If you are already a keen baker, many of the ingredients listed here will be familiar to you. They are no different from those used in home baking, but it is advisable to seek out the very best you can afford, and they are used in a slightly different way. Sugars are less used for sprinkling, more for caramelising and creating gossamer-thin threads of spun sugar. Butter is always unsalted, so you can add as much or as little as is required, and the type of flour used in a crème pâtissière varies from soft flour (cornflour) to strong bread flour, depending how firm the finished result should be. It would be difficult for a patisserie chef to work without pectin and gelatine – they're essential in several recipes to help set certain ingredients. There are also different varieties to choose from (powdered versus leaf gelatine, for instance), depending on which you prefer to use, or which is necessary for the particular recipe.

Below are all the ingredients included in this book, with hints and tips as to how they are used. Along with those that form the backbone of recipes and provide structure, a collection of those that create the finishing touches are useful too. For example, edible gold dust, gold leaf and other powdered colours will add a starry note to the final flourish of any patisserie.

SUGAR

In most baking books a general ingredient list would start with flour, which is the building block of most baked goods. Patisserie is a little different. While flour is, of course, still a major component, the key ingredient here is sugar.

Sugar is enormously versatile for pastry chefs. It is a sweetener, adds flavour and can dramatically alter the texture of a bake. Whip it with egg whites and you have a meringue; beat it with eggs and flour and you have a sponge; heat it until it browns and you have a caramel; heat it with cream and you have a fudge. You can model it, spin it or sprinkle it over pastries. It comes as granules – white to dark brown, very fine to pearl – or as a liquid.

Below is a list of the different types of sugar and how they are used in patisserie.

White sugars are pure sucrose and contain no molasses, a sticky by-product of the refining process. *Caster sugar* is the most commonly used type in patisserie. It has a fine granule so that it dissolves easily when mixed with other ingredients for baking and patisserie. It's also used to make caramel – either wet (heated with a little water), or dry (heated on its own). *Icing sugar* is used for dusting finished cakes, for glazes, and in baking that requires a finer sugar, such as smooth powdery meringues and dacquoises. *Confectioner's sugar* is a 50:50 mixture of icing sugar and cornflour that pastry chefs make themselves for dusting marshmallows.

Granulated sugar has a bigger crystal than caster sugar, and is great for preserves, as it prevents mould from forming in jams, jellies and marmalades. *Pearl or nibbed sugar* is compressed nuggets of white refined sugar, often used to decorate cakes and breads. It is very sweet, but also adds texture to the finished bake.

Invert sugar is used a lot in patisserie kitchens. It can be a clear, thin and liquid, just like the consistency of runny honey, or opaque and thick. It works alongside sugar as it helps to control crystallisation, so it may be used in fudges, caramels, ice creams and sorbets. In addition it is used in baking to add moisture and provide flavour, and to intensify flavours in ganaches. It also helps to prolong the freshness of certain patisserie. However, both *runny honey*, which is a natural invert sugar, and *liquid glucose* do a very similar job and can be substituted in most instances.

Brown sugars contain varying quantities of molasses (partially evaporated sugar cane syrup). They are less often used in patisserie because the recipes tend to be lighter, more delicate sponges and biscuits, so call for a fine caster sugar. *Light soft brown* has a soft texture and dissolves easily when combined with other ingredients. It contains a little molasses, so there is some body in the flavour but it is also quite sweet. *Light muscovado* is a shade darker, with a mellow toffee taste. It has a pleasing, fudge-like texture and gives a subtle butterscotch flavour to bakes. *Dark muscovado* is a dark, fudgy sugar that contains quite a large amount of molasses. It is less bitter than molasses and is used in fruit cakes and other dark bakes that call for flavour over sweetness. *Molasses* is the darkest of all the sugars and has a rich, bitter flavour. Use sparingly to avoid overpowering other ingredients.

Malt extract is a syrup made from barley. It is most often used in breads to add flavour and produce a golden colour in the bake.

◆

FLOUR

Fine patisserie sponges and pastries are most often made with strong flour or soft flour. Both cornflour and strong flour are used to stabilise creams that need a firm structure.

Plain flour is made from soft wheat and contains no raising agent, so it can be used in conjunction with a whisked egg and sugar mixture to give structure to bakes.

Strong bread flour is made from a variety of hard wheat and is used mostly in breads and pastry. It can also be used to give crème pâtissière a firmer texture.

Cornflour is a fine, flavourless flour made from dried corn/maize. It is used in crème pâtissière and meringues as a stabiliser.

VANILLA

Vanilla extract is a liquid made by macerating vanilla pods in water and alcohol. This process extracts their natural flavour.

Vanilla bean paste is a syrupy mixture dotted with the seeds of the vanilla pod. It is made with a higher percentage of sugar than vanilla extract and adds more flavour and sweetness to creams and custards. Use one tablespoon in place of one vanilla pod.

Vanilla pod – the whole pod is sold in its dried form. It contains slightly sticky seeds that can be used to flavour cakes, custards and creams. To use, run the tip of a small sharp knife down the length of the pod to split it open, then scrape the blade or the tip of a teaspoon handle along the inside to extract the seeds. The empty pod, if not used in a recipe, can be inserted into a jar or bag of caster or granulated sugar to flavour it.

Vanilla powder is a pure extract made from ground vanilla pods. It contains no sugar or alcohol, and its purity means that the flavour is very strong. Use sparingly – about one scant teaspoon in place of a pod – but it's worth experimenting to find the ratio that suits you.

◆

CHOCOLATE

Chocolate has many uses in patisserie – it can be melted and moulded for decoration, whipped with cream as a filling or topping, or mixed into a batter for a chocolate sponge. However, it must be tempered (heated) first if making chocolates or moulding decorations in order to make it more stable (see pages 33–4). When tempering chocolate, it's generally easier to work with a larger quantity than the recipe requires (about 300g), but any excess can be set and reused another time.

Cocoa and cocoa powder are made from cocoa mass by roasting the nibs of the cocoa bean and pressing it into a block. The block is then compressed to extract the cocoa butter, which is used for making chocolate, and the remaining 'mass' left over is ground into a powder to produce cocoa. Pastry chefs follow the rule that the darker the colour, the better the flavour and the quality will be.

Dark chocolate has a high percentage of cocoa solids (50–100%). Flavour notes can vary from rich to bitter, nutty to fruity.

Milk chocolate – a good-quality milk chocolate contains 30–40% cocoa solids. Its creamy flavour is softer than that of dark chocolate and adds sweetness rather than richness.

White chocolate is made from cocoa butter, sugar and milk solids. Use at least 25–35% cocoa solids for the best flavour.

DAIRY AND FATS

Eggs are used as a raising agent in meringues and sponges, to set custards, and to enrich pastries. They are also used to glaze pastry. Pastry chefs use medium eggs and measure them by weight for accuracy. The weight of eggs does vary, though, so the following is just a rough guide.

1 medium egg = 50g; yolk = 20g; white = 30g
Egg yolks are used to enrich a recipe, such as crème anglaise or sabayon, whereas egg whites are used to provide structure, as in meringues and dacquoises.

Milk – use full-fat for the best flavour and to make silky smooth crème pâtissière. *Milk powder* is sometimes used as it's a cheaper alternative to milk and stores well for longer periods of time too.

Butter adds a rich, creamy flavour to bakes and ganaches, and gives crispness to pastries. It is usually unsalted. Pastry chefs use *dry butter* to make laminated puff and croissant pastries. It has a lower percentage of buttermilk than ordinary butter, and a much higher percentage of fat (typically 84% and over). It can be bought from supermarkets and delicatessens or online, but it can be easily replicated by adding a little flour to normal butter. Patisserie chefs always use *unsalted butter*, as it allows them to control a bake's salt content, and ultimately the overall flavour. *Clarified butter* has a higher smoke point than ordinary butter (about 250°C as opposed to 160°C). It is made by heating butter in a pan, then skimming off the froth that rises to the surface, and discarding the solids that settle at the bottom. The result is a clarified (clear) liquid that will also keep for longer in the fridge.

Cream is used extensively in patisserie for toppings and fillings, and is also cooked with sugar to make fudge. *Double cream* contains a high percentage of fat (over 47%) and can be boiled without splitting. Although pastry chefs do use it, they tend to favour *whipping cream* as it contains less fat (35–38%), giving a lighter flavour, and keeps for longer at room temperature. *Single cream* contains a lot less fat than double or whipping cream (about 18%), so it can be warmed but not boiled, or it will split. It is most useful for drizzling over tarts. *Clotted cream* is made from full-fat milk that is heated, then slowly cooled. It has a very rich flavour, can be heated to a high temperature, and even boiled without splitting. This makes it useful in recipes such as fudge (see page 32).

Soft cheeses also play an important role in patisserie. One of the richest is Italian *mascarpone*, which is used for its high fat content, and as an alternative to cream for fillings and toppings. It can be cooked without splitting, and also be combined with double cream to make a more stable mixture for piping and decorating, as in the Gâteau St Honoré on page 153. *Ricotta* is an Italian full-fat soft cheese that can also be baked. It has a slightly acidic flavour, so counter-balances sweet ingredients, such as the dried fruit used in the Sfogliatelle on page 61.

Lard is a solid animal fat derived from pigs, and produces deliciously crisp shortcrust pastry.

STORE CUPBOARD

Raising agents produce gas inside sponges and breads, which is trapped and creates a rise in the batter or dough. *Baking powder* is made from a mixture of cream of tartar and bicarbonate of soda, and there are two types. The double-action type works first when liquid is added, then again when the bake goes into the oven. The lesser-known single-action baking powder activates only with heat. Use 5g baking powder for every 125g of plain flour. *Cream of tartar* is a natural raising agent, and helps to prevent sugar from crystallising. It can also be used to stabilise egg whites in meringues. *Yeast*, perhaps the best-known raising agent, is available in fresh and dried forms. It is a single-cell living organism and in order to work, it requires 'food' (found in sugar and sometimes flour), moisture (water or milk) and warmth (the heat of the oven). It is used mostly in breads and sweet bakes, and produces carbon dioxide bubbles that are trapped in the dough and create the rise.

Setting agents help sauces, jellies and glazes to become firm so that they hold their shape. *Gelatine* is a product derived from the bones of animals. It helps to set mousses and glazes and is available in two forms. *Powdered gelatine* must be covered in five times its weight of cold water and left to absorb it. *Leaf gelatine* can simply be covered in cold water and left to soak until it feels like a jelly, then the excess water is squeezed out before use. Gelatine is sometimes added in tiny quantities that must be measured precisely as they can have a dramatic effect on the texture of a finished cake – too much and it will set too firm, too little and it won't set properly. *Pectin powder* occurs naturally in certain fruits, and is often used to set jams and jellies. It is also used to help glazes firm up, and usually needs sugar and an acid, generally citric acid, to start activation. Before being used in a recipe it must be mixed with sugar. For some recipes the pectin needs to be thermo-reversible, which means that the mixture containing it can be heated again after it's cooled and will remelt evenly. This is particularly useful when glazing petits gâteaux, for instance. For these recipes pastry chefs use a product called *NH pectin*, which can be purchased online. *Agar agar*, derived from seaweed, is a vegetarian alternative to gelatine, and helps to thicken and emulsify certain ingredients. It is available as a powder or flakes, and both need to be dissolved in a hot liquid before use.

Ground almonds are used in patisserie to replace flour, or sometimes combined with it. They provide moisture and texture in certain meringue sponges, such as dacquoise.

Citric acid is a white powder that is sometimes used in place of lemon juice. It acts as a preservative, is used to activate pectin and and also helps to keep fruit firm.

Colours are used to represent the flavour of particular dishes. Green, for example, suggests pistachio or mint, while pink could be strawberry or any other red berry fruit. Of course, colours are also used for decoration. *Edible paste colours* are the most reliable; they are used for macarons (as on page 311), as they mix well into the meringue mixture. *Lustres and powders*, on the other hand, are used brushed or sprinkled for finishing touches. *Gold leaf and flake* are expensive, but take the ordinary to the extraordinary.

Egg white powder is a product that can be stored at room temperature without going off. It is useful for for giving more volume to meringue-based recipes, and also when an acidic fruit is being used in the meringue (see Lemon Meringue Pie, page 259).

Fruit purées are generally used by pastry chefs to flavour crème pâtissière and jellies. They are made by whizzing puréed fruit with a certain quantity of sugar. If making a large quantity of patisserie and you require a lot of a particular fruit purée, you can purchase it online. Otherwise, making your own will achieve an equally efficient result (see page 25).

Glaze, known as *nappage* by pastry chefs, adds a finishing gloss to fruit or a distinctive finish when used with a coloured edible powder. *Fruit glaze* is usually made with apricot conserve. Nappage, also known as 'writing gel', is a clear glaze, usually made from pectin or other thickeners, and can be purchased online.

EQUIPMENT

The patisserie chef's *batterie de cuisine* or equipment includes a variety of specialist tools – frames and ring moulds, for instance – that transform an everyday bake into exquisite perfection.

Home bakers won't need quite so many gadgets, but using the right kit for a particular recipe improves the efficiency of the method and cuts down on time too. Patisserie involves preparing several elements sequentially, and sometimes you'll be juggling two or three elements at the same time. For pastry chefs it's all about efficiency, and they will use tools that help them prepare the various parts of each recipe as quickly as possible.

The recipes in this book each include an equipment list, and the items found in them are outlined below. These are the minimum you'll need to make each dish, but you'll find it easier if you have a few spares to call upon. Extra bowls and baking sheets, for example, will free you from having to keep washing up in the middle of making something.

MIXERS, BLENDERS AND PROCESSORS

Alternative methods of mixing are provided throughout this book, but a *stand mixer with whisk, paddle and dough hook attachments* makes light work of the job, and can save time when creaming ingredients for cakes, whisking whites for meringues, and mixing and kneading dough for bread. An *electric hand whisk* is a good alternative for creaming and whisking cake mixes.

A *food processor* is ideal for blitzing fruit to a smooth purée, while a *mini food processor* is great for grinding nuts.

Using a *stick blender* ensures ganaches are smooth but not aerated, and it's also used in conjunction with a *cream whipper* to make espuma microwave sponges (see page 256).

An *ice-cream machine* is a quick and efficient way of churning ice creams and sorbets, as in the recipes on pages 23–4, but is not essential.

FRAMES, TINS AND MOULDS

For poker-straight lines and neat edges, patisserie chefs prefer to bake layered slices in frames set on baking sheets rather than in tins. A *stainless steel 28 x 18cm rectangular frame* is used throughout this book and will give you many options for trimmed sizes and shapes.

Where *cake tins* are required, it's worth using heavy-duty metal ones that can be used again and again without scorching or warping.

Silicone moulds are often used by pastry chefs for making sponges and moulded chocolates and jellies, but must sit on a baking sheet for stability.

Each recipe specifies the correct frame or tin for that particular bake.

SCALES, THERMOMETERS AND TIMERS

It's worth investing in an accurate set of *digital scales* that measures grams and millilitres in increments of 1g up to 5–6kg. You will also need a set of *microscales* in 0.5g increments for tiny quantities of ingredients, such as gelatine.

A *digital thermometer* is essential for checking the temperature of liquids, for cooking sugar and for chocolate work.

As analogue and oven timers may be inaccurate, it's worth getting a separate *digital timer*.

OTHER SPECIALIST EQUIPMENT

Acetate can be bought in A4 sheets and is used for shaping tempered chocolate.

A *cook's blowtorch* will caramelise toppings and fruit. It can also be used for quickly heating pans and tools.

A *heat gun*, rather like a powerful blow-dryer, is used for directing heat where it is specifically needed, such as melting just-set chocolate.

You'll need a selection of *disposable piping bags* in small, medium and large sizes and a *variety of piping nozzles*. See page 29 for more on the piping techniques and nozzles you'll need for the recipes in this book.

A *cream whipper*, also known as an espuma gun, makes sponges that can be microwaved and baked in a matter of seconds (see page 256). It's quite an investment, but can also be used to aerate creams and sauces.

A *metal ruler* is essential for accurate measuring and cutting.

A tiler's *notched adhesive spreader* is useful for scraping along tempered chocolate to make chocolate curls (see pages 33 and 151).

A *poker or skewer* can be heated up and used for branding the top of pastries in attractive patterns (see page 143).

———◆———

EVERYDAY EQUIPMENT

Aluminium foil

Baking trays and sheets – both lipped and unlipped for sliding bakes off easily

Balloon whisk – a medium head balloon whisk is most useful

Bowls in a variety of sizes

Cake lifter – fits underneath whole cakes for safe transfer from rack to plate

Chopping boards – keep one separate for baking and patisserie tasks

Citrus reamer – for juicing citrus fruits

Clingfilm

Cook's tongs – for transferring hot ingredients

Cut-off whisk – as seen on page 267, for making spun sugar

Cutters – preferably plain round metal ones in varying sizes

Dough scraper – metal or plastic

Funnel – for transferring liquids and smooth-running mixtures

Grater

Knives – a variety of sizes

Large metal spoon – for folding dry mixtures into wet

Measuring jug

Measuring spoons

Microwave

Palette knives – large for smoothing glazes and icing and a small offset palette knife for working on delicate patisserie

Parchment paper – also known as baking parchment, is coated so that meringues, biscuits and cakes don't stick to it. *Silicone paper* is also very effective, or invest in reusable *silicone mats*.

Peeler – for cutting fruit skins and zests in large pieces for decoration

Pizza wheel – for slicing easily through raw dough

Rolling pin

Saucepans – a range of small, medium and large stainless steel pans with lids. For patisserie and sugar work stainless steel allows you to see the colour of the sugar as it cooks

Scissors

Sealable containers

Skewers

Spatulas

Tea towels

Wire rack

Zester – preferably a fine one, also known as a canelle knife. It has five sharp round blades on its head to extract superfine zest from citrus fruit without the pith, and a larger hole to peel away strips for decoration.

MASTERING
THE
BASICS

There are certain basic recipes that all chefs have in their repertoire, and they form the foundation and building blocks of a great piece of patisserie. Take puff pastry and crème pâtissière, for example: if you know the ingredients and methods for making these, you can translate them into all sorts of fantastic bakes, including Mille Feuilles, Gâteau St Honoré and Fig Tart (see pages 141, 153 and 233).

The recipes included here are used either as part of a main recipe, in which case you will be referred back to this section to follow the relevant technique, or they are used as accompaniments. Quantities and ingredients, though, are as listed in the main recipe you're making.

The great thing about these basic recipes is that, apart from providing you with essential skills, they build up your confidence to experiment and create new flavour combinations. For example, add an alternative fruit to a crème pâtissière and use it to fill an éclair. Or swap the flavour profiles around in a layered slice to produce a totally different outcome. Once you've mastered the essentials, you'll go on to create more and more interesting patisserie and challenge your culinary awareness in many different directions.

SAUCES

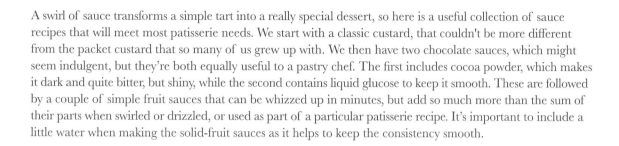

A swirl of sauce transforms a simple tart into a really special dessert, so here is a useful collection of sauce recipes that will meet most patisserie needs. We start with a classic custard, that couldn't be more different from the packet custard that so many of us grew up with. We then have two chocolate sauces, which might seem indulgent, but they're both equally useful to a pastry chef. The first includes cocoa powder, which makes it dark and quite bitter, but shiny, while the second contains liquid glucose to keep it smooth. These are followed by a couple of simple fruit sauces that can be whizzed up in minutes, but add so much more than the sum of their parts when swirled or drizzled, or used as part of a particular patisserie recipe. It's important to include a little water when making the solid-fruit sauces as it helps to keep the consistency smooth.

CRÈME ANGLAISE
SERVES 6

Although the name of this recipe translates as 'English cream', it is actually the pastry chef's traditional sweet pouring custard. Milk and cream are heated together, poured over a mixture of egg yolks and sugar, then returned to the pan and heated gently until a custard forms and coats the back of a spoon.

Crème Anglaise is excellent served with Blackberry, Apple Yogurt and Walnut Tart, Chocolate Tart and Pithivier (see pages 205, 213, and 237). Or use it as a base for a mousse, *crémeux* or a bavarois, as in Trifle (see page 269).

60g egg yolks (3 medium)
40g caster sugar
½ vanilla pod (from a pod split lengthways)
100g milk
100g double cream

1. Fill a large bowl with iced water. Place a medium bowl in it, making sure none of the water gets inside. Rest a sieve on top and set aside.
2. Put the egg yolks and sugar into another medium bowl and quickly stir them together with a balloon whisk, taking care not to introduce too much air.
3. Using the tip of a knife, scrape the seeds out of the vanilla pod and put both pod and seeds into a pan. Pour in the milk and cream and bring to the boil over a high heat.
4. As soon as the mixture comes to the boil – there'll be bubbles around the edge and the mixture will just be starting to rise in the pan – pour it over the eggs and sugar, whisking all the time until combined. Return the mixture to the pan and cook very gently over a low heat until the mixture reaches 85°C. Cook at this temperature for just 3 seconds. The mixture should be smooth and coat the back of the spoon.
5. Strain the mixture through the sieve and into the cold bowl to stop it from cooking any further. Serve warm or, to serve cold, leave it over the ice bath and stir to cool it down quickly, then transfer to the fridge to chill.
6. Store in an airtight container, with clingfilm placed directly on the surface of the custard to prevent a skin from forming. Chill for up to 3 days.

CHOCOLATE SAUCE
SERVES 8

This sauce can be served warm or cold, and is useful as an accompaniment to ice cream, to enhance arrangements of patisserie on a plate, or to provide a decorative base for a tart. For ease of use, it can be transferred to a squeezy bottle or applied with a brush.

50g cocoa powder, sifted
100g chocolate (55% cocoa solids), chopped
200g water
100g caster sugar

1. Put all the ingredients into a heavy-based pan and warm gently over a low heat to dissolve the cocoa.
2. Increase the heat and bring to the boil, gently whisking the mixture to prevent the cocoa powder from burning. Simmer for 1–2 minutes still whisking gently, then strain through a sieve into a clean bowl.
3. Store in an airtight container in the fridge for up to 7 days, or freeze for up to 1 month. Defrost and reheat in a pan over a low heat before serving.

WARM CHOCOLATE SAUCE
SERVES 8

Although this sauce uses just three ingredients, it is richer than the previous chocolate sauce, and has to be served warm or it will set. It contains glucose to prevent crystallisation and keep it smooth. Again, it's a great partner for ice cream and would provide a rich finish to the Chocolate Tart on page 213.

160g dark chocolate (55% cocoa solids), very finely chopped
200g milk
40g liquid glucose

1. Put the chocolate into a large bowl.
2. Put the milk and liquid glucose into a medium pan over a high heat and bring to the boil. Slowly pour the liquid over the chocolate, stirring all the time until the chocolate has melted and the mixture is smooth.
3. Store in an airtight container in the fridge for up to 5 days, or freeze for up to 1 month. The sauce thickens once it has cooled, so spoon it into a bowl and reheat in a microwave on low, or in a bowl set over a pan of simmering water.

SIMPLE FRUIT SAUCE
SERVES 6

As the fruit is the star turn in this recipe, use the best seasonal offerings you can – berries during the summer, and tropical fruits later in the year when they're at their peak – otherwise the end result will be lacking in flavour. We've listed raspberries in the ingredients below, but you could also use mangoes, strawberries, blackberries or blueberries.

Match like with like and serve a blackberry sauce with the Blackberry, Apple Yogurt and Walnut Tart on page 205, or experiment to find other interesting combinations. The raspberry sauce, for example, goes brilliantly with Hazelnut Chocolate Dacquoise, Chocolate Tart and Peanut Butter Tart (see pages 127, 213 and 217). And, of course, the sauces can also be served with ice cream.

250g raspberries
100g caster sugar
juice from ½ lemon
50g water

1. Put the fruit into a food processor or blender and whizz until smooth.
2. Transfer the purée to a medium pan and add the sugar, lemon juice and water. Bring to the boil over a high heat and simmer for 3–4 minutes, until the mixture starts to thicken.
3. Strain through a sieve into a clean bowl.
4. Store in an airtight container in the fridge for up to 5 days, or freeze for up to 1 month.

PASSION FRUIT SAUCE
SERVES 6–8

Everybody loves the flavour of passion fruit, but the seeds are less popular, so they are usually sieved out and discarded. Please don't do that – keep them to make a crunchy topping for decorating ice cream and cakes. Put them into a pan over a high heat and cover with lots of water. Bring to the boil and cook for 10–15 minutes. Drain well, then run under cold water to wash away all the fibres, leaving just smooth seeds. Wrap in clingfilm and freeze for up to 1 month.

200g passion fruit pulp (from about 10 fruits)
100g mango, peeled, stoned and roughly chopped
150g caster sugar
40g water
6g cornflour

1. Put the passion fruit pulp into a sieve resting over a medium pan. Stir furiously with a spatula or dough scraper to extract the juice. Reserve the seeds to make a crunchy topping (see introduction above).
2. Place the mango in a food processor or blender and whizz to a purée.
3. Add the mango purée and caster sugar to the pan of passion fruit juice and heat gently to dissolve the sugar.
4. Combine the water and cornflour in a small bowl and stir this into the pan. Bring to a simmer to thicken the sauce.
5. Store in an airtight container in the fridge for up to 5 days, or freeze for up to 1 month. Thaw before using, then place in a pan over a high heat and bring to the boil, whisking well until smooth.

ORANGE SAUCE
SERVES 8

200g freshly squeezed orange juice
  (from about 4 oranges)
40g caster sugar
¼ vanilla pod (from a pod split lengthways)
6g cornflour

1. Put the orange juice and caster sugar into a pan. Scrape the vanilla seeds into the pan, and add the pod too. Heat gently to dissolve the sugar, then bring to the boil.
2. Combine the cornflour with 1 tablespoon water in a small bowl and stir this liquid into the pan. Bring back to a simmer to thicken the sauce, then strain through a sieve into a bowl.
3. Store in an airtight container in the fridge for up to 5 days, or freeze for up to 1 month.

◆

SABAYON SAUCE
SERVES 6–8

A light, mousse-like sauce, sabayon has to be served hot as soon as it's made. It works well with a fruit-based pudding because the hint of fortified Marsala wine brings out the flavour of the fruit. You can replace the Marsala with port, orange liqueur or any other flavour if you prefer.

80g egg yolks (4 medium)
50g orange juice
10g lemon juice
20g Marsala wine
50g caster sugar

1. Put the egg yolks in a heatproof bowl. Add the remaining ingredients and sit the bowl over a pan of simmering water.
2. Using a balloon whisk, beat all the ingredients together for about 10 minutes until the mixture is light and fluffy and the temperature reaches 60°C. The mixture will be hot and the eggs will have cooked through.

CARAMEL SAUCE
SERVES 6

Here it's important to ensure the sugar is sufficiently caramelised. Too light and the result will be over-sweet; too dark and the caramel might taste bitter.

The sauce can be served warm, poured over desserts such as sticky toffee pudding. When cold, it's thicker, so is best used for decorating plates. To do this, take a small amount on the end of a palette knife, press it on to a plate and smooth it out into an attractive pattern.

100g caster sugar
200g whipping cream

1. Put the sugar in a heavy-based pan and place over a medium heat until it reaches a deep golden colour. Watch carefully as it dissolves, shaking the pan now and then, to ensure the sugar cooks evenly and doesn't burn. If you can smell a smokey aroma, it's gone too far, so start again.
2. Standing back from the stove as the mixture will sizzle and spit, carefully pour in the cream. Stir well to make a smooth sauce.
3. Store in an airtight container for up to 5 days. To serve warm, gently reheat in a pan until liquid.

◆

STOCK SYRUP

To make a stock syrup, stir together equal quantities of caster sugar and water (for example, 50g of each) in a bowl and set aside for 5 minutes. Stir again to make sure all the sugar has dissolved.

This is a useful recipe to have up your culinary sleeve as it is used to moisten dry sponges. For extra flavour, stir in a little vanilla extract, citrus zest or fruit purée and set aside to marinate for 20–30 minutes before using.

ICE CREAMS AND SORBETS

◆ ◆ ◆

A quenelle of ice cream or sorbet can add the finishing touch to a perfect tart or a deconstructed patisserie recipe, providing balance or contrast as required. A spoonful of raspberry sorbet with a crème brûlée, for example, adds a fruity acidic contrast to the rich creaminess of the dessert. Serve vanilla ice cream alongside a warm fruit tart, however, and it counterbalances the texture and temperature. Each serving is around 40–60g.

An ice cream machine makes light work of the churning required in these recipes, but is not essential. The mixing can be done equally well by hand.

◆

VANILLA ICE CREAM
SERVES 10

40g egg yolks (2 medium)
90g caster sugar
2g (½ tsp) vanilla extract
1 vanilla pod, split open lengthways
200g whipping cream
150g full-fat milk
20g milk powder

1. Fill a large bowl with iced water. Place a medium bowl in it, making sure none of the water gets inside. Rest a sieve on top and set aside.
2. Put the egg yolks, sugar and vanilla extract into a medium bowl. Using a balloon whisk, quickly mix them together, taking care not to introduce too much air.
3. Scrape the vanilla seeds into a medium pan. Add the pod too, then pour in the cream, milk and milk powder. Bring to the boil over a high heat, stirring continuously.
4. Pour the mixture over the eggs and sugar, whisking all the time until combined. Return to the pan and cook very gently until the mixture reaches 85°C. Cook at this temperature for just 3 seconds. The mixture should be smooth and coat the back of the spoon.
5. Strain through the sieve and into the cold bowl to stop it from cooking any further.
6. Transfer to an ice-cream machine and churn according to the manufacturer's instructions. Alternatively, place the mixture in a bowl (preferably metal, as this speeds up the freezing process) and put over a larger bowl filled with 8 trays of ice cubes and 500g salt (this mixture lowers the freezing point). Press the ice cream bowl down so that it is completely surrounded by the ice and salt mixture. Stir until frozen.
7. Store in an airtight container in the freezer for up to 1 month.

◆

FRUIT ICE CREAM
SERVES 8

Incredibly simple to make, this recipe calls for just three ingredients. The relatively small quantity of sugar helps to bind the other ingredients together, also enhancing rather than overpowering the fruit flavour in the purée.

150g fruit purée, such as mango, banana, strawberry, raspberry, or cherry
150g whipping cream
75g caster sugar

1. Put all the ingredients into a bowl and stir together. Transfer to an ice-cream machine and churn according to the manufacturer's instructions. Alternatively, use the ice and salt method as in Vanilla Ice Cream (see left).
2. Store in an airtight container in the freezer for up to 1 month.

CHOCOLATE ICE CREAM
SERVES 8

200g full-fat milk
10g milk powder
50g whipping cream
20g caster sugar
60g dark chocolate (65% cocoa solids), finely chopped
20g liquid glucose, honey or invert sugar

1. Fill a large bowl with iced water and set aside.
2. Pour the milk into a pan and add the milk powder, cream and sugar. Heat gently, stirring continuously until the mixture reaches 85°C.
3. Put the chocolate in a bowl with the liquid glucose and pour in the hot milk mixture, stirring well as you do so.
4. Place this bowl in the iced water to cool quickly, then transfer to an ice-cream machine and churn according to the manufacturer's instructions. Alternatively, use the ice and salt method as in Vanilla Ice Cream (see page 23).
5. Store in an airtight container in the freezer for up to 1 month.

———◆———

SORBET SYRUP
MAKES ABOUT 175G

This recipe can be scaled up if you want to make a large batch of a sorbet, or perhaps several sorbets in different flavours. It can also be stored in the fridge for up to two weeks in an airtight container.

35g water
90g caster sugar
50g liquid glucose

1. Pour the water into a pan, add the sugar and glucose and bring to the boil. There's no need to stir it at this stage.
2. Set aside to cool, then transfer to a covered container and chill.

FRUIT SORBET
SERVES 8

175g fruit purée, such as mango, raspberry, strawberry, banana or apricot
175g sorbet syrup (see previous recipe)

1. Combine the fruit purée and sorbet syrup in a bowl and stir together.
2. Transfer to an ice-cream machine and churn according to the manufacturer's instructions. Alternatively, use the ice and salt method as in Vanilla Ice Cream (see page 23).
3. Store in an airtight container in the freezer for up to 1 month.

CITRUS SORBET
SERVES 12

For an alternative tang, this recipe can also be made with passion fruit rather than lemon juice.

180g lemon juice
2 quantities Sorbet Syrup (see left)

1. Combine the fruit juice and sorbet syrup in a bowl and stir together.
2. Transfer to an ice-cream machine and churn according to the manufacturer's instructions. Alternatively, use the ice and salt method as in Vanilla Ice Cream (see page 23).
3. Store in an airtight container in the freezer for up to 1 month.

FRUIT PURÉES

◆ ◆ ◆

A fruit purée adds zing to mousses and crèmes pâtissières (as in the Croquembouches on page 135), and is also used to decorate plates of patisserie. Most pastry chefs buy purées from their favoured supplier (it will have 10% added sugar to preserve it and will also be pasteurised). Not only does buying ready-made save time, it also guarantees that the flavour will be consistently good no matter what time of year it's being used.

The key point when making your own fruit purées is to use good-quality seasonal ingredients so the flavour is top notch.

◆

PASSION FRUIT PURÉE
MAKES 125G

5 large passion fruit
15g sugar

1. Place a sieve over a pan. Cut the passion fruit in half and scoop the pulp into the sieve. Stir furiously with a spatula or dough scraper to extract all the juice. Reserve the seeds to make a crunchy topping (see page 21).
2. Add the sugar to the juice and place over a medium heat. Bring to a simmer and cook, stirring until the mixture reaches 85°C. Take off the heat and set aside to cool.
3. Store in an airtight container in the freezer for up to 1 month or in the fridge for up to 5 days.

RASPBERRY PURÉE
MAKES 240G

300g raspberries
40g caster sugar

1. Place a sieve over a pan. Whizz the raspberries in a food processor or blender until smooth. Tip the purée into the sieve and stir furiously with a spatula to extract the juice – you'll need 240g.
2. Add the sugar and place the pan over a medium heat. Bring to a simmer, stirring, and cook until the mixture reaches 85°C. Take off the heat and set aside to cool.
3. Store in an airtight container in the freezer for up to 1 month or in the fridge for up to 5 days.

◆

MANGO PURÉE
MAKES 125G

1 large mango, peeled and stoned (about 125g of flesh)
20g sugar

1. Whizz the mango flesh in a food processor or blender until smooth.
2. Transfer to a pan, add the sugar and bring to a simmer over a medium heat, stirring. Cook until the mixture reaches 85°C, then take off the heat and set aside to cool.
3. Store in an airtight container in the freezer for up to 1 month or in the fridge for up to 5 days.

CREAMS AND FILLINGS

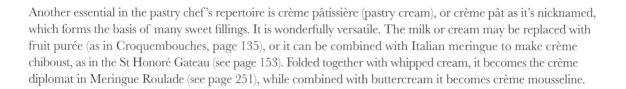

Another essential in the pastry chef's repertoire is crème pâtissière (pastry cream), or crème pât as it's nicknamed, which forms the basis of many sweet fillings. It is wonderfully versatile. The milk or cream may be replaced with fruit purée (as in Croquembouches, page 135), or it can be combined with Italian meringue to make crème chiboust, as in the St Honoré Gateau (see page 153). Folded together with whipped cream, it becomes the crème diplomat in Meringue Roulade (see page 251), while combined with buttercream it becomes crème mousseline.

CRÈME PÂTISSIÈRE (PASTRY CREAM)
MAKES ABOUT 300G

This recipe is made with cornflour, but plain flour or strong flour can be used if you wish. Just remember that you need double the quantity of these wheat flours to thicken the sauce. The addition of butter at the end gives it a richer flavour and silkier texture.

40g egg yolks (2 medium)
30g caster sugar
2g (½ teaspoon) vanilla extract
16g cornflour
200g milk
½ vanilla pod (from a pod split lengthways)
40g butter, at room temperature, cubed

1. Combine the egg yolks, caster sugar, vanilla extract and cornflour in a medium heatproof bowl and stir until smooth.
2. Pour the milk into a medium pan. Scrape in the vanilla seeds, add the pod itself and bring to the boil. Strain into the egg mixture, discarding the pod. Whisk thoroughly.
3. Return the mixture to the pan and slowly bring to the boil, stirring constantly. If it starts to turn lumpy, beat well until smooth. Simmer for 1–2 minutes to thicken the mixture, then remove from the heat and beat in the butter a piece at a time until thick, smooth and shiny.
4. Spread the mixture on a baking tray lined with clingfilm and cover the surface with more clingfilm to prevent a skin from forming. Set aside to cool.
5. Store in the fridge for up to 3 days.

CHANTILLY CREAM
SERVES 6

Plain whipped cream can sometimes taste cheesy if served with a sweet pudding, so this light, flavoured version is often served instead. Try it with the Blackberry, Apple Yogurt and Walnut Tart (see page 205).

100g whipping cream, chilled
25g icing sugar
1 tsp vanilla extract or ½ vanilla pod, split lengthways

1. Put the cream in a bowl and whisk it until thick and mousse-like.
2. Add the icing sugar and vanilla extract (or scrape in the seeds from the vanilla pod) and continue whisking until the mixture is just stiff. Serve straight away.

CHOCOLATE CRÉMEUX
MAKES ABOUT 700G

A crémeux, which translates as 'creamy', is made from a crème anglaise base (or with eggs, sugar, fruit purée and butter). As patisserie chefs say: 'It's not a mousse, it's not a cream – it's something in between.'

Smooth, rich and dense, crémeux can be used in many ways – piped, quenelled or spread – and it's a lovely indulgence on a croissant.

Take care when making the crème anglaise base that the mixture doesn't overcook and split or curdle.

200g dark chocolate (70% cocoa solids), very finely chopped
80g egg yolks (4 medium)
40g caster sugar
200g milk
200g double cream

1. Put the chocolate into a large bowl and set aside.
2. Put the egg yolks and sugar into another large bowl and mix with a balloon whisk until just combined. Try not to introduce too much air.
3. Pour the milk and cream into a medium heavy-based pan and bring just to the boil. Add 2 tablespoons of the hot liquid to the egg yolks and mix well. Slowly pour the remaining milk mixture into the egg yolks, stirring constantly with a spatula to keep it smooth.
4. Return the mixture to a clean pan and stir constantly over a low heat until it coats the back of a wooden spoon, about 5–6 minutes. Take care not to let it boil – if you want to test it with a digital thermometer, the temperature should be 83–85°C.
5. Strain the mixture through a fine sieve, then pour about a third of it into the chocolate. Working from the centre outwards, stir with a spatula to make a smooth emulsion. Add the remaining mixture in two separate batches, stirring until smooth and shiny.
6. Whizz the mixture with an electric hand blender to ensure it's very smooth, keeping the blade below the surface so that it doesn't incorporate too much air. Cover with clingfilm and chill for at least 6–8 hours or preferably overnight.
7. Store in an airtight container in the fridge for up to 3 days.

PEACH CRÉMEUX
MAKES ABOUT 500G

Any fruit purée can be used for this recipe, but here we've used peach to go inside the crisp éclair (see page 165). The texture is pipeable, but a little gelatine is included so that the crémeux keeps its structure while retaining a fresh flavour and silky smooth consistency.

5g powdered gelatine
25g cold water
160g peach purée (from about 1 whole peach)
60g egg yolks (3 medium)
50g egg (1 medium), beaten
100g caster sugar
120g butter, at room temperature and chopped
15g peach schnapps (optional)

1. Put the gelatine in a small bowl with the water and set aside to soften.
2. Put the peach purée into a pan, add the egg yolks, egg and sugar and stir well. Place the pan over a medium heat and bring just to the boil. Take care not to overheat it otherwise you'll end up with peach-flavoured scrambled eggs.
3. Add the gelatine, stir until melted, then allow to cool to 60°C.
4. Whisk in the butter, then whizz with a hand blender until smooth and creamy, taking care not to introduce too much air. Transfer to a bowl, cover with clingfilm and chill for at least 1 hour.
5. Store in an airtight container in the fridge for up to 3 days.

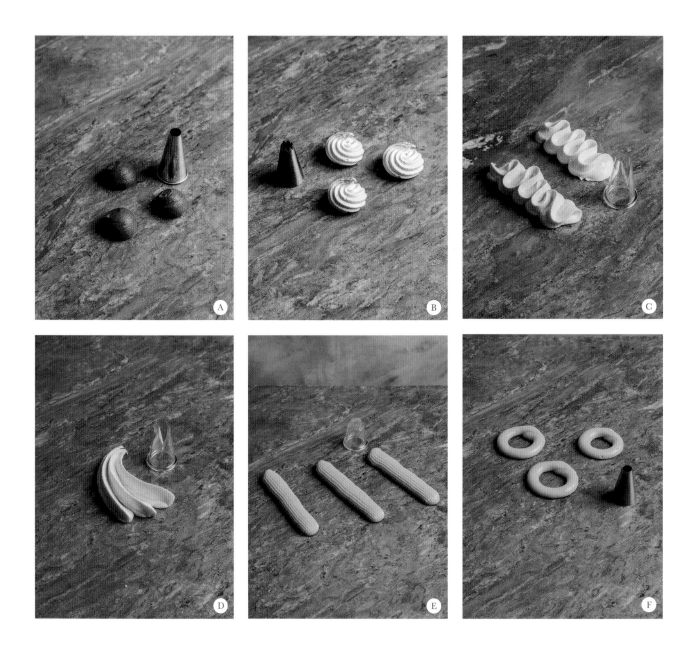

PIPING

◆ ◆ ◆

The art of piping is the pastry chef's equivalent of the sous chef's filleting skills. It's important not only for the finished appearance, but sometimes for structure too.

Piping takes practice. It's about knowing how to squeeze your bag, when to stop squeezing, when to cut the cream off with a flick to the side, when to pull up and how much pressure to apply. The angle of your piping bag or nozzle is key. If you need to practise first, pipe the mixture onto parchment paper, then scoop it back up and into the piping bag to reuse.

◆

TO PIPE A BALL

Use a piping bag fitted with a plain nozzle, hold it vertically and apply pressure evenly, squeezing gently to create a perfect sphere (A). This technique is used for choux buns and for shaping the Chantilly cream in Le Petit Antoine layered slice (see page 103).

◆

TO PIPE A ROSETTE

Use a piping bag fitted with a star nozzle, hold it at a slight angle and squeeze gently to give a pretty swirl effect (B).

◆

TO PIPE A WAVY PATTERN

To create the design seen on the Lemon Meringue Pie (see page 259), use a St Honoré nozzle. Hold the bag at a slight angle and pipe the mixture in a smooth zigzag motion from left to right (C).

TO PIPE THE CLASSIC ST HONORÉ DESIGN

It's essential to use a St Honoré nozzle for the recipe on page 153. Hold the bag upright but slightly angled towards you. Pipe and pull in a curved sweep, working from the outside towards the centre (all the joins meet in the middle and are piped over to hide them). You need to ease off the pressure as you approach the centre because the wave becomes finer and finishes with a point at the end (D).

◆

TO PIPE CHOUX PASTRY

If piping éclairs (see page 165), a special éclair nozzle should be used. Hold the bag at a slight angle and pipe evenly and steadily in straight lines (E).

If piping a circle with a hole in the middle (as needed for Paris–Brest, see page 173), hold the bag almost vertical and pipe a ring, squeezing from one side of circle and working round to meeting the other side (F).

SUGAR CONFECTIONERY

◆ ◇ ◆

Boiling sugar with water (or a variety of other liquids and ingredients) is the first step in creating a wealth of sugar confectionery. It can be used for making petit fours, as in Fudge and Caramels, or it can be the finishing touch to a patisserie recipe, such as a sprinkling of nut brittle over a layered slice.

STAGES OF COOKING SUGAR

When heated to gradually increased temperatures, sugar changes in appearance and its physical properties are altered. At each stage it is suitable for different purposes, as explained below.

◆

107°C THREAD
Place a dry finger on the surface of the syrup, join finger to thumb and a thread should form when they are separated. Used for making glacé and candied fruits.

112°C STRONG THREAD
Test as above, but the thread is thicker. Used for fudge, caramel and fondants.

118°C SOFT BALL
Spoon a small amount of the syrup onto a plate and set aside for a minute or two. Meanwhile, hold your fingers under cold water to make sure they're cool. When the syrup is cool enough to handle, roll a small amount between your fingers and it should set into a soft ball shape. Used for fudge and fondant recipes.

125°C HARD BALL
Test in the same way as soft ball, but this time the syrup sets into a hard ball. Used in marshmallow recipes.

140°C SOFT CRACK
Drop a teaspoonful into a glass of cold water. It's at soft crack stage when the sugar hardens immediately. Used for nougat and toffee.

150°C CRACK
Test in the same way as soft crack. When the ball is cold, the sugar will break and be crumbly. It's good for hard sweets and spun sugar.

155°C HARD CRACK
Test in the same way as soft crack. This time the ball will be amber, the colour will intensify when cold and the sugar will crumble because its water content has reduced. It's perfect for nut brittle, pralines and lollipops.

PASSION FRUIT CARAMELS

MAKES 40 PIECES

Every budding pastry chef needs a basic caramel recipe. It involves cooking cream and various sugars together until the mixture caramelises, then whisking in two different butters. The secret of success is getting the mixture to just the right temperature so that when it has cooled and firmed up, it has a pleasing, malleable consistency.

Before you start, cover your arms and wear rubber gloves as the mixture can spit. Also, use a long-handled balloon whisk if you have one so that your hands are clear of the pan while whisking.

300g whipping cream (35% fat)
200g caster sugar
210g liquid glucose
30g invert sugar, or liquid glucose or honey
½ vanilla pod (from a pod split lengthways)
90g passion fruit purée (see page 25), or ready-made frozen purée, thawed
10g salted butter, plus extra for greasing
8g cocoa butter

1. Pour the cream into a large, heavy-based pan and add the caster sugar, glucose and invert sugar. Scrape in the vanilla seeds and add the pod too.
2. Place the pan over a medium heat and bring to the boil, stirring gently with a spatula to dissolve the sugar. Cook until the mixture reaches 112°C.
3. Meanwhile, pour the passion fruit purée into a small pan over a high heat and bring to the boil.
4. Using a slotted spoon, scoop the vanilla pod out of the cream mixture, then very carefully and slowly pour in the hot passion fruit purée, taking care that it doesn't splash. Whisk continuously to combine the two mixtures.
5. Continue to cook until the temperature reaches 120°C, whisking constantly and checking the thermometer carefully as it will heat up quite fast. Immediately take the pan off the heat and quickly stir in both butters.

6. Pour the caramel into a 20cm square silicone mould or greased and lined cake tin and set aside at room temperature to set.
7. Turn the set caramel out on to a marble slab or a board lined with parchment paper and use a long, sharp knife to cut a lengthways strip about 4cm wide. Cut this strip into 2cm rectangles, keeping the individual sweets separate so that they don't stick together. Repeat this cutting process with the remaining caramel.
8. Wrap the caramels in cellophane squares, moulding them into neat shapes.
9. Store in an airtight container in a cool, dry place for up to 12 weeks.

CLOTTED CREAM FUDGE

MAKES 30 PIECES

Fudge is made by boiling a large quantity of sugar and liquid glucose with cream and butter. The tricky bit is getting the right level of crystallisation: too much and the texture will be gritty and hard; too little and the fudge won't set. That's why you need to keep a close eye on the temperature, which mustn't rise any higher than 118°C – soft ball stage (see page 30).

The perfect fudge is not too sweet and has a firm but yielding texture that's not at all grainy. If your fudge looks shiny and chewy, the crystallisation process hasn't fully developed, so leave the fudge in a cool dry place for another day and eventually it will seed and crystallise. If the fudge is too soft, it's undercooked, but still enjoyable – it just won't keep its shape when cut. If the fudge is crumbly and difficult to cut, it is overcooked and you will have to start again.

20g butter, chopped, plus extra
  for greasing
100g double cream
125g clotted cream

250g caster sugar
100g liquid glucose
vanilla extract
15g icing sugar, sifted

1. Butter a 15cm square tin and line it with parchment paper.
2. Put both the creams into a large, heavy-based pan and whisk in the caster sugar. Place the pan over a medium heat and add the glucose, butter and a few drops of the vanilla extract. Stir until the sugar has dissolved, then bring the mixture to the boil. Reduce the heat to a steady simmer, stand a sugar thermometer in the mixture and cook until the temperature reaches 118°C, whisking continuously to ensure the sugar doesn't catch on the bottom of the pan or become too dark.
3. Take the pan off the heat and whisk vigorously again, making sure you scrape the bottom of the pan and any corners where the mixture may have

set. Add the icing sugar and continue to whisk for 2–3 minutes. It's ready when the mixture becomes thicker and slightly loses its gloss but is still pourable.
4. Pour the mixture into the prepared tin and set aside for 24 hours at room temperature.
5. Using the parchment paper to help you, lift the fudge out of the tin, then peel off the paper. Lay the fudge on a clean chopping board and cut it into neat lozenge shapes using a small sharp knife. You need to drag the blade through the mixture to make a clean cut, rather than chopping straight down, which would make the fudge stick to the knife. Use a damp cloth to clean your knife between cuts.
6. Wrap the fudge pieces in plastic sweet wrappers or squares of cellophane.
7. Store in an airtight container in a cool, dry place for up to 6 weeks.

CHOCOLATE

◆ ◆ ◆

Chocolate plays a major part in the patisserie kitchen, adding flavour to a wide range of recipes, and body to ganaches, mousses and *crémeux*. It must be tempered (heated and cooled – see page 34) before use so that it will be shiny and have a good snap. The process also adds structure, texture and finish to such things as moulded chocolates and decorations.

There are two distinct categories of chocolate: real, and the lesser-known compound chocolate. Both are available in dark, milk and white varieties.

Real chocolate, also known as *couverture*, contains cocoa butter, which is extracted from the cocoa or cacao bean, and is the best for tempering. In recent times it's become fashionable to buy chocolate made from a single type of bean grown on a particular estate – this is known as single origin. However, chocolate can be made from a mixture of bean varieties from the same country or several different countries. The price is determined by the calibre of the producer, the place of origin and the quality of the product. The higher the percentage of cocoa solids it contains, the more expensive it will be.

Couverture is the main chocolate used in the patisserie kitchen. There are three types, each with the following percentages of cocoa solids:

dark chocolate: 50–100%

milk chocolate: 30–40%

white chocolate: over 32%

Compound chocolate, also known as baker's chocolate or pâte à glacer, contains vegetable oil rather than cocoa butter. This means it does not need tempering, but it is rarely used in the patisserie kitchen as it lacks the depth of flavour, bitterness and smoothness of real chocolate. Compound chocolate tends only to be used when a soft topping (less prone to cracking than real chocolate) is required for decoration. To decorate fudge, for instance, compound chocolate would be spread sparingly over the surface using a comb scraper to create ultra-fine lines. The fudge would then be cut into squares.

It's very important that chocolate intended for tempering doesn't come into contact with any moisture. Just a small amount, such as steam clinging to a hot spoon, can cause contamination that will make the chocolate seize and thicken. If this happens, all is not lost because the chocolate can still be used for making a sauce, ganache or cream, as more liquid has to be added anyway. Leave it to set, wrap well and store in a cool, dry place until needed. To use next time, simply chop it up and put it into a bowl, pour the specified boiling liquid on to it and stir slowly from the middle outwards until smooth.

Chocolate's sensitivity to water means that pastry chefs usually prefer to temper it in a microwave rather than a bain-marie. They believe it gives a better finished product without any risk (see overleaf).

HOW TO TEMPER CHOCOLATE

Real chocolate needs to be tempered – heated, then cooled to a particular temperature before use to give it a good sheen, snap and taste.

Tempering must be done slowly with lots of stirring or the set chocolate can bloom (develop a whitish coating) – a sign that the cocoa butter has separated from the cocoa solids.

Both microwave and bain-marie methods are given below, so use whichever you prefer. For complete accuracy, a digital thermometer is needed, but do not let it touch the bottom of the bowl.

1. Take about 300g chocolate drops, or finely chopped pieces that are more or less uniform in size.
2. Put 200g into a heatproof bowl and melt on high in a microwave, stirring it every 20–30 seconds and making sure the temperature does not rise any higher than 45–50°C.

Alternatively, place the bowl over a pan of simmering water and stir until the temperature reaches 45–50°C.
3. Remove from the heat, stir well and mix in the remaining 100g of chocolate. (This part of the process is called 'seeding'.) Stir continuously until melted and the temperature is 31–32°C for dark chocolate, 29–30°C for milk chocolate, or 28–29°C for white chocolate. If it drops below those temperatures and still contains lumps, put the bowl back in the microwave and heat for 5 seconds at a time until it reaches the right temperature. Alternatively, place it back over the pan of simmering water or use a heat gun – the sort that's used for paint stripping – to gently warm it. Remember to keep stirring.
4. To test if chocolate is adequately tempered, place a 5cm square of parchment paper on the melted chocolate. Transfer it to a cold surface to cool and if it sets within 2 minutes, the chocolate is tempered. The surface should be shiny, free of streaks and peel cleanly away from the parchment. If there are streaks or it hasn't set within 2 minutes, the chocolate is too warm. Stir it slightly or add more chocolate pieces to cool it down.
5. If the chocolate is too thick for your purpose, stir in some warm melted chocolate, or use a heat gun to increase the temperature by 1 or 2 degrees. Stir each time you do this.
6. Use the tempered chocolate as required. Decorations or chocolates can be placed in the fridge for 5–10 minutes, until firm.
7. Once set, store in an airtight container in a cool, dry place (no more than 21°C) and use within 2–3 months. Any leftover chocolate that isn't used can be left to set, remelted and used again.

MELTING CHOCOLATE FOR PATISSERIE

As chocolate melts just below body temperature (37°C), melting it in a pan over direct heat carries a risk that it will become grainy and burn. For that reason, use this method only if there is another ingredient (butter, cream or milk, for instance) in the pan with the chocolate. Keep the temperature low, watching carefully and shaking or stirring the pan from time to time.

If the chocolate does burn in the microwave, you will know from the smell. To rescue it, try removing the burnt bits and sieving the remainder.

GANACHE
MAKES ABOUT 650G

Equal parts chocolate and cream, ganache is used for truffles, sandwiching dacquoise and joconde in a layered slice, and decorating cakes and desserts.

300g dark chocolate (55% cocoa solids), finely chopped
300g whipping cream
50g liquid glucose or invert sugar

1. Put the chocolate into a bowl. Pour the cream and glucose into a pan and heat gently until the mixture comes to the boil.
2. Slowly add the cream mixture to the chocolate, stirring from the middle outwards to create a smooth, shiny emulsion. Allow to set at cool room temperature.

PASTRY

◆ ◆ ◆

There are four main types of pastry used in patisserie: sweet pastry (pâte sucrée) and its more luxurious cousin – enriched shortcrust (pâte brisée); almond sablé, puff pastry and choux. However, some basic rules apply, whatever type of pastry you're making. First, make sure your hands, kitchen and all your ingredients are cool before you start. Second, take care not to overwork or overstretch the dough as it might shrink down and away from the sides of a tin during baking.

◆

PÂTE SUCRÉE (SWEET PASTRY)
MAKES 440G

Known by pastry chefs as sweet 'paste', this is unlike ordinary shortcrust used for savoury bakes. This recipe includes egg, milk and sugar for a rich flavour and more crumbly texture. From start to finish, this pastry needs a light touch, so take care not to over-aerate the creamed butter and sugar, and don't overstretch the pastry when rolling it out. Chilling it before rolling prevents shrinkage during baking.

100g butter, softened
100g caster sugar
40g beaten egg (about 1 small)
200g plain flour, plus extra for dusting

1. *Mixer method:* Put the butter and sugar into a mixer and beat together at a low speed until the mixture looks pale and creamy. Add the egg and mix again until just combined. Sift in the flour and mix again at a low speed to make a rough dough.
  Hand method: Beat the butter and sugar together in a large bowl using a wooden spoon. Beat in the egg, then sift in the flour a bit at a time and fold in using a spatula. Work the mixture until it forms a rough dough.
2. Using your hands, knead the dough very gently until smooth.
3. Wrap the pastry in clingfilm and chill for 1 hour to firm up and relax before rolling out with short strokes on a lightly floured work surface.

PÂTE BRISÉE (ENRICHED SHORTCRUST)
MAKES ABOUT 540G

While made in the same way as pâte sucrée, this version includes less sugar, but more egg and milk, so it has a richer, more melt-in-the-mouth texture.

180g butter, chilled and cut into cubes
20g caster sugar
3g salt
50g egg (1 medium), beaten
20g milk
270g plain flour, plus extra for dusting

1. *Mixer method:* Put the butter, sugar and salt into a mixer fitted with a paddle attachment and beat together at a low speed to avoid incorporating any air. Add the egg and milk and continue to mix at a low speed for about 10 seconds. Sift in the flour and mix until a dough forms and starts to come away cleanly from the sides of the bowl.
  Hand method: Rub the butter into the sifted flour in a large bowl. Stir in the sugar and salt, then make a well in the centre. Slowly add the egg and milk and mix with a spatula until the mixture comes together. Knead lightly to form a smooth dough.
  Food processor method: Mix together the butter and flour, then add the remaining ingredients and mix until a dough forms.
2. Transfer the dough to a clean work surface and knead very gently until smooth. Shape into a circle, wrap in clingfilm and chill for 1 hour before rolling out.

ALMOND SABLÉ

The French word sablé means 'sandy', and that exactly describes the dry mixture used for this pastry. The traditional method involves the butter and icing sugar being 'pecked' together between fingers and thumbs, like a bird eating crumbs, then the egg is worked in, and finally the dry ingredients. The fat content from the butter and almonds imparts a lovely rich flavour. This recipe calls for a relatively large quantity of baking powder, which gives the pastry a light biscuit texture, rather like shortbread.

200g plain flour
125g butter, cubed
65g icing sugar
0.5g salt
50g ground almonds
4g baking powder
50g egg (1 medium), beaten

1. *Mixer or food processor method:* Put all the ingredients, apart from the egg, into a mixer or food processor. Mix at a low speed until the mixture resembles fine breadcrumbs. Add the beaten egg and mix again until a dough forms.

Hand method: Put the butter and icing sugar into a large bowl and 'peck' them together between fingers and thumbs until the mixture looks creamy. Work in the egg with a spoon, then stir in the flour until a dough forms.

2. Tip the dough onto a lightly floured work surface and bring together with your hands. Wrap in clingfilm and chill for 20 minutes before rolling.

HOW TO LINE A TART TIN

1. Butter a tin of the appropriate size/shape.
2. Place your pastry on a clean work surface dusted with a little flour. Rolling in one direction only and giving the pastry a quarter turn after each stroke, roll it out to a thickness of 2mm.
3. Drape the pastry over the rolling pin and lay it loosely over the tart tin. Using your fingers, smooth out the pastry, easing out any trapped air and gently pressing it into the corners of the tin, leaving a centimetre overhang. Carefully trim off any large pieces with kitchen scissors and prick the base with a fork. Cover with clingfilm and chill for 20 minutes.

HOW TO BLIND BAKE A TART

1. Preheat the oven to 200°C/180°C fan/gas mark 6.
2. Line the chilled pastry case with baking parchment and fill with baking beans. Bake blind for 15 minutes, until the edges are just golden.
3. Reduce the temperature to 180°C/160°C fan/gas mark 4. Remove the paper and baking beans, then return the pastry case to the oven for another 12–15 minutes, until golden brown.
4. Remove from the oven and use a small serrated knife to trim the pastry so that the edge is neatly flush with the rim of the tin. Set aside to cool.

PÂTE À CHOUX (CHOUX PASTRY)

Unlike other pastries, choux pastry requires very little hands-on work as it is stirred in a pan, spooned into a piping bag and squeezed into the required shape(s). Most important is to measure the ingredients accurately or the mixture will end up too soft or too firm. It must be baked in a hot oven so that the water evaporates and becomes steam, which crisps the outer shell of the pastry.

125g cold water
65g butter, chopped
7g caster sugar
1.5g table salt
125g strong bread flour, sifted
125g eggs (about 2½ medium), beaten

1. Place the water, butter, sugar and salt in a heavy-based pan and place over a medium heat to melt the butter.

2. As soon as the butter has melted, increase the heat slightly and bring the mixture almost to boiling point. (Take care not to let the liquid actually boil or too much water will evaporate.)

3. Take the pan off the heat, add the flour and mix quickly with a wooden spoon to make a paste. Put the pan back on a low heat and cook until the mixture forms a ball and leaves the sides of the pan clean (A).

4. *Mixer method:* Transfer the paste to a mixer fitted with a paddle attachment and mix at a slow speed for 2 minutes in order to cool down the mixture. With the motor still running at the same speed, slowly mix in enough egg to make a smooth and shiny mixture (B). Use immediately.

Hand method: Transfer the paste to a clean bowl and beat hard with a wooden spoon. Slowly add the eggs, as above, and beat until you can run the spoon through the mixture and it folds back on itself.

PÂTE FEUILLETÉE (PUFF PASTRY)

◆

There are several stages to making puff pastry. First a *détrempe* (dough envelope) is wrapped around a *beurrage* (slab of butter) to make a *paton* (block), which is repeatedly rolled and folded to distribute the butter evenly. This is what creates the numerous leaves or layers in the pastry. Note that lemon juice is added to the *détrempe* to strengthen the gluten in the flour, and this improves the elasticity and texture of the pastry.

420g strong bread flour, plus extra to dust
9g salt
a few drops of lemon juice
180–195g iced water
40g butter, softened
375g cold butter, cubed (for the beurrage)

TO MAKE THE DÉTREMPE (BASE DOUGH)

1. *Mixer method:* To make the *détrempe*, put 350g of the flour into a mixer with the salt, lemon juice, iced water and the softened butter. Mix at a slow speed for 2 minutes, then at a medium speed for another 4 minutes. Scoop out of the dough, wrap in clingfilm and rest in the fridge for 45 minutes.

Hand method: To make the *détrempe*, tip the 350g flour and 40g butter into a large bowl and rub together until the mixture resembles fine breadcrumbs. Add the salt, iced water and lemon juice and mix together with a wooden spoon. Knead lightly to make a dough. Wrap and chill.

TO MAKE THE BEURRAGE

1. *Mixer method:* Put the cold butter into a mixer fitted with a paddle attachment. Mix at a medium speed for 30 seconds, until the butter is smooth, then reduce the speed and add the remaining 70g flour. Mix to combine, then transfer the mixture to a chopping board lined with clingfilm. Shape into a 10cm square block, wrap tightly and chill for 45–60 minutes.

Hand method: Put the butter cubes and remaining 70g flour into a clean bowl and beat together. Shape into a 10cm square block, wrap tightly and chill for 45–60 minutes.

TO FOLD AND ROLL THE PASTRY

It's essential to complete the following steps quickly and keep everything cool so that the pastry doesn't become warm and sticky.

1. Unwrap the *détrempe* and place it on a lightly floured work surface. Using short, sharp strokes and taking care not to overwork the dough, roll it into a square measuring 22 x 22cm (A).
2. Turn the dough so it makes a diamond shape on the work surface. Place the *beurrage* squarely on it and fold the corners of the dough over it (B) so they meet in the middle and look like an envelope (C). Press the edges together with your fingers, then press the rolling pin along the bottom edge, in the middle and at the top edge to secure. Roll into a rectangle measuring 60 x 20cm (D). With the longest edge horizontal, fold the right-hand side in by a third (so the size is now 40 x 20cm), then flap the left-hand side over it (so the size is now 20 x 20cm).
3. Roll out again and repeat the folding process. You've done 2 turns and folds, so press your finger on it twice to make 2 light indents as a reminder. Wrap loosely in clingfilm and chill for 30 minutes.
4. Take the dough out of the fridge and put it on the board once more. With the main join to the left-hand side (it should be on the side rather than facing you each time it's rolled), roll and fold the pastry twice more, chilling in between. Press 4 indents on top as a reminder of how many you've done. If you prefer, the dough can be left overnight and the last stage completed in the morning.
5. Repeat the rolling and folding process once more so that the pastry has had a total of 6 folds and rolls. Wrap loosely in clingfilm and chill for 30 minutes. Use as required.

BAKERY AND VIENNOISERIE

COCONUT BUTTERKUCHEN

BRIOCHE NANTERRE

CRÈME DE PARISIENNES

SALTED CARAMEL BABKA KNOTS

SFOGLIATELLE

CROISSANTS

PAINS AUX RAISINS

PAINS AU CHOCOLAT

DANISH PINWHEELS

BAKERY AND VIENNOISERIE

The *tourier*, as it's known by classical patisserie chefs, is the area in the kitchen where the chefs specialise in all boulangerie, enriched dough and pastry products. It's slightly cooler than the other areas, which it needs to be for bakery items.

In the traditional pastry kitchen, a wooden table known as a 'dough roller' is the preferred surface for making and working with dough because the dough doesn't stick to it. Also, in the cool atmosphere, the wooden surface keeps the dough warm, which helps when it's being kneaded and shaped in between rising and proving.

The *tourier* is an important section for trainee patisserie chefs, as all the basics are learnt here. Their training involves not only practising the recipes, but honing techniques too. Working with various doughs, knowing when they've risen sufficiently, when they need to be knocked back, or if they've finished proving and are ready to bake are key skills. We hope you will enjoy discovering the skills and secrets of the *tourier* and trying them for yourself through the range of recipes in this chapter – from simple Coconut Butterkuchen to Croissants and Danish pastries (see pages 45, 67 and 79).

COCONUT BUTTERKUCHEN

Buttery buns topped with a scattering of desiccated coconut, a whipped butter glaze and crunchy pearl sugar

Butterkuchen, or 'butter cake', is a traditional sweet cake so called because its dimpled surface is dotted with butter before baking. It is a popular pastry in German bakeries and an essential recipe for German pastry chefs, often made in huge trays and cut into squares. This recipe is made into individual buns, but the principle is the same. The key is to make sure the dough rises evenly and that the butter sinks in to it so that you have a moist bun with a texture a little bit like a doughnut.

The all-important ingredient here is the yeast. It's a living organism that needs food, moisture and warmth to activate it. If any of these elements aren't just right, the yeast will die and the dough won't rise efficiently. Once the yeast is fed with sugar, the two ingredients combine to produce carbon dioxide, which is trapped in the dough, creating the bubbles that give the cake its wonderful texture and also contribute to its flavour. This recipe uses malt to assist the rise, although it isn't essential. The malt helps to convert the starch in the dough to sugar, which in turn feeds the yeast.

Serve these light buttery bakes at teatime or for a very indulgent breakfast treat.

MAKES 8

TIMING

Hands-on time: *20 minutes, plus rising and proving time*
Cooking time: *15 minutes*

PREPARE IN ADVANCE

These can't be prepared or baked ahead –
   they're best served fresh from the oven.

HAVE READY

Stand mixer, if using, fitted with the dough hook.
Eggs at room temperature and butter softened.
Baking sheet lined with parchment paper or
   a silicone mat.

EQUIPMENT

stand mixer, optional
  – dough hook
  – paddle attachment
baking sheet
parchment paper or a silicone mat
digital scales
medium bowl
large bowl, optional
clingfilm
rolling pin
piping bag
pastry brush

FOR THE DOUGH

14g milk powder

175g tepid water

7g dried yeast

50g caster sugar

350g strong bread flour

6g salt

40g softened butter

20g beaten egg

6g malt extract, optional

FOR THE TOPPING

150g butter, softened and whipped

25g butter, melted

50g desiccated coconut

15g pearl sugar

THE SECRETS OF SUCCESS

◆

If the kuchen don't rise…
You've probably killed the
yeast. Make sure next time
round when you activate
the yeast that the water is
just warm – it should be
blood temperature.

MAKE THE DOUGH

The yeast is first mixed together with milk powder, water and sugar.
This gives it time to activate before it's added to the rest of the ingredients,
which will slow it down and inhibit the rise. By dissolving the yeast in
liquid first it's better distributed throughout the dough too.

1. To activate the yeast put the milk powder into a medium bowl with the
water and stir to dissolve the grains. Sprinkle over the yeast and a pinch
of sugar. Stir everything together then set aside for 10–15 minutes to allow
the yeast to activate. It's ready when bubbles appear on the surface and
the mixture looks frothy.

2. Sift the flour into a large bowl or the bowl of a stand mixer and stir
in the salt. Make a well in the centre and pour in the yeast mixture, then
add the butter, egg and malt extract. Mix everything together on a low
speed for 3 minutes, then increase the speed to medium and continue to
mix for 6 minutes until smooth and no longer sticky. If you're doing this
by hand, use a table knife to cut the ingredients together to combine them,
then tip onto a clean work surface and knead until smooth.

3. Transfer the dough to a clean bowl, cover with clingfilm and allow
to rise for 15 minutes until doubled in size.

4. Cut the dough evenly into 80g pieces (you may have about 10g leftover).
Weighing each piece ensures that every *kuchen* bakes to the same size. Roll
each one into a round between the palms of your hands, then place them
on a clean work surface and use a rolling pin to roll them into discs about
15cm in diameter and 3–5mm thick. Place on the prepared baking sheet
and leave to prove for 30 minutes.

BAKE THE BUTTERKUCHEN

Whipping the butter makes it easier to pipe into the little holes in the
dough. You need to pipe only a hazelnut-sized nub into each one.

5. Preheat the oven to 180°C/160°C fan/gas mark 4.

6. Spoon the whipped butter into the piping bag and snip off the end.
Brush the tops of the buns with the melted butter, then use the tips of
your fingers to make little holes all over the top of each round. Pipe a
little butter into each hole, sprinkle with desiccated coconut and set aside
to prove for a further 15 minutes. To test if the dough is ready, press the
top lightly with a finger – it's ready when it springs back.

7. Bake for about 12 minutes, or until golden, then take out of the oven
and scatter over the pearl sugar and serve warm.

◆ ◆

BRIOCHE NANTERRE

A light, buttery breakfast loaf with a soft golden crust

Brioche is made from what's known in the trade as a super-enriched dough, so named because it contains extra milk, eggs, butter and sugar. It's as easy as a regular loaf to make – you just need to make sure that all the butter (almost a whole pack) is incorporated into the soft dough to create its unique buttery flavour.

Each additional ingredient serves a purpose: milk helps to make the bread soft, while sugar adds flavour. Butter helps this too, and produces a pleasing golden crust and soft yellow crumb. The egg – another form of fat – also helps the flavour and texture. Once the dough is made, it is refrigerated overnight to slow down the rise. It needs this slightly longer rising time as the extra ingredients slow down the action of the yeast.

Unlike an ordinary loaf, which has a simple curved 'roof', Brioche Nanterre has an interesting 'knobbled' surface, created by rolling the dough into eight balls and arranging them in rows in the baking tin. Pastry chefs ensure the balls are perfectly even by weighing the pieces of dough to make sure they are equal before placing them in the tin.

Serve for breakfast, in slices with a soft-set apricot or blackberry conserve.

MAKES 1 LOAF

TIMING

Hands-on time: *55 minutes, plus overnight chilling, rising and proving time*
Cooking time: *35 minutes*

PREPARE IN ADVANCE

Make the dough up to the end of step
5 up to 1 day ahead.

HAVE READY

Stand mixer, if using, fitted with the dough hook.
Baking sheet lined with parchment paper
and lightly dusted with flour.
Loaf tins greased and lined with parchment
paper, or brioche tins well buttered.

EQUIPMENT

stand mixer, optional
– dough hook
baking sheet
parchment paper
900g loaf tin
digital scales
small pan or microwavable bowl
microwave, optional
digital thermometer
small bowl
sieve
large bowl and wooden spoon, optional
plastic bag or damp cloth
pastry brush

FOR THE BRIOCHE DOUGH

15–30g milk

4g dried yeast

200g strong bread flour, plus extra
for dusting

15g caster sugar

85g eggs (about 1½ medium), beaten

2g salt

80g butter, softened, plus a little
extra for greasing

TO FINISH

25g egg (about ½ medium), beaten

THE SECRETS OF SUCCESS

If the mixture looks oily
and chewed-up rather than
smooth and shiny…
The mixture is too warm.
This can happen when the
friction of the mixer causes
the butter to leach out of
the dough. To rescue it,
pat it out flat and chill the
dough to allow the butter
to set, then mix again.

MAKE THE BRIOCHE DOUGH

You must start by mixing the milk and yeast together to make a ferment for the dough. The milk should be just at blood temperature, otherwise it might kill the yeast. Leaving the dough to rise gives the yeast a chance to work with the other ingredients and create the all-important carbon dioxide, which gives bread its light texture and develops the flavour.

1. Put the milk in a small pan or microwavable bowl and warm just to blood temperature (37°C).
2. Put the warm milk and the yeast in a small bowl and mix together. Set aside to allow the yeast to activate. It's ready when bubbles appear on the surface and the mixture looks frothy.
3. Sift all the flour into a large bowl or the bowl of a stand mixer. Make a well at one side and pour the yeast and milk mixture into it. Gently stir the yeast mixture, incorporating a little flour from the sides of the well until it forms a soft batter consistency. Take a spoonful of flour from the bowl and cover the batter as if you're burying it. Set aside and wait for bubbles to crack the surface – it will depend on the heat in your kitchen, but this will take about 15–30 minutes.
4. Add the sugar, eggs and salt to the bowl and first mix the mixture on a slow speed for 2 minutes then increase the speed to medium and mix for a further 8 minutes. Alternatively mix the ingredients together with a wooden spoon, then tip on to a lightly floured work surface and knead for 10 minutes.
5. Slowly beat in or knead the pieces of butter until incorporated and the dough is smooth and elastic.
6. Cover with a plastic bag or damp cloth and set aside to rise for about 1½ hours, until the dough has doubled in size. Turn the risen dough on to the prepared baking sheet and press it out flat to the size of the sheet. Cover with clingfilm and chill overnight.

SHAPE AND BAKE THE LOAF

Take care when brushing the loaf with the egg wash that you don't put too much on and it runs down the outside, otherwise the egg will cook and you'll end up with an omelette sticking to the sides of the tin.

7. Weigh the rested dough and cut it into equal pieces weighing about 50g. Roll each one into a ball and arrange them side-by-side in one of the tins. Leave to prove for 35 minutes, or until doubled in size and nearly to the top of the tin.
8. Preheat the oven to 200°C/180°C fan/gas mark 6.
9. Brush the beaten egg very lightly over the loaf. Bake for 10 minutes, then reduce the temperature to 180°C/160°C fan/gas mark 4 and bake for a further 25 minutes, or until golden. Remove from the tin and cool on a wire rack.

CRÈME DE PARISIENNES

*Soft, pillowy buns filled with sweet vanilla **crème pâtissière***

Rich brioche dough, often described as a cross between a cake and a bread, forms the base of these breakfast buns. To ensure success, each piece of dough must be rolled out thinly and evenly, then filled with a strip of crème pâtissière. One side of the dough is then cut into 'fingers', which are pulled across the filling to create the interesting shape. It's important to roll out the dough evenly so that the fingers bake uniformly and have the correct appearance. On baking, the dough becomes soft and fluffy, while the crème pâtissière just sets inside.

MAKES 16

TIMING

Hands-on time: *1 hour 15 minutes, plus overnight chilling, rising and proving time*
Cooking time: *40 minutes*

PREPARE IN ADVANCE

Make the brioche dough up to the end of step 2 at least 8 hours ahead or overnight.
The crème pâtissière must be made the day before and can be made up to 3 days ahead. Store, sealed with clingfilm, in the fridge.

HAVE READY

Stand mixer, if using, fitted with the dough hook.
Baking sheet lined with parchment paper.
Baking tray lightly greased.

EQUIPMENT

stand mixer, optional
  – dough hook
baking sheet
parchment paper
baking tray
digital scales
small pan or microwavable bowl
microwave, optional
digital thermometer
small bowl
sieve
large bowl and wooden spoon, optional
medium bowl
small whisk
medium pan
clingfilm
rolling pin
ruler
disposable piping bag
pizza cutter or sharp knife
pastry brush
wire rack

FOR THE DOUGH

75g warm milk

10g fresh yeast or 5g dried yeast

375g strong bread flour,
   plus extra for dusting

35g caster sugar

150g eggs (3 medium)

2.5g table salt

185g unsalted butter,
   at room temperature

a little oil, for greasing

FOR THE CRÈME PÂTISSIÈRE

80g egg yolks (4 medium)

85g caster sugar

30g cornflour

325g milk

seeds from ½ vanilla pod

½ teaspoon vanilla extract

FOR THE EGG WASH AND TO DECORATE

25g egg yolk, beaten (1 large)

1 tablespoon water

50g pearl sugar

MAKE THE BRIOCHE DOUGH

Start by fermenting the yeast to give it a head start before it is mixed with the other ingredients. First it's mixed with warm (not hot) milk until the mixture bubbles, then it is added to flour and left to activate before the enriching ingredients are mixed in. It has two provings to give the yeast time to develop fully and create the airy interior to the buns.

1. Make the brioche dough following the instructions for the Brioche Nanterre on page 49 up to the end of step 5.
2. Cover and set aside to rise in a warm place for about 1½ hours or until doubled in size. Press the dough out onto the lightly greased tray and leave to rest in the fridge for 8 hours or overnight.

MAKE THE CRÈME PÂTISSIÈRE

3. Put the egg yolks and sugar into a bowl and whisk together, then add the cornflour. Whisk lightly again.
4. Pour the milk into a medium pan and add the vanilla seeds and extract. Bring to the boil, then, as soon as the milk is boiling, pour it onto the egg yolk mixture, stirring all the time until smooth.
5. Pour the mixture back into the pan and bring it to a simmer, stirring continuously to prevent any lumps from forming. Cook for a couple more minutes until the mixture thickens but still drops easily from the spoon.
6. Spoon into a bowl, cover the surface with clingfilm and chill overnight.

SHAPE THE INDIVIDUAL BUNS

The pastry is first rolled into ovals. Each is piped at one end with cream and sliced at the other end into finger strips of pastry, which are then folded over the crème pâtissière and tucked carefully underneath the buns to neaten them. As the dough expands in the oven, the cream is sealed within the pastry.

7. Take the brioche dough out of the fridge, weigh it, and divide it into 16 even-sized pieces, each about 50g.
8. Roll out one piece on a very lightly floured work surface until it measures about 5mm thick and is a rough oval shape about 14cm long and 12cm wide.
9. Spoon the crème pâtissière into a piping bag and snip off the end. Pipe a thick line of crème pâtissière around the curve of one end of the oval, 2cm in from the edge and about 8cm long.

10. Use a pizza cutter or sharp knife to make 6–8 cuts at the other end of the dough, towards the centre (A). They should stop halfway into the dough so that it looks like a hand with a cream edge and pastry fingers.

11. Beat the egg yolk with the water and brush over the exposed dough. Fold the dough fingers neatly over the crème pâtissière and tuck them underneath the dough at the other side (B). Transfer to the lined baking sheet and repeat until you've shaped and filled all the buns. Leave to prove for 45 minutes.

12. Preheat the oven to 200°C/180°C fan/gas mark 6.

13. Brush the remaining egg wash over the buns and sprinkle them with the pearl sugar. Bake for 17 minutes, or until golden. Cool on a wire rack before serving.

THE SECRETS OF SUCCESS

If the bread has a tough texture…
Either the buns have not been proved for long enough, or they have been baked for too long. Make sure when you're proving the buns in step 11 that they feel soft and pillowy before you put them in the oven. To check they're baked, tap the base of one – it should sound hollow.

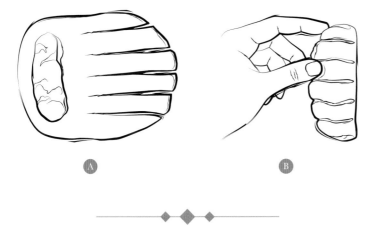

A   B

SALTED CARAMEL BABKA KNOTS

Deliciously nutty and sweet twisted buns

These little buns are named after the large Babka loaf, which is traditionally eaten across Eastern Europe at Easter, Christmas and New Year. A brioche dough forms the base of the buns, which are rippled with salted caramel and pecan nuts.

The skill here is in shaping the dough. It needs to be rolled, then sliced to reveal the filling, then shaped into a knot so that the ripple of flavouring is displayed and caramelises during baking. To finish, a glaze of vanilla syrup keeps the knots moist.

The quantity of water a flour will absorb varies from packet to packet and with the age of the flour, so add the liquid slowly when combining the ingredients together to make sure the dough isn't too wet. If it looks as if it might be dry, add a little more, tablespoon by tablespoon, until it forms a soft dough.

MAKES 8

TIMING

Hands-on time: *3 hours, including rising and proving time*
Cooking time: *12–14 minutes*

PREPARE IN ADVANCE

The salted caramel filling can be made up to 3 days ahead, stored in the fridge. Bring back to room temperature before using.

HAVE READY

Stand mixer, if using, fitted with the dough hook.
Baking sheet lined with parchment paper or a silicone mat.

EQUIPMENT

stand mixer, optional
  – dough hook
baking sheet
parchment paper or a silicone mat
digital scales
small pan or a microwavable bowl
microwave, optional
digital thermometer
whisk
large bowl
wooden spoon
small roasting tin
medium bowl
mini food-processor
medium pan
rolling pin
sharp knife
ruler
spatula
pastry brush
clingfilm
wire rack

FIRST MAKE THE DOUGH

It's important to have all the ingredients at room temperature before you start work. If the dough is too hot, it will kill the yeast. If it's too cold, it won't be warm enough to activate it.

1. Put half the milk into a microwavable bowl or small pan and warm it in the microwave on low, or over a low heat, until it reaches 34°C. Whisk in the yeast and a teaspoon of the sugar and set aside to allow the yeast to activate. It's ready when the yeast has dissolved and the mixture looks frothy on top.

2. *Mixer method:* Put the remaining ingredients into a stand mixer fitted with the dough hook and mix to combine. Make a well in the middle and add the yeasted mixture and continue to mix, adding the remaining milk to make a soft dough. Mix on a low speed for 3 minutes. Increase the speed to medium and continue to knead the dough for 5 minutes until smooth and elastic . Scrape the dough onto a lightly floured surface and knead to form a smooth even ball.

Hand method: Put the remaining ingredients into a large bowl and mix with a wooden spoon to combine. Make a well in the middle and add the yeasted mixture. Continue to mix, adding the remaining milk to make a soft dough. Tip onto a lightly floured work surface and knead until smooth and elastic, about 10-15 minutes. Form into a smooth even ball.

3. Place in a large clean bowl, cover and set aside to rise for about 50 minutes, until the dough has doubled in size.

MAKE THE SALTED CARAMEL FILLING

While the dough is resting, you can make the filling and syrup.

Toasting the nuts first boosts the flavour. Make sure the butter is softened so that it's easier to incorporate the remaining ingredients.

4. Put the pecans in a small roasting tin and toast for 4 minutes, then remove from the oven and cool on the tray. Turn the oven off for the time being.

5. Put the butter, sugar and salt into a medium bowl and cream together until the mixture is paler in colour and looks creamy.

6. Blitz the pecans in a mini food-processor until they're finely chopped and look like small crumbs. Beat them into the butter mixture then set aside at room temperature until ready to use.

Continued…

FOR THE DOUGH

85g whole milk

15g instant dried yeast

40g light brown soft sugar

40g unsalted butter, softened

210g strong bread flour,
   plus extra for dusting

40g egg yolks (2 medium)

½ teaspoon vanilla extract

½ teaspoon table salt

FOR THE SALTED CARAMEL FILLING

50g pecans

25g salted butter, softened

40g dark brown sugar

½ teaspoon sea salt flakes

FOR THE SYRUP GLAZE

½ vanilla pod, split lengthways

100g water

135g granulated sugar

MAKE THE SYRUP

7. Use a knife to scrape down the middle of the vanilla pod to extract the seeds then put them into a medium pan over a low heat with the pod, water and sugar.

8. Heat gently to dissolve the sugar then bring to a boil. Simmer for 1 minute until a thick syrup forms, then take off the heat and set aside to infuse at room temperature until required.

ROLL OUT AND SHAPE THE DOUGH INTO 'KNOTS'

The knot effect is created by rolling and twisting the dough to get as much shape and texture as possible.

9. Once the dough is rested, roll it out very thinly to a 40 x 60cm rectangle, with the shortest edge nearest you.

10. Cut the rectangle in half lengthways, then cut each half in half again to make 4 strips of dough, each measuring 10 x 60cm.

11. Spoon a quarter of the filling over each piece of dough, then use a palette knife to spread it out in a fine layer (A). Pinch one long edge of the first strip and carefully roll up the strip into a long sausage shape (B). Brush along the long edge with water and pinch the join to seal. Repeat so that all 4 strips are rolled up and sealed. Cut each roll in half to make eight 30cm rolls (C).

12. Take one piece and roll it on the work surface so that it's a little thinner and longer than before, about 40 cm (D), then take a sharp knife and split it down the middle, leaving a 1cm join at one end (E). Take the two 'fingers' of dough and twist them gently so that one end is smooth and further along you can see the cut dough. Plait the two ends around each other to make a long braid (F), then roll up the plait to make a coil shape (G). Neaten the end by tucking it underneath the roll (H). Repeat until you have 8 knots.

13. Transfer to the prepared baking sheet, cover with clingfilm and leave to prove for 40 minutes until doubled in size.

14. Preheat the oven to 220°C/200°C fan/gas mark 7 and bake the proved knots for 12–14 minutes until golden.

GLAZE THE KNOTS

15. Bring the syrup back up to the boil and, as soon as the babkas come out of the oven, brush the syrup all over them so that they infuse with the syrup and glaze evenly. Allow to cool and set on a wire rack before serving.

SFOGLIATELLE

*Crisp, flaky Italian pastries filled with a
ricotta cream scented with citrus*

These little Italian pastries are typically eaten at breakfast time with a shot of hot espresso. The unique fan-shaped layers are made from a simple dough, which is rolled out and brushed with clarified butter or lard to give the pastry its wonderful crispness. The base of the filling is created by cooking semolina until very thick. It is then lightened with ricotta and flavoured with citrus zests and sultanas.

Although the dough is a fairly simple one, the technique for rolling and shaping the pastries is a perfect way to show off your skills, as each piece is moulded into a cone by hand. The perfect *sfogliatella* should have a crunchy outer shell and even fanning throughout the cone.

It's important to use '00' flour for the pastry, which is the same flour used to make pasta, because it's very fine and will give a lighter finish. Be patient when rolling the dough through the pasta machine, and make sure you have plenty of space clear in the kitchen before you start.

MAKES 10–15

TIMING

Hands-on time: *1 hours 15 minutes,*
  plus 1 hour resting
Cooking time: *30–35 minutes*

PREPARE IN ADVANCE

The dough can be made and rolled up
  to the end of step 9, up to 2 days ahead.
The filling can be made and chilled up
  to 1 day ahead.

HAVE READY

Stand mixer, if using, fitted with
  the dough hook.
Baking sheets lined with parchment paper.

EQUIPMENT

stand mixer, optional
  – dough hook
  – paddle attachment
baking sheet
parchment paper
digital scales
zester
large bowl, optional
pasta machine or rolling pin
clingfilm
small pan
wooden spoon
sharp knife
pastry brush

250g '00' flour

2.5g honey

a good pinch of salt

140g water

125g clarified butter or lard, chopped

FOR THE FILLING

45g water

20g caster sugar

a pinch of salt

18g semolina

50g ricotta

10g egg yolk (½ medium)

seeds from ¼ vanilla pod

zest from ¼ orange

zest and juice from ¼ lemon

25g sultanas

FOR DECORATING

icing sugar, to dust

MAKE THE DOUGH

The technique here is all in the rolling. If you don't have a pasta machine, roll by hand, but give yourself a bit more time.

1. *Mixer method:* Put the flour, honey and salt into the bowl of a stand mixer and mix briefly with the dough hook to combine. Gradually pour in the water and continue to mix for 2–3 minutes until the mixture starts to come together. Continue to mix for a few minutes to knead the dough until the mixture starts to look smoother.

Hand method: Put the ingredients, except the clarified butter, into a large bowl and stir with a wooden spoon until a rough dough forms. Bring together with your hands, tip onto a lightly floured work surface and knead together until smooth.

2. Take the dough out of the mixer and flatten it slightly, then roll it through the pasta machine on the widest setting (A). Fold one third of the flattened dough over and the third at the other end over the top (B). Roll it four more times on the widest setting, folding it into three each time. If you don't have a pasta machine you can roll the pastry using a rolling pin.

3. Wrap in clingfilm and leave to rest at room temperature for 30 minutes.

MAKE THE BASE OF THE FILLING

This needs to be a good thick consistency so that it holds its shape in the sfogliatelle and doesn't ooze out.

4. Pour the water into a small pan over a high heat. Add the sugar and salt, bring to the boil, then gradually add the semolina, stirring all the time with a wooden spoon to make a smooth mixture. Continue to cook for about 30 seconds, or until very thick.

5. Take the pan off the heat, cover it with clingfilm, sealing the top of the mixture to prevent a skin from forming, and set aside to cool.

SHAPE THE DOUGH

It's easier to roll the dough with someone to help you – one person holds it flat to create tension so it rolls even tighter.

6. Cut the dough in half. Take one half and roll it through the pasta machine several times, starting at the thickest setting and rolling right through to the thinnest. If you're doing this with a rolling pin, roll to about 1mm thick.

Continued…

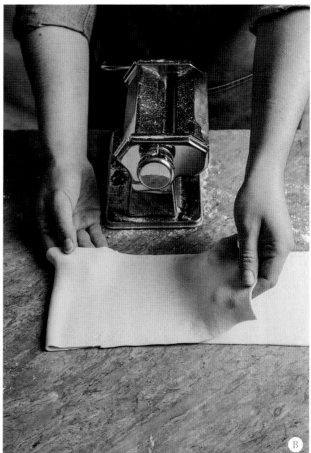

7. Stretch the rolled dough even further by gently pulling it until it's approximately 20–22cm wide and over a metre long – it will be easy to do this as it's soft and stretchy. Brush all over with a layer of clarified butter or lard and roll up from the shortest edge along the length of the dough until you have a thick log shape.

8. Roll out the second piece of dough to about the same size as the first one and brush all over with clarified butter or lard. Place the rolled piece at one end and wrap the flat piece around it. Roll up all the pastry (C) so that you have a log about 6cm wide and 23cm long.

9. Wrap in clingfilm and refrigerate for 1 hour.

FLAVOUR THE FILLING

10. Spoon the cooled semolina mixture into a stand mixer. Beat with the paddle attachment to break up the mixture and soften it. Add the ricotta, egg yolks, vanilla seeds, orange zest and lemon zest and juice. Beat until smooth. Add the sultanas and beat again on a low speed so that they don't break up. You can also do this step by hand with a wooden spoon.

ASSEMBLE THE SFOGLIATELLE

The pastry slices need to be really cold before you shape them. If they start to get warm, put the unshaped ones in the fridge while you make the others.

11. Cut the chilled roll into slices no more than 1.5cm thick.

12. Take one of the slices and gently flatten it between your fingers and thumbs into a flat disc about 1–2mm thick (D). Rub a little clarified butter or lard all over one side with your finger (E).

13. Gently press into the centre of the disc to make a cone shape, about 4–5cm from the point to the flat edge of the opening (F). It should be a rough triangle with a point at one end and a space at the top to spoon the filling into.

14. Spoon about a tablespoon of the filling into the cone so that it fills right to the tip (G), then pinch together the edges to encase the filling (H). Repeat until you've shaped and filled all of the slices (I). Place on the lined baking sheet and chill for at least 20 minutes. Preheat the oven to 190°C/170°C fan/gas mark 5.

15. Bake for 30–35 minutes until golden brown, dust with icing sugar and serve warm.

◆◆◆

CROISSANTS

Golden, flaky crescents that pull apart
to reveal soft layers of dough within

The perfect croissant is the mark of a great pastry chef – each one must have a golden crust and, when broken open, reveal soft honeycomb layers. These are achieved by incorporating a large quantity of butter into the dough using a rolling and folding technique known as the lamination process. Too little butter and the dough will be tough. Care must also be taken not to crush the layers while rolling the dough into the crescent shape that gives the pastry its name.

Patisserie chefs prefer to use what is called a 'dry butter' for the dough. It has a higher fat content (84%) and lower percentage of water than normal butter, thus producing a crisper croissant. It's not as easy to find, so check the label before buying and pick any butter that contains over 82% fat. For this recipe the butter is blended with a small amount of flour to achieve the same properties as a dry butter and produce the crisp layering.

MAKES 14

TIMING

Hands-on time: *1 hour 30 minutes, plus 24 hours*
  resting time and extra chilling time
Cooking time: *15–20 minutes*

PREPARE IN ADVANCE

The rolled, unbaked croissants can be
  prepared up to a day ahead and chilled
  before baking the next day, or frozen for
  up to 1 month and thawed before baking.
The base dough must be made 24 hours ahead.

HAVE READY

Stand mixer, if using, fitted with the dough hook
Baking sheets lined with parchment paper.

EQUIPMENT

stand mixer, optional
  – dough hook
2 baking sheets
parchment paper
digital scales
large bowl and wooden spoon, optional
large sealable freezer bag
clingfilm
rolling pin
ruler
pizza wheel or sharp knife
wire rack

250g strong bread flour,
    plus extra for dusting

100g plain flour

25g caster sugar

5g (1 teaspoon) table salt

8g dried yeast

25g butter, at room temperature

25g eggs (about ½ medium)

55g milk

100g iced water

FOR THE BUTTER
INCLUSION (BEURRAGE)

40g strong bread flour

200g chilled butter (82–84% fat
    content)

FOR THE EGG WASH

50g beaten egg (1 medium)

MAKE THE BASE DOUGH

Once prepared, the base dough is refrigerated for 24 hours to give it time to get a really good rise before the butter is incorporated, which slows down the proving.

1. *Mixer method:* Put the flours into the bowl of the mixer. Add the sugar, salt, yeast, the 25g butter, egg, milk and iced water and mix on a slow speed with the dough hook for 10 minutes. Increase the speed to medium and continue to mix for 10–15 minutes until smooth.

Hand method: Rub the butter into the flours in a large bowl, then add the sugar, salt and yeast. Make a well in the centre of the mixture and add the egg, milk and water. Stir to make a rough dough, then gather up and knead on a lightly floured work surface for 12–15 minutes until smooth.

2. Cover the bowl and leave the dough to rest for 10 minutes, then tip onto a lightly floured work surface, flatten slightly and shape into a rough square. Wrap in a large sealable plastic bag and refrigerate for 24 hours.

LAMINATE THE DOUGH

The lamination process involves folding in butter, then folding and rolling several times until the butter is incorporated in thin, alternating layers with the dough. The process is the same as that used for puff pastry (see page 38). Use short, quick strokes and make sure the butter doesn't break through the dough. Keep the room cool if possible so that the butter doesn't soften and start to leak out.

3. Knead the flour into the butter with a mixer or wooden spoon. Shape it into a block, wrap in clingfilm and chill, ideally overnight, or for at least 30 minutes to harden. At this point you're not creaming the two ingredients together, you're just incorporating the flour into the butter evenly.

4. Lay a large square of clingfilm on a work surface and place the block of butter in the centre. Lay another large piece of clingfilm on top. Beat out and flatten the butter evenly using a rolling pin until it's about 2cm thick. Shape into a 12cm square, then wrap the clingfilm around it and refrigerate again while you roll out the dough.

5. Take the dough out of the bag and place it on a lightly floured work surface. The dough will have risen overnight, so reshape it into a square, then roll it out to a 25cm square that is 1cm thick. Lay the dough with one corner pointing towards you to make a diamond shape. Peel the clingfilm away from the butter and lay the butter in the centre of the dough, with one flat edge towards you so that you have a square of butter inside a pastry diamond.

Continued…

6. Fold the pastry corner furthest from you down over the butter so that the point reaches the middle of the dough. Fold the bottom corner up to the centre, then fold in the sides so that the pastry encases the butter like an envelope. Seal the joins by pressing down with the rolling pin.

7. Using short, quick strokes, roll the pastry into a rectangle measuring 22 x 40cm, or slightly larger, and 1cm thick. Keep the work surface lightly floured, give the dough a quarter turn occasionally so that it doesn't stick, and try not to let any butter escape. You want to end up with the rectangle lying horizontally on the work surface.

8. Starting at one end, fold over one third of the dough, then fold over the third at the opposite end to cover it. Return the dough to the plastic bag and chill in the fridge for 30 minutes.

9. Once the dough is rested, roll it out again to make a rectangle the same dimensions as before, then repeat the folding and chilling process twice more. Refrigerate again for 30 minutes.

CUT OUT AND SHAPE THE CROISSANTS

A small notch is made in the base of the triangle to help the pastry spread out when you roll it up to create the crescent shape.

10. On a clean work surface lightly dusted with flour, roll out the dough to a rectangle about 31 x 41cm and about 6mm thick (A). Use a ruler to trim the edges to a neat 30 x 40cm, then cut down the length to make two long strips of pastry, each measuring 15 x 40cm.

11. Use a pizza wheel or sharp knife and a ruler to cut 14 equal-sized triangles (B). Take a strip of pastry and make tiny notches every 10cm along one long edge. Lay the ruler along the opposite edge and make one notch at 5cm, then notches every 10cm. Cut across the pastry in neat zigzags to join up the notches and cut out the triangles. They should be 10cm wide at the base and 20cm from the point to the base. Repeat with the second strip.

12. Take one triangle and use a sharp knife to make a 1cm cut, at a right angle to the base, halfway along the edge, to stretch and lengthen it slightly. Roll up the triangle from the flat edge to the point, taking care not to damage the layers as you roll (C).

13. Lay the rolled croissant on one of the lined baking sheets with the join underneath, then repeat with the remaining triangles. Cover loosely with clingfilm and leave to prove for about 2 hours until almost doubled in size. About 20 minutes before the croissants look as though they're ready to go in the oven, preheat it to 200°C/180°C fan/gas mark 6.

14. Glaze the croissants with the egg wash (D) and bake for 20 minutes until golden. Remove and transfer to a wire rack to cool.

PAINS AUX RAISINS

Glazed rounds of enriched pastry filled with vanilla-scented crème pâtissière and raisins, topped with slivers of almond

This moist, fruit-filled pastry uses a croissant dough that is rolled out flat, slathered with vanilla crème pâtissière and sprinkled with raisins. The dough is then rolled up tightly and, for a neat finish, pastry chefs pull out the end of the spiral a little and tuck it underneath.

As with croissants, the skill in this recipe lies in the lamination process, ensuring that the butter is properly layered throughout the dough by rolling and folding multiple times.

Note that the raisins must be softened before being baked so that they don't burn or dry up. This is best done overnight in boiling water.

MAKES 16

TIMING

Hands-on time: *1 hour 30 minutes, plus rising and proving time*

Cooking time: *1 hour*

PREPARE IN ADVANCE

Make the dough and roll up the *pains aux raisins* up to a day ahead, then chill before baking the following day.

HAVE READY

Raisins soaked overnight in a bowl of boiling water, then drained.

Stand mixer, if using, fitted with the dough hook

Baking tray lined with clingfilm.

Baking sheets lined with parchment paper.

EQUIPMENT

stand mixer, optional
  – dough hook

baking tray

clingfilm

2 baking sheets

parchment paper

digital scales

large bowl and wooden spoon, optional

large sealable freezer bag

rolling pin

ruler

medium heatproof bowl

medium pan

sieve

sharp knife

balloon whisk

pastry brush

chopping board

wire rack

FOR THE BASE DOUGH

250g strong bread flour,
    plus extra for dusting

100g plain flour

25g caster sugar

5g (1 teaspoon) table salt

8g dried yeast

25g butter, at room temperature

25g eggs (about ½ medium)

55g milk

100g iced water

FOR THE BUTTER INCLUSION

200g chilled butter
    (82–84% fat content)

40g strong bread flour

FOR THE CRÈME PÂTISSIÈRE

60g egg yolks (3 medium)

45g caster sugar

1 teaspoon vanilla extract

24g cornflour

300g milk

1 vanilla pod, split lengthways

60g butter, cut into cubes,
    at room temperature

FOR THE ASSEMBLY

100g raisins, soaked overnight
    in boiling water

2–3 good pinches of ground cinnamon

50g egg, beaten (1 medium)

MAKE THE DOUGH

As with all laminated doughs, fine layers of risen dough are achieved by repeatedly rolling and folding the dough to incorporate the butter.

1. A day ahead, make the dough using the method on page 68 up to the end of step 2. Wrap and chill overnight.
2. The next day, complete the recipe to the end of step 8 by laminating the dough with the butter.

MAKE THE CRÈME PÂTISSIÈRE

3. Make the crème pâtissière using the method on page 26. Spread it onto the baking tray lined with clingfilm and cover it with a second layer of clingfilm to prevent a skin forming. Set aside to cool.

FILL AND BAKE THE PAINS AUX RAISINS

4. Take the dough out of the fridge and roll it out on a lightly dusted work surface to a rectangle measuring about 61 x 31cm, with the long edge nearest you. Trim the edges with a sharp knife so that it measures a neat 60 x 30cm.
5. Unwrap the crème pâtissière and put it into a bowl. Use a balloon whisk to gently beat it until smooth, then spread it over the dough rectangle, leaving a border of about 5cm along the top long edge of the dough, and a smaller border of about 5mm around the other edges.
6. Spoon the drained, soaked raisins evenly over the top, then sprinkle over the cinnamon.
7. Brush the edges with water, then roll up the dough evenly, from the long edge at the bottom towards the top.
8. Transfer the rolled pastry to a chopping board and use a sharp knife to carefully slice 3cm rounds from the dough. Lay them on their sides on the prepared baking sheets and leave to prove for about 1½ hours until nearly doubled in size. Preheat the oven to 200°C/180°C fan/gas mark 6.
9. Bake the *pains aux raisins* for 20 minutes until golden brown, then transfer to a wire rack to cool.

> ### *FINISH IT LIKE A PASTRY CHEF...*
> An Apricot Glaze really enhances both the flavour and final look of the pains aux raisins. Heat *3 tablespoons apricot jam* in a small pan over a low heat. Gently brush the glaze all over the pastries and serve warm.
> Additional equipment: *small pan.*

PAINS AU CHOCOLAT

*Crisp flakes and soft layers of buttery dough
surrounding a bitter dark chocolate centre*

Known as a *chocolatine* in south-western France, this is the rich, dark chocolate cousin of
the simple croissant, shaped by rolling up squares rather than triangles of yeasted dough.
It is another star of the bakery and viennoiserie world, as the skill lies in incorporating the
butter into the base dough to create its light, crisp layers, and in tempering the chocolate
to give it better colour and texture and to stop it melting and running into the dough.

Take care when arranging the chocolate pieces into the folds of dough – they shouldn't
lie directly on top of one other, but rather be spaced apart so that, when you bite into the
pastry, the chocolate is evenly distributed throughout. The perfect pain au chocolat should
look like it has two chocolate-brown eyes peeping out of the baked dough at either end.

MAKES 8

TIMING

Hands-on time: *about 1 hour 30 minutes,*
   plus chilling overnight
Cooking time: *20 minutes*

PREPARE IN ADVANCE

Can be rolled and chilled up to 1 day ahead,
   or frozen and thawed, before baking.

HAVE READY

Make the base dough the day before
   and refrigerate overnight.
Stand mixer, if using, fitted with the dough hook.
Baking sheets lined with parchment paper.

EQUIPMENT

stand mixer, optional
   – dough hook
2 baking sheets
parchment paper
digital scales
large bowl and wooden spoon, optional
large sealable freezer bag
clingfilm
rolling pin
ruler
microwavable or heatproof bowl
microwave, optional
medium pan, optional
digital thermometer
disposable piping bag
sharp knife or pizza wheel
pastry brush
wire rack

FOR THE BASE DOUGH

250g strong bread flour,
plus extra for dusting

100g plain flour

25g caster sugar

5g (1 teaspoon) table salt

8g dried yeast

25g butter, at room temperature

25g eggs (½ medium)

55g milk

100g iced water

FOR THE BUTTER INCLUSION

200g chilled butter
(82–84% fat content)

40g strong bread flour

FOR FINISHING

120g dark chocolate (70% cocoa solids)

50g egg (1 medium), beaten

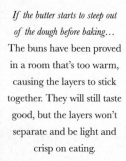

THE SECRETS OF SUCCESS

◆

If the butter starts to steep out of the dough before baking…
The buns have been proved in a room that's too warm, causing the layers to stick together. They will still taste good, but the layers won't separate and be light and crisp on eating.

MAKE THE BASE DOUGH

1. The day before you plan to bake, make the dough following the method on page 68 up to the end of step 2. Wrap and chill overnight.
2. The following day, complete the recipe to the end of step 8.

TEMPER THE CHOCOLATE

Draw 16 straight lines 10cm long on the underside of the parchment, then flip it over and use the lines as a guide when piping the chocolate.

3. Temper the chocolate following the instructions on page 34.
4. Spoon the tempered chocolate into a piping bag and snip off about 3mm from the end. Pipe 16 strips of chocolate onto a piece of parchment paper and leave them to set.

ROLL OUT THE DOUGH AND CUT IT TO SIZE

5. Take the chilled dough out of the fridge and roll it out on a lightly dusted clean work surface to about 41 x 31cm and 6mm thick.
6. Trim the edges of the rectangle to a neat 40 x 30cm. Use a pizza wheel or sharp knife and a ruler to cut down the length to make two long strips, each measuring 40 x 15cm, then cut out four rectangles from each strip measuring 10 x 15cm. You should get 8 rectangles.

FILL AND SHAPE THE PAINS AU CHOCOLAT

Pressing the dough together after you've rolled the pastries keeps them sealed while they bake so that the chocolate doesn't leak out. You can also gently roll the filled pastries again on the work surface to help them plump and shape up. Baking them seam-side down helps to stop them from bursting open.

7. Take a rectangle of dough and place a chocolate baton widthways a third of the way from the short edge of the dough. Fold over the pastry to the middle of the rectangle and put a second chocolate baton on top, a little away from the other stick of chocolate. Fold the other end of the dough over the top and gently press it down to seal.
8. Turn over the dough so that the seam is underneath, then roll it slightly, if you think it needs it, to plump it up. Place on a baking sheet with the sealed edge underneath. Repeat steps 7 and 8 to make 8 pains au chocolat, then set aside to prove for about 1½ hours until the dough has almost doubled in size. Preheat the oven to 200°C/180°C fan/gas mark 6.
9. Brush the pastries with egg wash and bake in the oven for 20 minutes until golden. Remove and cool slightly on a wire rack before serving.

DANISH PINWHEELS
WITH PEACH, ORANGE AND HONEY

*Catherine-wheel pastries filled with peach jam and topped
with syrup-soaked fresh fruit and streaks of white icing*

What other countries know as Danish pastry is known in Denmark as *wienerbrød* (bread from
Vienna), as that is where it originated. Traditionally filled with fruit jams and custard, the
pastries can also be filled with chocolate, fruit, sweet cheeses or nuts, and the dough can be
flavoured with spices such as cinnamon, cardamom and allspice.

The pastry should have multiple layers – 27 being the ideal – an airy texture and be strong
enough to hold the filling without losing its shape. The skill is in ensuring that the butter is
folded and rolled evenly throughout the dough.

In this recipe, the pinwheels are baked with a quick home-made jam, garnished with fresh
peaches macerated in vanilla syrup, and given a final flourish of white icing.

MAKES ABOUT 12

TIMING

Hands-on time: *2 hours 30 minutes,*
  plus resting overnight
Cooking time: *10–15 minutes*

PREPARE IN ADVANCE

The dough for the Danish can be made
  and rolled up to 1 day ahead, chilled
  and baked the following day.

HAVE READY

Stand mixer, if using, fitted with the
  dough hook.
Make the base dough the day before
  and refrigerate overnight.
Baking sheets lined with parchment paper.
Piping bag fitted with the nozzle.

EQUIPMENT

stand mixer, optional
  – dough hook
large bowl and wooden spoon, optional
large sealable freezer bag
clingfilm
rolling pin
ruler
2 baking sheets
parchment paper
piping bag
  – 3mm nozzle
digital scales
small pan
medium bowl
mini food-processor or blender
small bowl
sharp knife
pastry brush
wire rack

FOR THE BASE DOUGH

400g strong bread flour,
    plus extra for dusting

40g caster sugar

8g table salt

10g dried yeast

45g butter, at room temperature

50g egg (1 medium)

160g milk

FOR THE BUTTER INCLUSION

250g chilled butter
    (82–84% fat content)

60g strong bread flour

FOR THE PEACH JAM

125g peach, chopped

35g granulated sugar

juice from 1 orange

1 tablespoon honey

FOR THE ICING

25g water

100g icing sugar

FOR THE EGG WASH

50g egg (1 medium), beaten

FOR THE MACERATED PEACHES AND DECORATING

2–3 fresh peaches, peeled,
    stoned and sliced

25g caster sugar

15g water

3g vanilla extract

125g fresh raspberries, halved

FOR THE GLAZE

50g apricot jam

15g water

MAKE THE BASE DOUGH

The secret to a good Danish is in the lamination – the folding and rolling of the dough to incorporate the butter. The dough must be chilled between each rolling to prevent the butter becoming soft and absorbing into the dough. The ideal temperature is between 15°C and 20°C.

1. The day before you plan to bake, make the dough following the method on page 68, up to the end of step 2. Wrap and chill overnight.
2. The next day, complete the recipe to the end of step 8 by laminating the dough with the butter.

MAKE THE PEACH JAM

The jam needs to be be thick enough so that it sets neatly in the centre of the pinwheel.

3. Put the chopped peach in a small pan over a low heat. Sprinkle over the sugar, then add the orange juice and honey. Heat gently to dissolve the sugar.
4. Bring to a simmer and cook until the mixture becomes jam-like and has thickened. Transfer to a bowl to cool slightly, then blend until smooth. Set aside to cool.

MAKE THE ICING

You need to be able to control the icing when you pipe it later, so make sure you don't add too much water.

5. Mix together the water and icing sugar in a small bowl until combined. It should flow off the spoon steadily but not be too thick or too thin.

SHAPE AND BAKE THE PINWHEELS

While the pinwheel shape looks impressive, it is in fact quite easy to do. The squares of pastry are cut at each corner and alternate triangles of dough are folded over to the centre of the square so that you end up with 4 points and 4 folded pieces that will puff up in the oven.

6. Preheat the oven to 210°C/190°C fan/gas mark 6½.
7. Roll out the dough on a lightly floured work surface until it measures 40 x 30cm and cut into twelve 10cm squares.

8. Take one of the squares and make four 4cm diagonal cuts at each corner (A). Fold alternate points down to the centre of the pastry square (B) to create a pinwheel shape (C), then spoon a little peach jam onto the centre of each one. Repeat with the rest of the squares.

9. Brush the pinwheels all over with egg wash and transfer them to the prepared baking sheet. Bake for 10 minutes until golden and transfer to a wire rack to cool.

MACERATE THE PEACHES

10. Put the peach slices into a medium bowl.

11. Put the sugar, water and vanilla extract into a small pan and heat gently over a low heat so that the sugar dissolves. Spoon the mixture over the peaches.

GLAZE AND DECORATE THE PINWHEELS

12. Heat the apricot jam with the water in a small pan over a medium heat until soft. Gently brush over the pastries, then arrange a peach slice on top of each, followed by the halved raspberries.

13. Finally, spoon the icing into the prepared piping bag and pipe the icing in a zigzag pattern over each pinwheel. Allow to set before serving.

THE SECRETS OF SUCCESS

*If there aren't any layers
to the dough…*
It has been rolled with a
heavy hand and the layers
have been crushed during
this process. Use a lighter
touch next time.

*If the dough hasn't
risen sufficiently…*
The room was too cold
when the dough was proving.
You don't want it to be
too cold or too warm,
and make sure you don't
leave it in a draft.

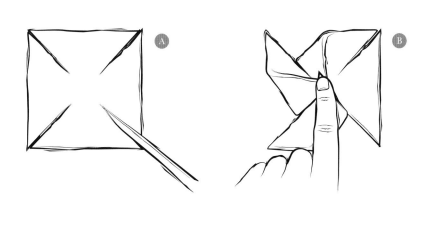

LAYERED SLICES

RASPBERRY AND ROSE
CHOCOLATE SLICES

SAINT MARC

MATCHA GREEN TEA AND
JASMINE DÉLICES

LES PETITS ANTOINES

OPÉRAS AUX FRUITS

FRAMBOISIERS

COCONUT
DACQUOISES

LAYERED SLICES

From the most simple confection, such as the alternating layers of sponge and ganache in the Raspberry and Rose Chocolate Slices (see page 87), to the more complex Coconut Dacquoise, a multi-tiered combination of textures and flavours (see page 117), the layered slice is an exercise in culinary harmony, and the budding pastry chef has much to learn from them.

The skill and secret to a successful slice is that all the components hold themselves individually, and that they are arranged in the right order. The base may consist of a light and airy sponge, or it might be a dacquoise (a fat -free whisked sponge, here made with coconut so that it has more flavour and significantly more texture). The next layer needs to be something firm, as it carries the weight of the others, which are arranged on top. Each recipe therefore becomes slightly lighter as it moves up towards the crowning layer. As long as this is achieved, slicing is easy and neat bars can be cut.

The finished pieces might look challenging, but they're a delight to make. Approach them with patience and precision, taking care to chill the recipe at the various stages, and success will be yours!

RASPBERRY AND ROSE CHOCOLATE SLICES

Layers of raspberry- and rose-flavoured sponge and dark chocolate ganache, topped with a thick chocolate glaze

This elegant chocolate slice consists of several layers of a thin flourless sponge that's soaked with a raspberry and rose syrup and spread with equal layers of dark chocolate ganache. The raspberry syrup is very light so that it soaks into the sponge evenly and provides an all-important subtle fruit flavour to offset the richness of the chocolate and cream.

This sponge doesn't use a traditional raising agent, such as baking powder. Instead, the base is a cold sabayon, made by whisking egg yolks and sugar until they increase in volume and become very mousse-like. Next a meringue is folded in, and finally the mixture is stabilised and flavoured with cornflour and cocoa powder. It's very light and soaks up the syrup, which adds additional moisture and flavour. You'll need two large baking trays in order to spread the sponge out very thinly, but if you have only one, bake one batch first as it cooks quickly and the other will be fine sitting for a short time before going into the oven.

The final flourish to this delicate cake is to top it with a fresh raspberry, dipped in gold dust and placed either in the centre or at one end of each slice.

SERVES 12

TIMING

Hands-on time: *about 2 hours 30 minutes, plus 4 hours freezing and chilling*

Cooking time: *12 minutes*

PREPARE IN ADVANCE

The sponge and syrup can be made a day ahead. Wrap the cake in clingfilm and store the syrup in an airtight container at room temperature.

HAVE READY

Stand mixer, if using, fitted with the whisk attachment.

Baking trays greased and lined with parchment paper.

Oven preheated to 200°C/180°C fan/gas mark 6.

EQUIPMENT

stand mixer, optional
 – whisk attachment
2 baking trays, each 40 x 30cm
parchment paper
digital scales
long sharp knife
chopping board
sieve
heatproof bowl
small pan
wooden spoon or spatula
stick blender

electric hand whisk, optional
large bowl
balloon whisk
large metal spoon
2 wire racks
2 small bowls
ruler
palette knife
jug
digital thermometer
stainless steel frame,
optional

FOR THE RASPBERRY GANACHE

200g dark chocolate (55% cocoa solids), very finely chopped

200g whipping cream

50g raspberries, mashed with a fork and strained

20g invert sugar, or honey, or liquid glucose

25g butter, cut into cubes, at room temperature

FOR THE FLOURLESS SPONGE

150g egg yolks (about 7½ medium)

235g caster sugar

20g invert sugar, or honey, or liquid glucose

190g egg whites (about 6 medium)

35g cornflour, sifted

70g cocoa, sifted

FOR THE RASPBERRY AND ROSE SYRUP

70g raspberries, mashed with a fork and sieved

125g water

50g caster sugar

a few drops of rose essence

FOR THE CHOCOLATE GLAZE AND TO DECORATE

5g powdered gelatine

60g cold water

100g whipping cream

140g caster sugar

45g cocoa, sifted

edible gold powder, for dusting

12 fresh raspberries

MAKE THE RASPBERRY GANACHE

This is the smooth chocolate layer that's used to sandwich the sponges together.

1. Put the chocolate into a heatproof bowl.
2. Pour the cream into a small pan over a high heat. Add the strained raspberry purée and the invert sugar, or honey or glucose, and bring to the boil. Slowly pour this mixture over the chocolate and stir from the centre with a spoon or spatula until the mixture forms a smooth, glossy emulsion.
3. Add the butter cubes to the bowl and use a hand blender to very carefully blend the mixture until smooth, taking care to keep the blade below the surface so that it doesn't incorporate too much air into the mixture.
4. Set aside at room temperature for about 1½ hours to thicken, stirring occasionally to check when it is set and thick enough to spread.

MAKE THE FLOURLESS SPONGE

The first stage here is to make a cold sabayon – a whisked mixture made with egg yolks and sugar, which gives the sponge volume. Then you make a meringue, which is folded into the sabayon mixture along with the cornflour and cocoa powder to create the sponge.

5. Put the egg yolks, 140g of the caster sugar and the invert sugar, or honey or glucose, into the bowl of a stand mixer. Whisk until the mixture is thick and moussey – this will take about 12 minutes. It's important to get as much volume as possible here. You can also do this in a large bowl with an electric hand whisk, but it will take slightly longer – about 15 minutes. This is your sabayon.
6. Now make a meringue. Put the egg whites into a large, spotlessly clean bowl and whisk with an electric hand whisk until the mixture stands in soft peaks. You should be able to hold the bowl over your head without the mixture falling out. Slowly add the remaining 95g caster sugar, one tablespoonful at a time, until the mixture is smooth and glossy and all the sugar has dissolved with the egg whites.
7. Fold a large spoonful of the meringue into the sabayon to loosen the mixture, then fold in the rest of the meringue, along with the sifted cornflour and cocoa.
8. Spoon half the mixture onto each prepared baking tray and use a spatula to gently spread it right to the edge in thin, even layers, each about 40 x 30cm. Bake for 12 minutes, then allow to cool for a few minutes on the trays. They're ready when the tops spring back when you press them very lightly with a finger.
9. Lift the sponges out of the baking trays on the paper and transfer to wire racks to cool completely, leaving the parchment paper on for the time being.

MAKE THE RASPBERRY AND ROSE SYRUP

A flourless sponge requires a drizzle of syrup for moisture. Be sparing with the essence, as rose is a powerful flavour and can easily become overpowering.

10. Put all the ingredients for the syrup except the rose essence, into a small pan and slowly bring to the boil, stirring until the sugar dissolves.
11. Simmer for 2–3 minutes to make a thin syrup, then add a few drops of rose essence. Taste it to make sure you're happy with the flavour and add more essence if necessary, then strain through a sieve into a small bowl. Set aside to cool.

ASSEMBLE THE LAYERS

The assembled cake is frozen to firm up the fragile layers to make it easier to cut, and for the warm glaze to set evenly and quickly on top.

12. Turn one of the sponges onto a chopping board and carefully peel away the parchment paper. Cut the sponge in half widthways to make two sheets of sponge, each measuring about 30 x 20cm. Do the same with the second sponge.
13. Drizzle about a quarter of the syrup all over the top of one of the sponges and spoon over a third of the ganache, spreading it out to an even, flat layer with a palette knife. Place a second layer of sponge over the top. Repeat until all the sponge and ganache layers are in place. Press down gently to firm them up and make sure they are even. Drizzle a very fine layer of syrup over the top slice. Scrape the remnants of ganache from the bowl and spread thinly over the top to fill any holes.
14. Transfer the cake to the freezer for 4 hours.

MAKE THE GLAZE

Timing is important here, as you need to mix and heat the ingredients to 106°C, then cool the mixture to 40°C, at which point it's ready to use.

15. Half an hour before the cake is ready to come out of the freezer, make the glaze. Put the gelatine in a small bowl with 25g of the water. Set aside to allow the gelatine to absorb the water.
16. Put the cream, caster sugar and 35g water into a small pan and heat gently to dissolve the sugar. Bring to the boil and heat the mixture to 106°C. Stir in the cocoa powder and gelatine, then take off the heat and stir well to dissolve the gelatine.
17. Strain the mixture through a sieve into a jug. Set aside until the glaze has cooled to 40°C.

Continued…

GLAZE AND SLICE THE CAKES

To trim and slice the cake you need a hot, sharp knife that will easily cut through the sponge and ganache layers. Don't allow the knife to cool down or it might drag and cause the cake to collapse. Continue to run it under hot water whenever you need to, drying it before cutting the next slice.

18. Set a wire rack over a tray and place the cold cake on it. Lift up one end of the rack so that the cake is at an angle and pour over the glaze, letting it run down evenly and tipping the rack as needed for a smooth all-over finish. Rest it back on the tray, then chill for 5 minutes to set the glaze.
19. Transfer the cake to a board. Run a long sharp knife under hot running water, dry it well, then use it, along with a ruler or stainless steel frame, to trim the edges of the cake to make a rectangle measuring about 28 x 18cm. Discard the trimmings, or save them for nibbling with a cup of tea. Dust the top with gold powder.
20. Now slice the cake through the middle to get two long rectangles measuring 28 x 9cm. Cut each one into 6 rectangles, each measuring 9 x 4.5cm, making sure the knife stays hot.
21. Sprinkle a little gold powder over each raspberry before placing it on a slice, and serve.

———◆ ◆ ◆———

SAINT MARC

*Soft layers of almond-rich chocolate and vanilla joconde sponge
with a brûléed top, encasing smooth chocolate and vanilla mousses*

These classic French layered slices looks very impressive, but the process is, in fact, fairly straightforward. Once you've made each component part, carefully cut out the sponges using a frame, then layer up the individual elements, chilling the slices at certain stages.

A good frame is worth the investment. Pastry chefs prefer them for a neater, more precise finish to layered slices and desserts. One decent-sized frame will be most versatile because you can cut and trim the baked sponges into whatever size and shape you need.

If you've never attempted to make a layered slice before, this is a good recipe to start with. If you want to experiment at a later stage, introduce another layer of chocolate joconde sponge after chilling the chocolate mousse.

SERVES 12

TIMING

Hands-on time: *1 hour 50 minutes,*
  plus at least 6 hours 30 minutes chilling
Cooking time: *40 minutes*

PREPARE IN ADVANCE

The sponges can be made up to 1 day
  ahead and wrapped in clingfilm.

HAVE READY

Stand mixer, if using, fitted with the
  whisk attachment.
Baking tray lined with parchment
  paper.
Oven preheated to 220°C/200°C fan/
  gas mark 7.

EQUIPMENT

stand mixer, optional
  – whisk attachment
large baking tray
parchment paper
digital scales
2 medium bowls
large metal spoon or spatula
balloon whisk
wire rack
heatproof bowl
medium pan
electric hand whisk, optional
digital thermometer
1 or 2 large bowls
chopping board
28 x 18cm stainless steel frame
pastry brush
small bowl
palette knife, optional
small pan
long sharp knife
sieve
blowtorch, optional
ruler

FOR THE CHOCOLATE JOCONDE SPONGE

145g (about 5 medium) egg whites,
    measured into 2 separate bowls
    of 80g and 65g
50g icing sugar
50g ground almonds
25g plain flour
25g cocoa powder
25g caster sugar
25g butter, melted and cooled
    (but not set)

FOR THE VANILLA JOCONDE SPONGE

145g (about 5 medium) egg whites,
    measured into 2 separate bowls
    of 80g and 65g
50g icing sugar
50g ground almonds
50g plain flour
seeds from ½ vanilla pod
25g caster sugar
25g butter, melted and cooled
    (but not set)

FOR THE SUGAR SYRUP

70g almond-flavoured liqueur
30g water
30g caster sugar

FOR THE CHOCOLATE MOUSSE

100g dark chocolate (about 80%
    cocoa solids), finely chopped
45g caster sugar
20g egg yolk (1 medium)
50g egg, beaten (1 medium)
200g whipping cream

MAKE THE CHOCOLATE JOCONDE SPONGE

A joconde is a sponge cake made with almonds, which contain lots of fat. This gives the cake moisture and good structure.

1. Put the 80g egg whites into a medium bowl. Stir in the icing sugar, ground almonds, flour and cocoa powder and mix well until everything is combined and the mixture looks like a paste.
2. In a separate, spotlessly clean bowl, whisk the remaining 65g egg whites to soft peaks. Whisk in the sugar, a teaspoon at a time, to make a smooth and glossy meringue.
3. Fold a spoonful of the meringue mixture into the paste to loosen it. Fold in the remaining meringue and gently mix together. Fold in the butter.
4. Using a spatula, spread out the sponge thinly on the prepared baking tray to a rectangle about 30 x 20cm. Bake for 8–10 minutes, until the sponge feels firm to the touch. Lift the sponge onto a wire rack and leave to cool. Reline the baking tray with fresh parchment paper.

MAKE THE VANILLA JOCONDE SPONGE

5. Follow the method for the chocolate joconde sponge above to make the vanilla sponge, stirring in the vanilla seeds in place of the cocoa. Bake at the same temperature for 8–10 minutes then transfer to a wire rack to cool. Reline the baking tray with parchment paper.

MAKE THE SUGAR SYRUP

6. Stir together all the ingredients for the sugar syrup and set aside for about 10 minutes for the sugar to dissolve, stirring from time to time.

MAKE THE CHOCOLATE MOUSSE

7. Put the finely chopped chocolate into a heatproof bowl and set it over a pan of simmering water, making sure the base of the bowl doesn't touch the water. Allow to melt, then set aside to cool.
8. Place the bowl of the stand mixer over the pan of just-simmering water, making sure the base doesn't touch the water. Add the sugar, yolks and eggs to the bowl and cook for about 10 minutes, whisking continuously, until the mixture reaches 65°C.
9. Transfer the bowl to the mixer and whisk for about 5 minutes, until the mixture looks thick and moussey. Alternatively do this in a large bowl with an electric hand whisk. It will take about 10 minutes.
10. In a separate large bowl, whip the cream until it's thick and moussey.
11. Fold the warm egg mixture into the melted chocolate along with the whipped cream and mix until smooth.

START TO BUILD THE LAYERS

The chocolate sponge layer forms the base of the cake. Try to keep each layer perfectly flat and even.

12. Put the chocolate sponge on a clean chopping board, lay the frame on top and use it to cut the sponge so that it fits neatly inside. Remove the chocolate sponge and repeat with the vanilla sponge.

13. Put the frame onto the chopping board and lay the chocolate sponge into it (A, overleaf). Brush half the syrup over the top, then spoon the mousse on top. Level the surface with a palette knife or spatula (B, overleaf) and chill for 30 minutes to firm up the layers.

MAKE THE VANILLA CREAM

A small quantity of gelatine sets the cream so that it will hold its shape as an independent layer.

14. Put the gelatine into a small bowl with 20g water and set aside to allow the gelatine to absorb the water.

15. Heat 75ml of the cream in a pan until just warm, then stir it into the hydrated gelatine along with the liqueur.

16. Put the remaining cream, icing sugar and vanilla seeds into a medium bowl and whip until just thick. Whisk in the gelatine mixture.

FINISH BUILDING THE LAYERS

17. Spoon the vanilla cream onto the chocolate mousse and level the surface with a spatula or palette knife. Chill for 30 minutes.

18. Lay the vanilla sponge on top of the mousse, then brush with the syrup. Chill for at least 6 hours, or overnight.

MAKE THE CLEAR GLAZE

The liquid glucose stops the sugar from crystallising, so it is important for creating a clear glaze. The pectin and citric acid firm it up, and the acid also acts as a preservative.

19. Put the water and liquid glucose into a small pan and place over a medium heat. Stir together and heat until the temperature reaches 40°C.

20. In a small bowl, mix together the sugar and pectin, then add to the pan. Bring to a simmer and cook for 1 minute, then stir in the citric acid and cook for a further minute.

Continued…

FOR THE VANILLA CREAM

4g powdered gelatine

20g cold water

250ml whipping cream

15g almond-flavoured liqueur

25g icing sugar

seeds from ½ vanilla pod

FOR THE CLEAR GLAZE

100g water

70g liquid glucose

65g caster sugar

2.5g powdered fruit pectin

0.5g citric acid

FOR THE BRÛLÉED TOP

50g icing sugar

BRÛLÉE THE TOP OF THE CAKE

The top of the cake has a *brûléed* (burnt) effect that is achieved by dusting it with icing sugar, then using the base of a smoking hot pan to scorch and caramelise it. You will probably need to reapply heat to keep the pan hot enough to *brûlée* the whole of the top. You want it to be a golden colour and not burnt to dark brown or black.

21. Lift the frame with the sponge onto a clean board. Slide a sharp knife down the insides of the frame to loosen the edges, then remove the frame. Dust the top with the icing sugar (C).

22. Heat the base of a pan by putting it over a very high heat or by using a blow torch, until piping hot. Set the base of the pan down flat on top of the sponge – the sugar will caramelise underneath the pan (D). Don't leave the pan down for too long or the sugar will burn – lift it up after 1–2 seconds and move to the next section of the cake. Continue until the whole top is caramelised to an even colour.

23. Brush the glaze over the *brûléed* sugar and leave it to set.

CUT THE SLICES

24. Trim the sides until the cake measures about 27 x 17cm. Carefully cut it in half lengthways, then cut each rectangle into 6 slices, each measuring 8.5 x 4.5cm.

FINISH IT LIKE A PASTRY CHEF

Spun Sugar Balls are an elegant decoration for these sophisticated slices and perfectly complement their golden tops.

Follow the instructions on page 266 to make the spun sugar, then form it into small balls and use it to decorate one end of each layered slice before serving.

Additional equipment: *long-handled spoon, cut-out whisk or fork.*

MATCHA GREEN TEA AND JASMINE DÉLICES

Tea-infused slices with matcha green tea and jasmine white chocolate mousses sitting on a soft almond and matcha sponge base

A *délice* is another name for a layered slice that has a dense joconde sponge base topped with a smooth, light ganache or mousse filling.

Joconde is a traditional patisserie sponge made with ground almonds, which provide structure and moisture due to their high fat content. The finished sponge has a soft texture that complements the mousse layers and cuts cleanly when you're creating the *délice* slices.

Layered slices give pastry chefs the opportunity to experiment with different flavour and texture combinations. The green tea-flavoured joconde in this slice is topped with two different mousses, each made from a combination of white chocolate and cream, and set with gelatine. One is flavoured with earthy matcha green tea, the other with floral jasmine, to create a delightful afternoon tea dessert.

SERVES 12

◆ ◆ ◆

TIMING

Hands-on time: *1 hour 30 minutes*

Cooking time: *50 minutes*

PREPARE IN ADVANCE

The sponge can be made up
   to 1–2 days ahead, or frozen,
   well wrapped in clingfilm,
   for up to 1 month

HAVE READY

Stand mixer if using, fitted with
   the whisk attachment.
Baking trays lined with parchment
   paper.
Oven preheated to 200°C/
   180°C fan/gas mark 6.

EQUIPMENT

stand mixer, optional
   – whisk attachment
2 baking sheets
parchment paper
digital scales
balloon whisk
large bowl
electric hand whisk, optional
large metal spoon
ruler
spatula
2 small bowls

large pan and heatproof bowl
   or microwave and
   microwavable bowl
microwave, optional
digital thermometer
small pan
28 x 18cm stainless steel frame
long sharp knife
palette knife
large chopping board
tea strainer

150g ground almonds

40g plain flour

170g caster sugar

200g eggs (4 medium), beaten

30g butter, melted

5g (2 teaspoons) matcha
   green tea powder

140g egg whites (4–5 medium)

FOR THE GREEN
TEA MOUSSE

4g powdered gelatine

20g cold water

60g egg yolks (3 medium)

25g caster sugar

85g white chocolate, chopped

25g white wine

2g (scant ½ teaspoon) matcha
   green tea powder

250g whipping cream,
   whipped and chilled

FOR THE JASMINE
MOUSSE

6g powdered gelatine

30g cold water

125g white chocolate, chopped

3g jasmine tea

50g milk

200g whipping cream,
   whipped and chilled

FOR THE DECORATION

50g *nappage* (clear gel glaze, see
   page 15)

MAKE THE GREEN TEA JOCONDE SPONGE LAYER

The aim here is to create a thin layer of sponge that is firm enough to hold the mousse above.

1. Put the ground almonds into a large bowl with the flour and 100g of the caster sugar and mix together. Stir in the beaten eggs and whisk well by hand to form a batter. It should be smooth and without any lumps. Whisk in the butter and green tea powder.

2. Put the egg whites into a spotlessly clean bowl with the remaining 70g sugar and whisk until stiff peaks form. Fold the whisked mixture into the batter until combined, taking care not to knock out too much of the air.

3. Spread the mixture onto the prepared baking sheet, into a rectangle measuring about 30 x 20cm square. Use a spatula to spread the mixture into an even layer. It will be about 3–5mm thick. Bake for 12–15 minutes until golden.

MAKE THE MATCHA GREEN TEA MOUSSE

The base of the mousse is a sabayon. See page 22 for detailed instructions about how to make one.

4. First put the gelatine into a small bowl with the water. Set aside to allow the gelatine to absorb the water.

5. Put 5cm water into a large pan over a low heat and place a heatproof bowl on top. Add the egg yolks and sugar and whisk until the mixture reaches 78°C. Take the bowl off the heat. This is the sabayon base.

6. Melt the white chocolate using the instructions on page 34.

7. Warm the wine in a very small pan and stir in the gelatine to melt it.

8. Fold the green tea powder into the sabayon, followed by the wine, then fold the mixture into the melted white chocolate.

9. Finally, fold in a spoonful of the whipped cream to loosen the mixture, then fold in the rest of the whipped cream.

START BUILDING THE DÉLICE LAYERS

10. Lay the frame on top of the joconde sponge and run a sharp knife inside the edges to cut the sponge to size, removing the trimmings. Place the frame on the prepared baking sheet and lay the sponge into it to make the base of the cake. Pour the green tea mousse over the top of the sponge and level it using a palette knife. Transfer to the fridge to set for 20 minutes while you make the jasmine mousse.

MAKE THE JASMINE TEA MOUSSE

The chocolate mixture must be cooled to 35°C before you add the whipped cream, or the cream will melt.

11. Put the gelatine in a small bowl with the water. Set aside to allow the gelatine to absorb the water.

12. Put the chocolate into a microwavable bowl and melt it in the microwave on high in 30-second bursts, shaking the bowl after each one, until it is half melted.

13. Put the jasmine tea into a small bowl. Pour the milk into a small pan over a high heat and bring to the boil. Pour the hot milk over the tea and leave to infuse for 3 minutes.

14. Strain the tea-infused milk into a medium bowl and add the gelatine, then slowly pour the mixture into the white chocolate, in batches, stirring from the middle until the mixture forms a smooth emulsion. If there are some bits of chopped chocolate still remaining in the mixture, put the bowl in the microwave and melt on low in short bursts, stirring well between each one.

15. Allow the mixture to cool to 35°C, then fold in the cold whipped cream.

16. Take the set layers out of the fridge and pour over the jasmine tea mousse. Return to the fridge or freezer to set for a couple of hours.

DECORATE AND CUT THE SLICES

The cake is glazed with *nappage*, a thick, clear gel glaze (see page 15). The knife used for cutting it should be hot so that it slices through easily without the cake collapsing. Don't allow the knife to cool down – run it under hot water whenever you need to.

17. Put about 50g of *nappage* and a little green tea powder in a small bowl and mix together. Use a palette knife to spread it out thinly on a flat surface, such as a marble slab, then use the same knife to gently drag the mixture across the top of the cake to create a marbled effect. Finish with a smooth layer of clear gel.

18. Place the cake on the chopping board. Run a long sharp knife under hot running water and dry it well, then use it to slide down the side of the frame to release the cake. Remove the frame and trim the edges by 5mm all the way round to neaten it.

19. Now carefully slice the cake lengthways down the middle so that you have 2 long rectangles. Cut each one into 8 equal rectangles measuring 8.5 x 3.5cm and serve.

THE SECRETS OF SUCCESS

◆

If the cake doesn't slice cleanly and the mousses have sunk into each other... The individual mousse layers haven't chilled thoroughly and the gelatine hasn't set properly, so the mousses lack a distinct line between them. Ensure that each layer is completely set before adding the next.

LES PETITS ANTOINES

A chocoholic's dream – croquantine, dacquoise and mousse combine in this chocolate-rich confection

The celebrated French patisserie chef Stéphane Glacier created and named this thoroughly modern layered slice. This variation on his recipe features a hazelnut and wafer base called a *croquantine*, rich chocolate mousse, a nutty layer of *dacquoise* and light milk chocolate Chantilly cream. It is crowned with a fine bar of tempered dark chocolate, which sits like a roof on top of the Chantilly cream.

The *croquantine* layer includes only three ingredients – dark melted chocolate, a praline paste and *feuilletine*, which are made by crushing good-quality wafers into small, fine pieces. Both the praline paste and *feuilletine* can be made from scratch, but professional chefs buy them in as they need large quantities. You can find them easily online.

The challenge for this recipe is in the precision. Make sure you don't overwhip the chocolate Chantilly or the mixture will split and you won't be able to pipe small, neat domes. Similarly, they need to line up perfectly to achieve symmetry as they are the penultimate decoration before the gold-brushed bar of chocolate.

SERVES 14

◆ ◆ ◆

TIMING

Hands-on time: *3 hours 15 minutes, plus chilling*
Cooking time: *12 minutes*

PREPARE IN ADVANCE

The recipe can be made and semi-assembled up to the end of step 11, up to 1 day ahead. Store in the fridge.
The chocolate decoration can also be made 1 day ahead.

HAVE READY

Stand mixer, if using, fitted with the whisk attachment.
Baking tray lined with baking parchment.
Oven preheated to 200°C/180°C fan/gas mark 6.
Piping bag fitted with the nozzle.

EQUIPMENT

stand mixer
  – whisk attachment
baking tray
parchment paper
piping bag
  – 1cm plain nozzle
digital scales
long sharp knife
chopping board
2 large bowls
balloon whisk or electric hand whisk, optional
sieve
large metal spoon or spatula
ruler
wire rack
28 x 18cm stainless steel frame
microwave and microwavable bowl or medium pan and heatproof bowl

microwave, optional
digital thermometer
small pan
palette knife
A4 sheet of acetate
pastry brush

FOR THE DACQUOISE

110g egg whites (about 4 medium)

35g caster sugar

8g cocoa powder

90g icing sugar

45g ground almonds

45g ground hazelnuts

FOR THE CROQUANTINE

25g dark chocolate (70% cocoa solids),
    finely chopped

65g praline paste

65g feuilletine

FOR THE MILK CHOCOLATE CHANTILLY CREAM

100g milk chocolate,
    very finely chopped

250g whipping cream

FOR THE DARK CHOCOLATE MOUSSE

60g egg yolks (3 medium)

30g caster sugar

200g dark chocolate (70% cocoa solids),
    finely chopped

300g whipping cream

FOR THE CHOCOLATE DECORATION

115g dark chocolate (70% cocoa solids)

edible gold lustre

MAKE THE DACQUOISE LAYER

This layer is rich in both finely ground almonds and hazelnuts and provides that all-important texture to the finished patisserie, alongside the mousse and croquantine.

Any excess sponge can be stored in an airtight container for nibbling – chef's perk! – or chop it finely and sprinkle it over vanilla ice cream.

1. Put the egg whites in a large bowl or the bowl of a stand mixer and whisk until the mixture stands in stiff peaks, but isn't dry. Slowly add the caster sugar, a spoonful at a time, continuing to whisk until the mixture is thick and glossy.

2. Sift over the cocoa and icing sugar, then scatter over the ground nuts. Gently fold all the ingredients together until combined.

3. Spoon the mixture onto the prepared baking tray and spread it out to about 30 x 20cm. Level the surface with a spatula and bake for 12–15 minutes, until the cake feels firm when pressed lightly. Slide the sponge, still on the parchment paper, onto a wire rack to cool.

4. Once cool, slide the sponge onto a chopping board. Put the frame on top and slide a sharp knife down inside it to cut the sponge. Remove the excess sponge and reline the cooled baking tray with parchment paper.

MAKE THE CROQUANTINE

This forms the base layer of the slice. It is made by combining dark chocolate with hazelnut praline and flaky feuilletine and makes a rich, crispy layer.

5. Melt the dark chocolate using the instructions on page 34, making sure the temperature doesn't rise any higher than 45°C. Stir in the praline paste and feuilletine and mix well.

6. Set the frame on the parchment paper and spoon the croquantine into it. Use a small palette knife or the back of a spoon to ease it out and over the parchment to the edges of the frame. It will be a very thin layer, so just keep pressing it out until it covers it. Transfer to the fridge to chill while you make the other elements for the slice.

MAKE THE CHOCOLATE CHANTILLY CREAM

It's important to chill the mixture thoroughly before whipping it up, otherwise it will be too warm and won't produce the same effect.

7. Meanwhile, melt the milk chocolate as before.

8. Put the cream into a small pan over a medium heat and bring just to the boil. Pour it over the hot chocolate and stir gently to combine. Allow to cool, then cover and chill until completely cold.

MAKE THE DARK CHOCOLATE MOUSSE

It is important to get as much volume as possible when whisking the egg yolks and sugar together, as the mixture – called a *pâte à bombe* in the trade – forms the base of the mousse. It is also used for other mousse desserts.

9. Place the egg yolks and sugar in a bowl set over a pan of simmering water and whisk with a balloon whisk until the temperature reaches 60°C and the mixture leaves a trail when the whisk is lifted.
10. Melt the chocolate using the method on page 34, making sure the temperature doesn't rise any higher than 45°C, then set aside while you whip the cream.
11. Whip the cream in a large bowl until it forms soft peaks. Fold half the cream into the slightly cooled melted chocolate, then fold in the egg yolk mixture, followed by the remaining cream. Pour this mousse over the sponge and croquantine base and leave to set.

START TO ASSEMBLE THE LAYERS

A stainless steel frame is essential here, as is chilling the patisserie at every stage to firm up the different layers.

12. Once the mousse has chilled, take it out of the fridge along with the frame and spread a thin even layer of mousse over the chilled croquantine using a palette knife. You won't need to use it all.
13. Flip over the dacquoise and carefully peel off the parchment paper. Lay it into the frame onto the chocolate mousse, patting it in to fit snugly and make it level. Spread the remainder of the chocolate mousse evenly over the top. Chill to firm up while you prepare the ingredients for the next layers.

MAKE THE CHOCOLATE DECORATION

A simple bar made from tempered dark chocolate sits on top of the milk chocolate crème Chantilly domes.

14. Temper the dark chocolate following the instructions on page 34.
15. Lay the acetate sheet on a board and pour over the chocolate, spreading it thinly, to about 2mm, with a palette knife. While semi-set, use a sharp knife and a ruler to score the chocolate into 12 rectangles, each measuring 8.5 x 3.5cm, and leave to set at room temperature.
16. When the chocolate is fully set, carefully break it along the scored lines. Lift the rectangles off the acetate as and when needed. Brush the tops with edible gold lustre.

Continued…

ASSEMBLE THE FINAL LAYERS

The chocolate Chantilly must be piped evenly, not only to give a neat and even finish, but also to ensure the chocolate bars lie perfectly level on top of each slice.

17. Slide a hot, dry palette knife down inside the frame and lift it away from the layered chocolate cake. Slide the cake, on its paper, onto a large chopping board.

18. Trim the edges of the cake to neaten with a hot, dry, sharp knife, then slice into 14 bars, each measuring 8.5 x 3.5cm. The lining paper will easily fall away from each slice.

19. Whip the milk chocolate Chantilly to stiff peaks, then spoon it into the piping bag and pipe 10 neat, even domes onto each bar.

20. Place a chocolate bar on top of each slice and serve.

◆ ◆ ◆

OPÉRAS AUX FRUITS

A twist on the classic gâteau opéra featuring a pistachio joconde, cherry-rich buttercream and decadent dark chocolate ganache

This classic gateau is traditionally flavoured with coffee. The challenge here is to replace the coffee with a fruit that won't overpower the chocolate, but sit alongside and complement it. Similarly, the chocolate itself should not be so dark as to obscure the flavours of the fruit.

The finishing touches mirror the delights within. A star of pistachio Chantilly cream, a scattering of crunchy pistachios and a succulent Griottine® cherry sit on top of the shiny chocolate glaze.

If you can't get hold of pistachio paste, chop the pistachios until they're very fine, then grind to a paste using a mortar and pestle.

SERVES 14

TIMING

Hands-on time: *1 hour 45 minutes*
Cooking time: *10 minutes*

PREPARE IN ADVANCE

Both the sponge and glaze can be made
    up to 1 day ahead. Store the sponge
    wrapped in clingfilm and the glaze
    in an airtight container at cool
    room temperature, bringing it up
    to temperature before using.

HAVE READY

Stand mixer, if using, fitted with
    the whisk attachment.
Baking sheets lined with parchment paper.
Oven preheated to 200°C/180°C fan/
    gas mark 6.
Piping bag fitted with the star nozzle.

EQUIPMENT

stand mixer
    – whisk attachment
2 baking sheets
parchment paper
piping bag
    – 1cm star nozzle
digital scales
long sharp knife
chopping board
small pan
medium bowl
balloon whisk
electric hand whisk, optional
large metal spoon or spatula
palette knife
ruler
digital thermometer
large bowl
28 x 18cm stainless steel frame
pastry brush
medium pan
small bowl

MAKE THE PISTACHIO SYRUP

1. Put the sugar and water into a small pan over a medium heat and bring to the boil. Simmer for 1–2 minutes until the sugar dissolves and makes a syrup. Remove from the heat and stir in the pistachio paste. Set aside to cool.

MAKE THE PISTACHIO JOCONDE

This is made like a normal joconde sponge, with the addition of pistachio paste rather than additional almonds.

2. Put the 80g of caster sugar into a medium bowl with the ground almonds, plain flour, pistachio paste and egg. Whisk well to a smooth paste with the consistency of batter.
3. Whisk the egg whites in a large, spotlessly clean bowl with an electric hand whisk or in a stand mixer until they form stiff peaks, but aren't dry. Slowly add the 55g of sugar, one tablespoon at a time, and continue to whisk into a stiff and glossy meringue.
4. Fold the melted butter into the batter mixture and mix well, then fold in a spoonful of the meringue to loosen the mixture. Fold in the remaining meringue mixture to combine.
5. Divide evenly between the two prepared baking sheets and spread out with a palette knife until each measures 30 x 40cm. Bake for 8–10 minutes, until evenly baked.

MAKE THE CHERRY BUTTERCREAM

6. Put the sugar, liquid glucose and water into a small pan and heat gently to dissolve the sugar. Bring to the boil and cook until the mixture reaches 121°C. However, as soon as the temperature hits 116°C, start to whisk the eggs and egg yolk together. When the syrup has reached the correct temperature, slowly pour the syrup into the egg mixture at the edge of the bowl and whisk until thick and moussey. Continue to whisk until slightly cooled, then slowly add the cubed butter, piece by piece, to make a buttercream.
7. Continue to whisk until cool. Fold in the cherry purée, chopped cherries and kirsch.

Continued…

FOR THE PISTACHIO SYRUP
95g caster sugar
65g water
15g pistachio paste

FOR THE PISTACHIO JOCONDE
80g + 55g caster sugar, weighed
   separately
120g ground almonds
30g plain flour
50g pistachio paste
155g eggs (about 3 medium)
105g egg whites (3½ medium)
25g butter, melted

FOR THE CHERRY BUTTERCREAM
150g caster sugar
15g liquid glucose
35g water
35g egg (about ⅔ medium)
35g egg yolks (about 1½ medium)
200g butter, cubed
25g fresh or tinned cherries, puréed
100g Griottine® cherries, chopped
7g kirsch, from the jar of cherries

FOR THE DARK CHOCOLATE GANACHE
125g double cream
20g invert sugar, honey or glucose
125g dark chocolate (about 68%
   cocoa solids), finely chopped
Continued

FOR THE DARK CHOCOLATE GLAZE

2g powdered gelatine

65g cold water

105g caster sugar

35g cocoa powder

35g double cream

25g dark chocolate (about 68% cocoa solids), finely chopped

FOR THE PISTACHIO CHANTILLY CREAM

20g mascarpone

7g icing sugar

100g double cream

¼ vanilla pod, split lengthways

10g pistachio paste

FOR THE DECORATION

15g pistachios, finely chopped

12–14 Griottine® cherries

ASSEMBLE THE FIRST LAYERS

You will need to cut four rectangles from the sponge sheets. Use the frame as a template to make sure they're all the same size and fit snugly inside the frame when you build up the layers.

8. Lay the frame on top of one of the sponges and slide a sharp knife inside the frame edges to cut out a rectangle. Move the frame over and cut out a second rectangle. Remove the trimmings and slide a palette knife underneath each layer to loosen it from the paper. Repeat with the second joconde sheet and set aside.

9. Lay a clean piece of parchment paper on a baking sheet and put the frame on top. Lay one of the joconde layers into it to make the base of the cake. Brush about a quarter of the syrup over the top.

10. Spoon half the buttercream onto the sponge and spread it out evenly with a palette knife. Put the next joconde layer on top, brush again with a quarter of the syrup, then transfer to the fridge to chill and firm up while you make the chocolate ganache.

MAKE THE DARK CHOCOLATE GANACHE

When you spread the ganache over the sponge layers, make sure the top is spread evenly to give level finished slices.

11. Pour the double cream and invert sugar, or honey or glucose, into a medium pan and bring to the boil.

12. Put the chocolate in a medium bowl and pour the hot cream mixture onto it. Mix well, stirring from the middle to the outside until the mixture is smooth and glossy.

13. Spoon the ganache onto the joconde sponge and smooth it over with a palette knife. Slide the palette knife under a third joconde layer and carefully place it in the frame. Brush with more syrup.

14. Spoon the remaining buttercream on top and smooth it over. Lay the last piece of joconde sponge on top of the buttercream and brush it with the last of the syrup. Chill the cake while you make the dark chocolate glaze.

FOR THE DARK CHOCOLATE GLAZE

15. Place the gelatine in a small bowl with 10g of the water. Set aside to allow the gelatine to absorb the water.

16. Put the sugar, the remaining 55g of water, cocoa powder and cream into a small pan over a medium heat. Put the chocolate into a bowl. Bring the sugar mixture to the boil, then pour it on top of the chocolate and

mix well, stirring from the middle outwards until the mixture is smooth. Stir in the soaked gelatine, making sure it has all dissolved. Allow to cool to 44°C before using.

17. Pour the cooled glaze onto the joconde in the frame and smooth it with a clean palette knife, if necessary. Transfer to the fridge to chill and set for 30 minutes while you make the decoration.

TO MAKE THE PISTACHIO CHANTILLY

Be careful not to overwhip the cream or it will look as if it's split and won't produce a smooth star shape.

18. Beat the mascarpone and icing sugar together in a bowl until smooth, then slowly fold in the cream. Add the pistachio paste and vanilla seeds and whisk together quickly until it's thick enough to pipe, taking care not to overwhip. Spoon the mixture into the piping bag.

COMPLETE THE LAYERS

Patissiers always use the best-quality ingredients, so try to find Griottines® cherries, which are Morellos macerated in eau de vie or kirsch.

19. Take the gateaux out of the fridge. Slide a hot, dry palette knife down the edge of the frame and remove it. Trim the edges to neaten them and cut the cake in half lengthways. Cut each rectangle into 8.5 x 3.5cm bars. You should get 14 slices, with a little excess.

20. Pipe a star of Chantilly cream at one end of each slice, place a Griottine® cherry next to it and sprinkle with chopped pistachios.

FINISH IT LIKE A PASTRY CHEF

For extra pizzazz you could decorate the cherry with a little *gold leaf*. A pair of wooden tweezers is useful for handling this delicate substance.

FRAMBOISIERS

Layers of raspberry and yogurt mousse on a crisp pistachio joconde base with sweet raspberry jelly

Framboisier, meaning literally 'raspberry bush', comes in many forms, but the red berry fruit is a constant. Here the slices have a pistachio joconde base sandwiched together with a rich berry jelly, and topped with a Greek yogurt mousse followed by a raspberry mousse.

The layers are light, soft and summery to match the season in which raspberries are grown. Again, as with other slices, uniformity, consistency and precision are essential to get even layers. Each flavour should also harmonise with the others so that nothing overpowers the delicate taste of raspberries.

SERVES 12–14

TIMING

Hands-on time: *1 hour 45 minutes*

Cooking time: *20 minutes*

PREPARE IN ADVANCE

The chocolate garnish can be made and stored
in an airtight container for up to 3 days.

HAVE READY

Stand mixer, if using, fitted with the whisk attachment.

Baking sheet lined with parchment paper.

Oven preheated to 200°C/180°C fan/gas mark 6.

EQUIPMENT

medium bowl

balloon whisk

stand mixer

– whisk attachment

large metal spoon or spatula

2 baking sheets

parchment paper

digital scales

chopping board

zester

wire rack

medium pan

digital thermometer

28 x 18cm stainless steel frame

small bowl

small pan

large pan and heatproof bowl, or
microwave and microwavable bowl

acetate sheet, at least 45 x 21cm

palette knife

ruler

long sharp knife

1cm round cutter

50g pistachio paste, or see
   Secrets of Success (opposite)

85g ground almonds

85g icing sugar

25g plain flour

125g whole eggs (2½ medium)

25g butter, melted and cooled

160g egg white (just over 5 medium)

40g caster sugar

FOR THE RASPBERRY
PÂTE DE FRUIT

200g raspberries

180g caster sugar

8g yellow pectin

50g liquid glucose

1g citric acid

flowers from 1 stalk of dried lavender,
   finely chopped

FOR THE GREEK
YOGURT MOUSSE

7g powdered gelatine

35g cold water

20g honey

10g water

15g liquid glucose

40g egg yolks (2 medium)

160g Greek yogurt

zest from 1 lemon

150g whipping cream

50g wetproof crispy freeze-dried
   raspberries (available online)

MAKE THE PISTACHIO JOCONDE

1. Put the pistachio paste, ground almonds, icing sugar, flour, eggs and butter into a bowl and whisk together for about 3 minutes to make a smooth paste.

2. Whisk the egg whites into stiff peaks in a stand mixer. Gradually whisk in the caster sugar until a smooth and glossy meringue forms.

3. Fold a spoonful of the meringue into the pistachio mixture to loosen it, then fold in the remaining meringue. Spread out thinly on the lined baking sheet to an area of about 30 x 40cm. Bake for 12–15 minutes, until done. Transfer to a wire rack to cool.

MAKE THE RASPBERRY PÂTE DE FRUIT

A light jelly layer that sits between two layers of pistachio joconde sponge.

4. Put the raspberries in a medium pan with 60g of the sugar and bring to the boil. Mix the pectin with another 60g of the sugar stir into the raspberry mixture. Bring back to the boil, then stir in the remaining 60g sugar and return to the boil.

5. Add the liquid glucose and cook until the temperature reaches 108°C. Stir in the citric acid and lavender, then take off the heat.

START TO ASSEMBLE THE FRAMBOISIERS

6. Use the frame to mark and cut out two 28 x 18cm rectangles from the joconde. Line a baking sheet with fresh parchment paper and put the frame on it. Place one joconde inside it. Spoon over the hot raspberry pâte de fruit. Lay the second joconde on top, ensuring it's flat. Leave to set at room temperature.

MAKE THE GREEK YOGURT MOUSSE

7. Put the gelatine into a small bowl, add the water and set aside to soak.

8. Make a pâte à bombe by heating the honey, water and glucose in a small saucepan until the temperature reaches 120°C. Whisk the egg yolks in a stand mixer. Keep the machine running as you slowly pour the syrup down the edge of the bowl and whisk until the mixture becomes thicker and mousse-like.

9. Whisk in the gelatine and allow to cool to 45°C before folding in the yogurt and lemon zest.

10. Whip the cream until moussey, then fold a spoonful into the yogurt mixture to loosen it. Fold in the remainder until thoroughly combined. Stir in the freeze-dried raspberries.

11. Spoon this mixture over the joconde, then freeze for 1 hour.

MAKE THE RASPBERRY MOUSSE

Make sure the raspberries are beautifully ripe so that the full flavour carries through into the mousse.

12. Put the gelatine into a small bowl, add the water and set aside to soak. Meanwhile, heat the cream in a pan and set aside. Once the gelatine has absorbed all the water, stir into the cream.

13. Whisk the raspberry purée, egg white powder and sugar together in a stand mixer until the mixture is thick and glossy.

14. Whip the cream mixture until it's cool, but take care not to overwhip or it will be too thick to fold in. Fold the cream into the raspberry meringue mixture until smooth. Spoon over the Greek yogurt mousse, level it out with a palette knife and freeze until firm.

MAKE THE DECORATION AND FINISH THE SLICES

A ruler is essential to cut out the triangles from the white chocolate so that they're perfectly shaped on every piece.

15. Temper the white chocolate following the instructions on page 34.

16. Spread it onto the acetate sheet to cover an area about 44 x 20cm. Mark out 12 or 14 right-angled triangles measuring 8.5 x 3.5cm. Mark a circle in the right-hand corner of each slice using a 1cm cutter. Leave the chocolate to set.

17. Slide a hot, dry palette knife around the sides of the frame and lift it off. Trim the edges to neaten, then slice into 12 or 14 slices measuring 3.5 x 8.5cm.

18. Carefully extract each chocolate triangle and the circles from the acetate and arrange one of each on every slice.

FOR THE RASPBERRY MOUSSE

14g powdered gelatine

70g cold water

100g double cream

210g raspberry purée

15g dried egg white powder

15g caster sugar

FOR THE DECORATION

200–300g white chocolate (33% cocoa solids)

THE SECRETS OF SUCCESS

◆

If you can't get hold of pistachio paste… Chop the pistachios very finely, then grind in a mortar until they form a paste.

FINISH IT LIKE A PASTRY CHEF

Make marbled triangles by brushing the acetate sheet with melted red cocoa butter, then tempered white chocolate, then continue with step 16 as above. Arrange them on each slice and garnish with *a sprig of lemon balm*, *a halved raspberry*, *a sprinkling of chopped pistachio* and a touch of *gold leaf*.

Additional equipment: *pastry brush.*

COCONUT DACQUOISES

Irresistible slices of crunchy coconut dacquoise, creamy mango and coconut ganache and mousse, finished with a dark chocolate glaze

These classic patisserie slices, which originated in Dax, south-west France, are made by layering a combination of dacquoise sponges with mousse and ganache. A traditional dacquoise, which is essentially a meringue-based sponge, calls for chopped hazelnuts to provide both texture and flavour, but here this is swapped with desiccated coconut. It's important that the dacquoise is crisp on the outside to support the mousse or cream on top, but soft and chewy on the inside to marry with the texture of the other layers. There's an additional joconde layer that is lighter than the dacquoise but still provides that important texture and flavour to contrast with the other layers.

This dessert includes a variety of complementary textures and flavours, and there is significant skill in choosing just the right elements to achieve an overall balance.

SERVES 12

TIMING
Hands-on time: *3 hours, plus chilling*
Cooking time: *30 minutes*

PREPARE IN ADVANCE
The dacquoise and joconde sponges can be made up to 1 day ahead, wrapped in clingfilm and stored at room temperature.

HAVE READY
Stand mixer, if using, fitted with the whisk attachment.
Baking tray lined with parchment paper.
Oven preheated to 180°C/160°C fan/ gas mark 4.

EQUIPMENT
stand mixer, optional
 – whisk attachment
baking tray
parchment paper
sieve
large bowl
zester
balloon or electric hand whisk, optional
large metal spoon or spatula
ruler
palette knife
wire rack
2 or 3 medium bowls
1 or 2 small bowls
small saucepan
chopping board
28 x 18cm stainless steel frame
long sharp knife
microwave and microwavable bowl or large pan and heatproof bowl

FOR THE COCONUT DACQUOISE

160g egg whites (5–6 medium)

125g caster sugar

125g icing sugar

35g plain flour

5g cocoa powder

95g desiccated coconut

seeds from ¼ vanilla pod

FOR THE COCONUT JOCONDE

160g egg whites (5–6 medium whites)

125g caster sugar

125g eggs, beaten (2½ medium)

65g icing sugar, sifted

seeds from ¼ vanilla pod

95g desiccated coconut

25g plain flour, sifted

25g butter, melted and cooled slightly

FOR THE MANGO GANACHE

3g powdered gelatine

15g cold water

200g white chocolate,
   very finely chopped

100g mango flesh, chopped
   and puréed

20g blanched pistachios, finely chopped

finely grated zest and strained juice
from ½ lime

MAKE THE COCONUT DACQUOISE

This meringue sponge layer adds a little crispness to the final slice. It is lighter than the joconde, so it sits on top.

Take care not to knock out the air in the meringue when you fold in the dry ingredients.

1. Put the egg whites into the bowl of a stand mixer and whisk until stiff peaks form. Slowly whisk in the sugar a spoonful at a time until the mixture is smooth and glossy. You can also do this with a large bowl and a balloon or electric hand whisk.
2. Sift the icing sugar, flour and cocoa powder over the top and add the desiccated coconut and the vanilla seeds. Carefully fold all the ingredients together.
3. Spread the mixture out on the prepared baking tray to an even 30 x 20cm rectangle and level the surface with a palette knife. Bake for 18–20 minutes until the mixture feels firm to the touch, then slide the sponge on the parchment paper onto a wire rack and leave to cool.
4. Reline the tray with parchment and increase the oven temperature to 190°C/170°C fan/gas mark 5.

MAKE THE COCONUT JOCONDE

This is a moist and nutty sponge layer, the fat coming from ground almonds and a little butter. It is lighter than the dacquoise and forms a delicious texture in the middle of the slice.

5. Whisk the egg whites in the stand mixer until stiff peaks form, as above. Slowly whisk in the sugar a spoonful at a time until the mixture is smooth and glossy. Alternatively, use a large bowl and balloon or electric hand whisk.
6. Put the whole eggs in a separate medium bowl with the sifted icing sugar. Add the vanilla seeds to the bowl and whisk until pale, thickened and moussey, and the mixture leaves a ribbon-like trail when the whisk is lifted out of the mixture.
7. Fold the egg mixture into the meringue, then fold in the desiccated coconut, sifted flour and butter. Spread onto the tray to a 30 x 20cm rectangle and bake for 11–12 minutes. Slide the sponge on the parchment onto the wire rack and leave to cool.

MAKE THE MANGO GANACHE

8. Put the gelatine in a small bowl, add the water and set aside to soak.
9. Place the chocolate in a bowl. Pour the puréed mango into a small pan and bring to the boil. Take the pan off the heat and stir in the gelatine

until dissolved. Pour the hot mango mixture over the chocolate, stirring until melted. Add the pistachios, lime zest and juice. Cover and chill until starting to thicken, but not set, checking and stirring the mixture occasionally.

START TO ASSEMBLE THE LAYERS

The layers are chilled at each stage so that they are firm enough to support the next layer.

The trimmed sponge can be frozen for making a future trifle or simply nibbled while you bake. You can also crumble a little over the top of the finished slices (see the box overleaf).

10. Slide the joconde onto a chopping board. Lay the frame on top and use a knife to cut inside it so that your sponge is the same size and shape as the frame. Repeat with the dacquoise. Slide a palette knife underneath both sponges to release them from the parchment.

11. Re-line the tray with clean parchment paper and lay the dacquoise onto it. Fit the frame around the sponge. Spoon the mango ganache onto it and spread it up to the edges of the frame, then level the surface. Transfer to the fridge to set for 20 minutes.

MAKE THE COCONUT GANACHE AND BUILD THE SECOND LAYER

12. Meanwhile, warm the coconut milk in a small pan over a medium heat until almost boiling. Put the chocolate into a bowl and pour in the hot coconut milk, stirring slowly. Stir in the coconut liqueur, then cover and chill.

13. Take the joconde tray out of the fridge. Carefully slide a palette knife underneath the sponge, lift it up and fit it into the frame. Push down slightly so that it sits level. Spoon over the coconut ganache and spread it out until level. Chill for 30 minutes (or longer if necessary – it should be firm and not at all runny).

MAKE THE COCONUT MOUSSE AND BUILD THE THIRD LAYER

The coconut mousse mixture must be chilled when it's poured into the cream, but not thoroughly set so that it can still be spread over the surface. You might not need it all. Fill the frame until it's almost at the top, but leave enough space – about 1mm – for a thin layer of glaze.

14. Put the gelatine in a small bowl, add the water and set aside to soak.
Continued…

FOR THE COCONUT GANACHE

100g coconut milk

150g dark chocolate,
   very finely chopped

25g coconut liqueur, optional

FOR THE COCONUT MOUSSE

6g powdered gelatine

30g cold water

185g double cream

55g caster sugar

175g coconut milk

15ml coconut liqueur, optional

FOR THE CHOCOLATE GLAZE

2g powdered gelatine

10g cold water

175g dark chocolate,
   very finely chopped

175g double cream

15. Whisk together the cream and sugar in a large bowl until soft and moussey, but not too stiff.

16. Warm 60g coconut milk in a small bowl in the microwave or a small pan until nearly boiling. Remove from the heat and stir in the softened gelatine until dissolved. Mix in the remaining 115g coconut milk and the coconut liqueur, if using, until cooled slightly.

17. Pour the cooled coconut mixture into the cream and whisk for a few minutes until fully combined. Cover and chill until moussey and the mixture has thickened enough to pour in a thick layer. Stir occasionally to check.

18. Spoon or pour the coconut mousse over the coconut ganache and spread it out evenly right to the edges and so that it almost fills the frame. You need to leave space for the chocolate glaze, so you may not need it all. Chill again for at least 4 hours or until completely set.

MAKE THE CHOCOLATE GLAZE AND COMPLETE THE LAYERS

19. Put the gelatine into a small bowl, add the water and set aside to soak. Put the chocolate into a medium bowl.

20. Pour the cream into a small pan and bring it to the boil. Take the pan off the heat and stir in the gelatine to dissolve. Pour the mixture onto the chocolate and stir gently to make a smooth emulsion. Pour over the top of the coconut mousse, spreading it smooth with a palette knife. Chill for at least 30 minutes or until set.

21. To serve, slide a hot, dry palette knife down the sides of the frame and lift it away. Transfer the dacquoise to a board, still on the parchment. Trim the sides to neaten them, then slice into 12 equal bars, separating each as it's cut. You will have a little excess. Serve.

FINISH IT LIKE A PASTRY CHEF

These slices look pretty piped with a petite line of *Swiss meringue* domes. Carefully toast with a blowtorch and crumble a little *leftover coconut dacquoise* on top.
Additional equipment: *blowtorch*

PATISSERIE

HAZELNUT CHOCOLATE
DACQUOISE

CHOCOLATE-COATED FIG
AND PRUNE GUGELHUPF

MINI CROQUEMBOUCHES

MILLE FEUILLES

PINEAPPLE TIGER SKIN ROLL

WHITE CHOCOLATE
SACHERTORTE

GÂTEAU ST HONORÉ

PATISSERIE

Here we present a collection of recipes featuring patisserie classics – magical creations where pastry and cake combine. The glossy chocolate-coated Gugelhupf on page 131, for example, features macerated fruit and an almond-rich sponge made with *mandelmassa*, a rich almond paste favoured by pastry chefs. It's less sweet than ordinary marzipan, but gives a pleasing dense texture to the finished bake. The recipe for Sachertorte has also been given a twist – transformed into a white chocolate version with light sponge, white chocolate glaze and a slick of apricot conserve to bring it all together (see page 149).

Pastry creations include the chic Mini Croquembouches (see page 135), which are scaled down from the crowd-pleasing tower usually served at weddings. Here they are filled with a light, summery duo of crèmes patissière (passion fruit and raspberry), and each arrangement is enough to serve two people. The simple appearance of the Mille Feuilles (see page 141) belies the fascinating challenge within. Crisp squares of puff pastry are layered with a vanilla crème pâtissière that includes just a touch of gelatine to ensure it holds its shape, a technique used in several other creations and worth getting the hang of.

All these recipes are perfect for any celebration. There's something here to please everyone, and budding patisserie chefs will find a range of challenges to test their skills.

HAZELNUT CHOCOLATE DACQUOISE

Light almond meringue sponge layers filled with rich chocolate cream and berry compote

A dacquoise is a sponge made from a base meringue, with nuts and a little flour folded through it. The perfect dacquoise bakes to a thin layer that is crisp enough on the outside to hold a light inner sponge. The nuts are most commonly almonds or hazelnuts, and a good pastry chef will fold these in very gently until just combined so that very little air is knocked out of the mixture and the volume of the whisked egg whites is maintained.

Rosettes of rich chocolate *crémeux* – a delicious combination of crème anglaise and dark chocolate – are piped over the base sponge, and a delicately sweetened fruit compote is spooned in between so that there's an equal serving of both in each slice. A chocolate with about 70% cocoa solids is called for here to offset the fruit flavours in the compote and the nutty taste of the sponge.

Fresh fruit dusted with icing sugar finishes this extravagant, show-stopping centrepiece.

SERVES 14

TIMING
Hands-on time: *2 hours,*
    plus overnight chilling
Cooking time: *20 minutes*

PREPARE IN ADVANCE
Both the *crémeux* and compote must
    be made at least 8 hours ahead,
    and can even be made up to
    4 days ahead. Store each of
    them separately in airtight
    containers in the fridge.

HAVE READY
Stand mixer, if using, fitted with
    the whisk attachment.
Cake tins greased and base-lined,
    or flan rings sitting on baking sheets
    lined with parchment paper.
Piping bags fitted with the nozzles.
Oven preheated to 180°C/
    160°C fan/gas mark 4.

EQUIPMENT
stand mixer, optional
  – whisk attachment
2 shallow 18cm loose-bottomed
    cake tins, or 2 flan rings
2 baking sheets, optional
parchment paper, optional
2 piping bags
  – 1cm plain nozzle
  – 2cm star nozzle
fine sieve
digital scales
zester
sharp knife
chopping board
2 large bowls

balloon whisk
medium heavy-based pan
spatula
wooden spoon
digital thermometer
stick blender
clingfilm
2 small bowls
medium pan
2 medium bowls
electric hand whisk, optional
large metal spoon
wire rack
5cm plain cutter

FOR THE CHOCOLATE CRÉMEUX

200g dark chocolate (70% cocoa
   solids), very finely chopped

80g egg yolks (4 medium)

40g caster sugar

200g milk

200g double cream

FOR THE MIXED BERRY COMPOTE

8g powdered gelatine

40g cold water

190g frozen mixed berries,
   thawed and drained

65g fresh raspberries,
   mashed and sieved

finely grated zest of 1 lemon,
   plus 15g (1 tablespoon) juice

25g invert sugar or liquid glucose
   or honey

25g caster sugar

3g (1 teaspoon) fruit pectin
   powder

FOR THE HAZELNUT DACQUOISE SPONGES

150g caster sugar

140g egg whites (from about
   4½ medium)

30g plain flour

85g ground hazelnuts,
   plus extra for dusting

15g hazelnuts, chopped

icing sugar, to dust

FOR THE DECORATION

115g mixed fresh berries such
   as raspberries, strawberries
   and blueberries

icing sugar, to dust

MAKE THE CHOCOLATE CRÉMEUX

1. Make the chocolate *crémeux* using the method on page 27. Cover with clingfilm and chill for at least 6–8 hours or preferably overnight.

MAKE THE MIXED BERRY COMPOTE

Gelatine is mixed into the compote so that when it's piped into the dacquoise, it sets and doesn't seep into the meringue sponge.

2. Put the gelatine into a small bowl, add the water and set aside to soak.
3. Put the thawed berries into a medium pan with the mashed and strained raspberries, lemon zest and juice, and the invert sugar, or liquid glucose or honey. Place over a medium heat and cook gently and briefly to warm the mixture through.
4. Combine the caster sugar and pectin in a bowl, then stir this mixture into the fruit and bring to the boil. Take the pan off the heat and stir in the gelatine until it has dissolved completely. Transfer the mixture to a medium bowl. Allow to cool, then cover and chill for about 4 hours, or overnight until firm.

MAKE THE HAZELNUT DACQUOISE

The key to a great dacquoise is air. The egg whites and sugar are whisked until light and the dry ingredients are sifted to incorporate even more air. Use a light, careful touch when folding the two together so that you don't beat out all the volume created in the initial whisking.

5. Put 50g of the sugar and the egg whites into the bowl of a stand mixer or a large bowl. Whisk with the mixer or an electric hand whisk until the mixture stands in soft peaks.
6. Sift the flour and ground hazelnuts into a separate medium bowl, adding any bits leftover in the sieve at the end, then stir in the remaining 100g sugar. Gradually fold this into the meringue mixture using a large metal spoon until combined, taking care not to knock out too much of the air.
7. Spoon the mixture into a piping bag fitted with a 1cm nozzle. Pipe the mixture in spirals, working from the centre to the outside, to fill the base of each of the cake tins or flan rings. Sprinkle each with half the chopped hazelnuts, then dust with icing sugar.
8. Bake for about 20 minutes, until golden and firm. Loosen the edges from the tin to remove. Cool on a wire rack, then carefully peel off the parchment paper.

TO ASSEMBLE THE DACQUOISE

9. Put one of the sponges onto a serving plate. Take the other sponge and use the 5cm cutter to carefully cut a circle out of the middle.
10. Spoon the chocolate *crémeux* into a piping bag fitted with the 2cm star nozzle. Pipe a large rosette of *crémeux* onto the centre of the base layer and circle it with a border of large rosettes.
11. Spoon the berry compote into the second piping bag and snip 3–4cm from the end. Carefully pipe the compote in-between the piped *crémeux* border and the central rosette to fill any gaps.
12. Carefully place the second dacquoise on top and fill the hole with carefully arranged mixed berries. Dust lightly with icing sugar and serve.

FINISH IT LIKE A PASTRY CHEF

For a touch more glamour you can glaze the fruit on top of the cake. Put *50g apricot jam* into a pan and heat it up. Carefully brush the glaze over the fruits and leave to set a little on parchment paper before arranging them in the centre of the dacquoise. As the glaze gives a glossy finish, there's no need to dust with icing sugar.
Additional equipment: *pastry brush.*

CHOCOLATE-COATED FIG AND PRUNE GUGELHUPF

A dense, brandy-laced almond and fruit cake glazed with dark chocolate and decorated with crunchy almonds

This traditional central European cake is baked in a fluted ring tin of the same name. It is rich and dense and often served in slices with coffee.

Although some gugelhupf recipes call for yeast, this one uses baking powder to stimulate the rise. It is made by creaming the butter and sugar together with an almond paste called *mandelmassa*, which pastry chefs prefer because it has a high percentage of almonds to sugar (anything from 50%). Don't be tempted to use ready-made supermarket marzipan, as it is too sweet and won't cream together with the butter and sugar.

Although it looks simple, there is much skill here – the tin must be greased and floured evenly so that no part of the cake batter sticks to it and breaks up when later turned out of the mould; the *mandelmassa* must be warmed sufficiently to blend with the other ingredients; and the syrup must be just enough to moisten the dense sponge, but not too much for the cake to crumble on slicing.

This recipe is best kept for a few days for the flavour to develop. It can also be frozen up to a month ahead once it's been brushed with the syrup and has cooled. The secret to keeping it moist is to brush over a brandy syrup while the sponge is still warm, then wrap it in clingfilm so that the steam and brandy are trapped inside the cake.

SERVES 10

TIMING

Hands-on time: *50 minutes,*
  plus 24–48 hours marinating
Cooking time: *50–55 minutes*

PREPARE IN ADVANCE

The figs and prunes must be soaked in brandy 1 or 2 days ahead (see step 1).

The cake can be made up to 5 days ahead and stored in an airtight container, or frozen up to 1 month ahead.

The glaze can be made up to 7 days ahead and stored in an airtight container at room temperature.

HAVE READY

Figs and prunes soaked in brandy (see step 1).

Stand mixer, if using, fitted with the paddle attachment.

Bundt tin greased and lightly floured.

Baking tray lined with clingfilm.

Oven preheated to 190°C/ 170°C fan/gas mark 5.

EQUIPMENT

medium bowl
stand mixer, optional
– paddle attachment

16cm bundt tin
baking tray
clingfilm
sharp knife and chopping board
zester
microwave and microwavable bowl
  or heatproof bowl and pan
electric hand whisk, optional
sieve
large metal spoon or spatula
skewer or cocktail stick
wire rack
pastry brush
digital thermometer
jug

FOR THE CAKE

50g dried figs, chopped

50g prunes, chopped

25g brandy

90g mandelmassa almond paste
(50% ground almonds)

90g butter, softened

65g caster sugar

20g invert sugar, liquid glucose
or honey

5g vanilla sugar

zest from ½ lemon

a good pinch of salt

8g cornflour

100g eggs (2 medium)

20g egg yolk (1 medium)

90g plain flour

3g baking powder

15g candied peel

FOR THE SUGAR SYRUP

10g caster sugar

30g brandy

FOR THE GLAZE

200g dark chocolate (65% cocoa solids),
chopped

40g vegetable oil

FOR THE DECORATION

25g roasted almonds, chopped

SOAK THE FRUIT

1. One or two days before you plan to bake your gugelhupf, put the figs and prunes in a bowl and pour over the brandy. Set aside for 24–48 hours to marinate.

MAKE THE CAKE

Air is incorporated into the mixture during the whisking and sifting. Fold gently to keep it in the batter for a light cake.

2. Put the *mandelmassa* into a microwavable bowl and warm it in the microwave on medium for 30 seconds to 1 minute – it should feel warm and soft, but not hot. You can also do this in a bowl over a pan of simmering water.

3. Put the butter and sugar into the bowl of a stand mixer and add the *mandelmassa*. Mix until the mixture is fluffy and the sugar has dissolved. Add the invert sugar, or glucose or honey, vanilla sugar, lemon zest, salt and cornflour and beat the mixture until everything is combined. You can also do this in a large bowl with an electric hand whisk.

4. Gradually add the eggs, one at a time, beating well after each addition. Adding the eggs gradually helps to ensure that the cake mixture doesn't split. If it looks as if the mixture is about to curdle, beat in a tablespoon of flour. Once all the whole eggs have been incorporated, beat in the egg yolk.

5. Sift over the flour and baking powder, then add the strained fruit and the candied peel, folding everything together with a large metal spoon or spatula.

6. Spoon the mixture into the prepared tin and bake for about 50 minutes, or until a skewer pushed into the centre comes out clean. Leave in the tin to cool for 10 minutes, then invert onto a wire rack and sit the rack on the tray lined with clingfilm. Set aside while you make the syrup.

MAKE THE SUGAR SYRUP

The cake is wrapped in clingfilm to seal in the flavour and moisture from the syrup.

7. Mix together the brandy and sugar in a medium bowl, then brush the mixture all over the cake while it's still warm.

8. Place the warm cake on a square of clingfilm, then bring together the corners and fold them into the centre. Leave it to cool, then chill it in the fridge. If you're going to freeze it at this stage, wrap again in clingfilm before putting it in the freezer.

MAKE THE CHOCOLATE GLAZE

9. Melt the chocolate using the instructions on page 34, making sure it doesn't reach any higher than 45°C.
10. Stir in the oil – don't whisk it in as you don't want to introduce any air bubbles to the mixture. Transfer to a jug.

DECORATE THE CAKE

The sponge is drenched in the chocolate glaze and 'dipped' in chopped almonds.

11. Lay the wire rack on the baking tray lined with clingfilm. Unwrap the cake and place it on top of the rack. Pour the glaze carefully all over the cake. Start from the top and work around it until it's completely covered, making sure that none of the sponge is visible. Transfer the cake to a cake board and squeeze any glaze on the clingfilm back into the bowl. Use it to patch up any bits of sponge you may have missed.
12. With the cake on the board, use your hand to scoop up some of the chopped almonds and gently press them around the bottom of the cake. Continue to do this all the way round so that the cake looks like the base has been dipped in the nuts, then serve.

THE SECRETS OF SUCCESS

If the glaze is too thick and doesn't pour consistently...
It isn't hot enough. Warm it very gently in the microwave to melt it.

If the glaze is too thin and washes over the cake...
It's too hot to pour, so set it aside for a few minutes and allow it to cool and thicken up slightly.

FINISH IT LIKE A PASTRY CHEF

After coating, flick *tempered white, milk and dark chocolate* over the sides of the cake Jackson Pollock-style. To temper the chocolate, follow the instructions on page 34. For white chocolate, the temperature needs to be about 28–29°C, for milk chocolate 29–30°C, for dark chocolate 31–32°C.

Additional equipment: *paper piping bags or cornets.*

MINI CROQUEMBOUCHES

Toffee-coloured choux bun towers filled with raspberry, passion fruit and mango creams and coated with crisp caramel

Croquembouche is the traditional cake served at French weddings, First Communions and christenings. The name translates as 'crackle in the mouth', referring to the crunch from the golden caramel. Pastry chefs have updated the classic recipe by adding flavourings to the crème pâtissière.

Unlike other pastries, choux dough is piped rather than hand-shaped into delicate buns, then baked in a hot oven, where the water evaporates and the resulting steam creates crisp shells of pastry with hollow centres. It's important to cook the buns until they're firm and dry so that they hold their shape when filled and can be built into mini choux mountains.

This recipe has been scaled down to make miniature versions of the classic dessert, each enough for two people. The buns are filled with fruit-flavoured crèmes patissière that are just tart enough to balance out the sweet sugar coating. The purées can be made fresh, although pastry chefs tend to use ready-made frozen purées that are thawed before using.

MAKES 4 MINI CROQUEMBOUCHES TO SERVE 8

TIMING

Hands-on time: *1 hour 30 minutes*
Cooking time: *25–30 minutes*

PREPARE IN ADVANCE

The choux buns can be made ahead and frozen
  in an airtight container for up to 1 month.
The crème pâtissière can be made and chilled,
  covered in the fridge, up to 4 days ahead.

HAVE READY

Mixer, if using, fitted with the paddle attachment.
Baking sheets lined with parchment paper
  or silicone mats.
Piping bags fitted with the nozzles.
Sink half-filled with cold water.
Tea towel folded up into a square.
Oven preheated to 200°C/180°C fan/gas mark 6.

EQUIPMENT

stand mixer, optional
  – paddle attachment
2 large baking sheets
parchment paper or 2 silicone mats
3 large piping bags
  – 8mm and 5 mm plain round nozzles
tea towel
digital scales
sharp knife and chopping board
sieve
small pan, food-processor or blender
2 medium stainless steel pans
wooden spoon
2 medium bowls
pastry brush
sieve, optional
whisk
2 sealable containers
clingfilm
rubber gloves, optional

FOR THE CHOUX
PASTRY BUNS

125g cold water

65g butter, chopped

7g caster sugar

1.5g table salt

125g strong bread flour, sifted

125g beaten egg (about 2½ medium),
plus 25g (½ medium)

FOR THE MANGO
AND PASSION FRUIT
CRÈME PÂTISSIÈRE

125g fresh mango purée (see page 25),
or ready-made frozen purée, thawed

125g fresh passion fruit purée
(see page 25), or ready-made
frozen purée, thawed

50g caster sugar

¼ vanilla pod, split lengthways

60g egg yolks (3 medium)

20g strong bread flour

FOR THE RASPBERRY
CRÈME PÂTISSIÈRE

240g fresh raspberry purée
(see page 25), or ready-made
frozen purée, thawed

10g lemon juice

50g caster sugar

60g egg yolks (3 medium)

20g strong bread flour

FOR THE CARAMEL SUGAR

350g caster sugar

120g hand-hot water

65g liquid glucose

TO MAKE THE CHOUX PASTRY BUNS

The choux buns must be completely dried out and quite crisp so that they're strong enough to hold the structure of the tower. A hole is poked in the bottom of each hot bun so steam can escape and they don't get soggy.

Brushing the buns lightly with egg wash glaze gives them a shine and prevents cracking, while the criss-crossing helps them to puff up evenly.

1. Make the choux pastry using the method on page 37.
2. Spoon the mixture into the piping bag fitted with the 8mm nozzle and pipe balls 1.5cm wide onto the parchment paper or silicone mats, leaving enough space between each one for them to double in size. You'll need to pipe 56 balls.
3. Brush each bun very lightly with the 25g beaten egg, taking care not to flood the top, then press the back of the tines of a fork in a criss-cross pattern on top of the buns (A).
4. Bake for 10 minutes, then reduce the temperature to 180°C/160°C fan/gas mark 4 and continue to cook for a further 10–15 minutes, until the buns have dried out. Leave the buns to cool slightly on the trays.
5. Use a plain piping nozzle to make a small hole in the bottom of each bun. Set aside to cool completely.

MAKE THE FRUIT CRÈMES PATISSIÈRE AND FILL THE BUNS

Strong flour is added with the fruit purées to help thicken and give a firm texture to the pastry cream.

6. Put the mango and passion fruit purées into a medium pan with 25g of the caster sugar. Scrape in the vanilla seeds and add the pod too.
7. In a bowl, whisk together the egg yolks, the remaining 25g caster sugar and the flour until combined.
8. Place the pan over a medium heat and bring the fruit purée mixture to the boil. Whip out and discard the vanilla pod, then pour the purée over the flour mixture, whisking all the time until well combined.
9. Return the mixture to the pan and bring to the boil to thicken the sauce – it'll take about 2–3 minutes. Whisk constantly to ensure there are no lumps and to stop the mixture from burning.
10. Transfer to a sealable container and seal the top of the mixture with clingfilm to prevent a skin from forming. Allow to cool.
11. Repeat using the ingredients for the raspberry crème pâtissière, adding the lemon juice with the raspberry purée. If you're not using it immediately, store in a separate container and seal with clingfilm to prevent a skin from forming.
12. Whisk one of the creams again until smooth and spoon it into the piping bag fitted with a 5mm nozzle. Fill half the buns (B). Repeat with the second cream and fill the remaining buns. Set aside, keeping the two flavours separate, while you prepare the caramel.

Continued…

MAKE THE CARAMEL TOPPING

The key to making caramel is to avoid crystallisation. Any dirt on the sides of the pan, or splashed sugar, can fall into the mixture and create a chain reaction of sugar crystals that will seize it. Stirring would also encourage crystallisation. It is best to use a stainless steel pan so that you can clearly see the progress of the caramel – watch it carefully, it should be a light golden colour.

13. Put the sugar and water into a spotlessly clean, heavy-based stainless steel pan. Stir gently with your fingers until the mixture has the consistency of wet sand, taking care not to splash the sides of the pan. Clean any splashes by wetting your hands in cold running water and wiping the inside of the pan. Add the liquid glucose.
14. Place over a high heat and quickly bring the mixture to the boil. Continue to cook, without stirring, until it is a light caramel colour. Take the pan off the heat and plunge the base into the bowl or sink of cold water for a few seconds to halt the cooking. Place the pan on the folded tea towel so that it cools evenly and not too quickly.

CONSTRUCT THE CROQUEMBOUCHES

Choose even choux buns for each layer so that the towers are level. Use the biggest buns for the bottom layers.

If the caramel starts to cool and is too thick to dip the coated buns into, put the pan back over a very low heat. Gently tilt it around without stirring so that the mixture becomes liquid again without any further colouring or caramelising.

Wear rubber gloves to protect your hands when you dip the buns into the caramel. Alternatively, have a large bowl of iced water beside you while you work. If you touch the caramel dip, your hand immediately into the bowl to prevent the skin burning and blistering.

15. Carefully dip the top and side of one choux bun in the caramel, removing any excess by gently wiping against the rim of the pan. Place on the parchment paper or silicone mat. Take a second bun and dip it into the caramel, set it alongside the first bun so that the two buns stick together. Repeat until you have a circle of 5 buns, alternating the flavours as you go (C).
16. Dip a new bun into the caramel and place it on top of the first ring of buns. Repeat to make a second ring of 5 buns, followed by a ring of 3 buns (D). Finally, dip the top only of a bun into the caramel and place it on top of the tower to complete your croquembouche.
17. Repeat with the remaining buns to make 4 mini towers.

FINISH IT LIKE A PASTRY CHEF

Decorate the croquembouches by sticking *sugared almond dragees* and sugar flowers all around the towers.

To make the Sugar Flowers, roll out *150g sugar paste* on a board, lightly dusted with icing sugar, to 2mm thick. Stamp out 20 flowers using a 13mm daisy cutter and set aside to dry. If you want to shape the flowers, leave them to dry in a small half-sphere silicone mould. Mix together *120g icing sugar, 20g egg white (⅔ medium), a few drops of lemon juice* and a couple of drops of *yellow food colouring*. Spoon into a small piping bag and snip off the tip, or make your own bag by rolling up a square of parchment paper into a cone shape. Pipe a small dome in the centre of each flower and use the icing to stick them to the croquembouches. Stick the dragees in the same way.

Additional equipment: *rolling pin, 13mm daisy cutter, small half-sphere silicone mould, optional, small bowl, small disposable piping bag or parchment paper.*

MILLE FEUILLES

Crisp squares of golden puff pastry layered with rich cream and decorated with caramelised sugar

The name of this puff pastry tart translates literally as 'a thousand leaves', a reference to the many layers created by the butter in the puff pastry dough. It's sometimes also called a Napoleon, and traditionally consists of three layers of pastry filled with cream and fresh fruit.

This version is made in a square shape and filled with crème pâtissière, then dusted with icing sugar and finished by pressing a hot skewer onto the sugar to caramelise it, creating a striking pattern.

Make sure you follow the rules when making the puff pastry to ensure the butter is laminated throughout the dough (see page 38). The even, crisp sheets are achieved by pricking the pastry with a fork and baking it with a wire rack on top to control the rise. The pastry has to be baked thoroughly until it's dark golden with light buttery layers, so turn it over halfway through baking to ensure it cooks properly.

SERVES 8

TIMING

Hands-on time: *2 hours*
Cooking time: *20–30minutes*

PREPARE IN ADVANCE

The pastry can be made up to 2 days ahead.

HAVE READY

Stand mixer, if using, fitted with the dough hook.
Baking sheets lined with parchment paper.
Piping bag fitted with the nozzle.

EQUIPMENT

stand mixer, optional
 – dough hook and paddle attachments
3 baking sheets
parchment paper
piping bag
 – 1.5cm nozzle
small sharp knife
chopping board
large bowl, optional
wooden spoon, optional
clingfilm
rolling pin
ruler
3 x wire racks
small bowl
large bowl
balloon or electric hand whisk
medium pan
long sharp knife
sieve
metal skewer
tea towel
blowtorch, optional

FOR THE PUFF PASTRY

420g strong bread flour, plus extra
    to dust
9g table salt
a few drops of lemon juice
180–195g iced water
40g butter, softened
375g cold butter, cubed
50–75g icing sugar, plus extra to dust

FOR THE CRÈME PÂTISSIÈRE

3g gelatine
15g cold water
80g egg yolks (4 medium)
60g caster sugar
4g vanilla extract
32g cornflour
400g fresh milk
1 vanilla pod, split lengthways
80g butter

MAKE AND BAKE THE PASTRY

It's very important that the pastry is baked properly and is completely dried out and crisp, otherwise it will be claggy and soft once it is filled with the cream. If you don't have three racks, roll each layer out individually and place the rest of the dough in the fridge while the others bake.

1. Make the pastry following the method on page 38. Wrap and chill for 20 minutes.
2. Preheat the oven to 200°C/180°C fan/gas mark 6.
3. Split the dough into 3 equal pieces. Roll each piece out thinly on a work surface lightly dusted with icing sugar until it measures about 32 x 16cm and 5mm thick. Lay each on separate baking sheets and prick all over with a fork. Place wire racks on top so that the pastry is able to rise in the oven, but is kept even by the weight of the rack.
4. Bake for 20–30 minutes, or until golden brown, turning the pastry over once it's light golden, about 15 minutes, and continuing to bake until the pastry is completely dried out. If the temperature seems very hot at this stage, reduce it to 180°C/160°C fan/gas mark 4 for the remainder of the cooking time.

MAKE THE CRÈME PÂTISSIÈRE

The pastry cream is thickened with gelatine so that it is strong enough to maintain the structure of the pastry towers.

5. Put the gelatine into a small bowl, add the water and set aside to soak.
6. In a large bowl, whisk together the egg yolks, caster sugar and vanilla extract, then gently stir in the cornflour.
7. Pour the milk into a medium pan and place over a medium heat. Scrape in the vanilla seeds and add the pod too. Bring to the boil, then strain into the egg mixture, discarding the pod. Whisk continuously to mix everything together.
8. Return the mixture to the pan and bring it to the boil. Simmer for 1–2 minutes to thicken the mixture.
9. Take the pan off the heat and stir in the gelatine, then whisk in the butter. Lay a layer of clingfilm over the top to seal the cream and prevent a skin from forming. Set aside.

ASSEMBLE THE MILLE FEUILLES

10. Lay one sheet of puff pastry on a clean board and trim the edges, then use a ruler to carefully cut it into eight 7cm squares. Repeat with the other sheets of puff pastry.

11. Spoon the crème pâtissière into the piping bag and pipe 9 even-sized domes over one square of pastry. Top with another square of pastry and press down gently to secure it. Pipe 9 more cream domes and top with a third pastry square, pressing lightly to secure. Repeat until you have 8 tarts. Dust heavily with icing sugar.

DECORATE THE TOPS

The mille feuilles are decorated by caramelising a heavy dusting of icing sugar using a very hot skewer. Be very careful when handling the skewer as it might need to be wiped and reheated between tarts.

12. Wrap the handle of a metal skewer in a cloth and heat the skewer over a gas hob, or with a blowtorch, until it's smoking hot. Quickly burn 2 lines on top of one tart to make an off-centre cross pattern. Repeat with the remaining tarts. You may need to carefully wipe the skewer and reheat it if it cools down. Transfer to plates and serve.

PINEAPPLE TIGER SKIN ROLL

A marbled roll of light-as-air sponge filled with a smooth buttercream and caramelised pineapple pieces

This unique Chinese cake is a twist on a traditional Swiss roll. It's made with lots of egg yolks to produce a wonderfully soft sponge and a rippled 'tiger skin' effect when the cake is baked.

There is very little flour in the mix compared with the large quantity of yolks and sugar and this causes the rippling on the surface of the sponge during the baking. Normally it's the flour that creates the structure in a cake, but in this case the sponge is supported mainly by the cooking of the egg yolks. It's the perfect pudding to make after you've whipped up a batch of macarons, which use only egg whites.

The base of the buttercream is a simple meringue that's whisked together with boiled sugar before the butter is added. The result is a beautiful textured Italian meringue buttercream that perfectly complements the light and airy sponge. Finally, it's studded with nuggets of caramelised pineapple and carefully rolled up to serve.

SERVES 10

TIMING

Hands-on time: *1 hour 20 minutes*
Cooking time: *8–10 minutes*

PREPARE IN ADVANCE

The sponge can be baked and frozen
   up to 1 month ahead. Store it flat,
   wrapped well in clingfilm.
The buttercream can be made and chilled
   up to 3 days ahead. It needs to come
   back to room temperature and be
   whisked until soft and creamy (about
   8–10 minutes in a mixer) before use.

HAVE READY

Stand mixer, if using, fitted with the
   whisk attachment.
Tin lined with parchment paper.
Oven preheated to 240°C/220°C fan/
   gas mark 9.

EQUIPMENT

stand mixer, optional
   – whisk attachment
30 x 20cm Swiss roll tin
parchment paper
digital scales
blender
sieve
sharp knife
chopping board
large bowl and and electric hand whisk,
optional
large metal spoon
spatula
small heavy-based pan
digital thermometer
large frying pan
sharp serrated knife

FOR THE SPONGE

20g beaten egg (about ½ medium)

200g egg yolks (about 10 medium)

75g caster sugar

30g plain flour

FOR THE PINEAPPLE
BUTTERCREAM

60g egg whites (2 medium)

120g caster sugar

50g water

250g butter, softened

75g pineapple, blended and strained

FOR THE CARAMELISED
PINEAPPLE

¼ fresh pineapple, cut into small cubes

1 tablespoon caster sugar

MAKE THE SPONGE

1. Whisk the egg, egg yolks and sugar together in the bowl of a stand mixer until the mixture reaches the ribbon stage. You could also do this in a large bowl with an electric hand whisk. Gently fold in the flour.
2. Pour the mixture into the prepared tin, spreading it out to an even layer and right into the corners of the tin. Bake for 8 minutes. Allow to cool.

MAKE THE PINEAPPLE BUTTERCREAM

This step requires a bit of juggling. The meringue base is made while heating the sugar syrup to soft ball stage (see page 30). This is combined, cooled and beaten with butter, then the puréed pineapple is folded into the mixture.

Take care when boiling the sugar as it's a very small quantity and will burn easily. Have the thermometer next to you as it bubbles away so that you can easily check the temperature.

Whisking the egg white initially with a little sugar helps to stabilise it.

3. Put the egg whites into the bowl of a stand mixer with 30g of the caster sugar. Whisk until thick and foamy. You can also do this in a large bowl with a balloon whisk.
4. Meanwhile, put the remaining 90g caster sugar into a small heavy-based pan over a low heat with the water. Heat gently to dissolve the sugar, then increase the heat and cook until the sugar reaches 121°C (soft ball stage, see page 30).
5. With the motor running, pour the sugar syrup over the egg whites and whisk until cool.
6. Add the softened butter to the mixture and beat until smooth. Whisk in the puréed pineapple and set aside.

CARAMELISE THE PINEAPPLE

Do not attempt to use the diced pineapple until it is cold, or it will melt the buttercream.

7. Put the pineapple cubes into a large frying pan and sprinkle over the sugar. Place over a high heat and cook until the pineapple caramelises. It will look golden a glistening with slightly browned edges. Spoon onto a plate to cool.

ROLL AND SERVE

The roll should have even layers of sponge and cream, so be careful not to roll it up too tightly or you might squeeze out some of the filling.

By freezing the rolled sponge, you will be able to slice through it cleanly. Any leftover buttercream can be frozen in an airtight container.

8. Carefully lift the cooled sponge out of the tray by the paper. Invert onto a work surface lined with parchment paper so that the rippled skin is facing down, and the short end of the pastry is nearest you.
9. Spread the buttercream all over the sponge to about 8mm–1cm thick. Sprinkle with the cooled caramelised pineapple.
10. Use the paper to help you roll up the sponge tightly from the edge that's nearest you, keeping nice even layers of sponge and buttercream.
11. Chill the roll in the fridge for 1–2 hours (or put it in the freezer if you need it sooner). Use a serrated knife to trim the ends so that you see the lovely roll of buttercream and pieces of pineapple.

THE SECRETS OF SUCCESS

———◆———

If you don't achieve the tiger skin effect…
The eggs haven't been beaten enough. It is essential they reach the ribbon stage, when the mixture looks as though it falls in ribbons when the whisk is lifted.
It will still taste delicious, though.

WHITE CHOCOLATE SACHERTORTE

Thin layers of white chocolate sponge and apricot jam topped with a smooth white chocolate glaze and glazed fruit

This classic Austrian cake never goes out of fashion for patisserie chefs. Traditionally it is a cocoa-rich sponge layered with apricot jam and covered in a dark chocolate glaze. The original is a fairly dry sponge that is served with a large portion of sweet whipped cream to provide moisture.

The alternative version here, using white chocolate, is more delicate and moist because in place of the thick sponge in its dark chocolate counterpart, the sponge is baked in thin layers, which are then interspersed with a white chocolate glaze. The skill is in ensuring that the batter for the sponge is spread evenly in the tray before baking so that when the finished bake is sandwiched with the fruit conserve and white chocolate, it is perfectly even.

SERVES 10–15

TIMING

Hands-on time: *1 hour 30 minutes, plus overnight chilling*
Cooking time: *15–20 minutes*

PREPARE IN ADVANCE

The white chocolate glaze must be made at least 12 hours and up to 3 days ahead.

HAVE READY

Stand mixer, if using, fitted with the paddle attachment.
Baking sheets lined with baking parchment.
Frame greased.
Cut a few 20 x 5cm strips from the acetate sheet.
Oven preheated to 200°C/ 180°C fan/gas mark 6.

EQUIPMENT

stand mixer, optional
 – paddle attachment
2 large baking sheets
parchment paper
28 x 18cm stainless steel frame
A4 sheet of acetate
ruler
digital scales
small sharp knife
2 chopping boards
small bowl
2 or 3 large bowls
small pan
wooden spoon or spatula
microwave and microwavable
 bowl or medium pan and
 heatproof bowl
digital thermometer
electric hand whisk, optional

large metal spoon
sieve
palette knife
long sharp knife
pastry brush
curved mould, such as a
 terrine, bûche mould,
 or small cake tin
comb scraper
clingfilm
wire rack

FOR THE WHITE CHOCOLATE GLAZE

1.5g gelatine

7.5g cold water

300g white chocolate,
   very finely chopped

75g whipping cream

75g whole milk

FOR THE SPONGE

100g white chocolate,
   broken into pieces

110g butter, softened

35g icing sugar

100g egg yolks (5 medium)

150g egg whites (5 medium)

150g caster sugar

110g plain flour

FOR THE ASSEMBLY AND DECORATION

150–200g apricot conserve

200g dark chocolate

a few raspberries, strawberries
   and a string of redcurrants

15g pistachios, peeled, roasted
   and finely chopped

MAKE THE WHITE CHOCOLATE GLAZE

The tiny amount of gelatine in the glaze ensures that it's firm enough to stay on top of the cake. Too much gelatine and it would become a jelly.

1. Put the gelatine into a small bowl, add the water and set aside to soak.
2. Put the chocolate into a large bowl.
3. Pour the cream and milk into a small pan, place over a high heat and bring to the boil. Stir in the gelatine with a spatula until dissolved, then pour the mixture over the chocolate. Stir well, working from the inside of the mixture to the outside to make a smooth emulsion. Allow to cool, then leave to set in the fridge for at least 12 hours.

MAKE THE SPONGE

This sponge is a twist on the original Sacher sponge.

4. Melt the chocolate using the instructions on page 34, making sure the temperature doesn't rise any higher than 45°C.
5. Put the butter and icing sugar into the bowl of a stand mixer and cream together with the paddle attachment until the mixture looks pale and fluffy. Add the egg yolks, little by little, beating until completely combined before each addition. Slowly beat in the melted chocolate. You could also do this in a large bowl with an electric hand whisk.
6. Whisk the egg whites and caster sugar in a clean bowl until firm with smooth peaks, then fold into the butter mixture. Lastly, sift the flour into the bowl and fold it in, cutting through the mixture with a large metal spoon to ensure that all the ingredients are fully combined.
7. Divide the cake batter between the 2 baking sheets and spread out with a palette knife to rectangles measuring 30 x 40cm. Bake for 15–20 minutes, then remove from the oven and leave to cool on the sheets.

ASSEMBLE THE LAYERS

Keep a close eye on the glaze as you warm it – too runny and it will slip off the cake, too firm and it will be too thick to pour. It should be no hotter than 35°C.

8. Put one sponge layer on a board and cut it in half widthways so that you have two rectangles measuring 30 x 20cm. Trim each piece again to 28 x 18cm so that they will fit neatly in the frame. Repeat with the second sponge layer.

9. Put the frame on a clean sheet of parchment paper and lay one of the sponge rectangles inside. Spread the sponge with a thin layer of apricot jam and lay another sponge on top. Repeat until all the sponges are layered up and brushed with the jam, then transfer to the freezer for 1–2 hours until firm.

MAKE THE CHOCOLATE CURLS

The impressive-looking dark chocolate curls are, in fact, easy to do, but you need a curved mould such as a terrine or bûche mould, or even a small cake tin, as well as a comb scraper – like the ones tilers use.

This quantity of chocolate is easier to work with than smaller amounts, but you'll get more curls than you need. However, the curls can be kept in an airtight container for up to two weeks or melted down and used for something else – just make sure you re-temper the chocolate.

10. Lay the acetate strips on a board with your curved mould alongside.
11. Temper the chocolate (see page 34) and pour it over the plastic strips, spreading it out to thin, even layers with a palette knife.
12. Drag a comb scraper through the length of the chocolate to mark it into thin, strips. Curl the acetate inside the mould and leave the chocolate to set. Carefully peel away the acetate.

GLAZE AND DECORATE THE SACHERTORTE

The glaze must lie in a perfectly smooth, even layer over the cake.

13. Melt the glaze by gently warming it in the microwave or resting the bowl over a pan of just simmering water, making sure the base doesn't touch the water. Check the mixture as it melts and make sure it doesn't go any higher than 35°C.
14. Line a work surface with clingfilm and put a wire rack on top. Slide a palette knife down the sides of the cake to remove the frame, then slip it underneath the cake to loosen it from the parchment. Lay the cake on the wire rack and pour the glaze over it. Use a palette knife to spread the glaze quickly and evenly over the top to ensure it's smooth. Put the cake back on the board and chill for 30 minutes.
15. Trim the sides of the chilled cake so that there is a neat edge all around the edge. Pile the berries in one corner and sprinkle the finely chopped pistachios in neat curves over its length. Arrange the chocolate curls over the top and serve.

GÂTEAU ST HONORÉ

A classic patisserie made from a crisp puff pastry base, edged with craquelin-topped choux buns filled with vanilla-scented crème chiboust (crème pâtissière whipped with meringue) and a fresh mascarpone cream

Named after the French patron saint of pastry, this dessert includes choux buns that are traditionally dipped into caramelised sugar to provide a crisp contrast to soft pastry. Here the buns are coated in a craquelin topping and the whole tart is finished with a mascarpone cream.

Frozen puff pastry trimmings left over from, say, the Fig Tart on page 232, are ideal for using up in this recipe. To keep the layers intact, don't scrunch them up into a ball before rolling – lay them out on a board and fit them together like a jigsaw, with the bits slightly overlapping. Dust with a little flour, roll them flat and they will stick together.

If you have any choux pastry left over, you can pipe it into fingers (for éclairs) or into more rounds (for buns) and bake as before. Cool on a wire rack, then place in an airtight container and freeze. Use within three months.

SERVES 10

TIMING

Hands-on time: *3 hours 15 minutes, plus freezing, cooling and chilling*

Cooking time: *about 30 minutes*

HAVE READY

Stand mixer fitted with the paddle attachment

Baking sheets lined with silicone mats or parchment paper.

Piping bags, fitted with the nozzles.

Oven preheated to 220°C/ 200°C fan/gas mark 7.

EQUIPMENT

stand mixer
 – paddle and whisk attachments
2 baking sheets
parchment paper
3 piping bags
 – 8mm and 5mm plain nozzles
 – 14mm St Honoré nozzle
chopping knife and board
rolling pin
dinner plate
spatula
bowl
heavy-based pan
wooden spoon
2 medium bowls

pastry brush
2cm round cutter (or use the similar-sized wide end of a piping nozzle)
wire rack
medium heatproof bowl
sieve
clingfilm
skewer
microwave and microwavable bowl, or medium pan and heatproof bowl
digital thermometer
electric hand whisk
large bowl

FOR THE PUFF PASTRY BASE

a little flour, for rolling out

about 170g puff pastry (frozen trimmings are fine, see introduction)

FOR THE CRAQUELIN TOPPING

25g butter, at room temperature

30g demerara sugar

about ¼ teaspoon red edible paste colouring

30g plain flour

icing sugar, for dusting

FOR THE CHOUX PASTRY

125g cold water

65g butter, cubed

7g caster sugar

1.5g table salt

125g strong flour

125g eggs (about 2½ medium)

20g egg yolk mixed with 1 teaspoon water, for the egg wash

FOR THE VANILLA CRÈME PÂTISSIÈRE

3g gelatine plus 1 tablespoon cold water

60g egg yolks (3 medium)

35g caster sugar

3g vanilla extract

20g cornflour

270g fresh milk

½ vanilla pod, split lengthways

FOR STICKING THE BUNS

25g dark chocolate, finely chopped

FOR THE CRÈME CHIBOUST

60g caster sugar

25g water

45g egg whites (1½ medium)

FOR THE MASCARPONE CREAM

½ vanilla pod, split lengthways

250g good-quality mascarpone

50g caster sugar

250g whipping cream

PREPARE THE PUFF PASTRY BASE AND CRAQUELIN TOPPING

1. Lightly flour a clean work surface and roll the pastry into a circle 22–24cm in diameter and 4mm thick. Place a similar-sized dinner plate on top and cut around it to form a perfect circle.
2. Prick the pastry all over with a fork (this prevents it from rising too much), then transfer to the lined baking sheet and chill while you make the craquelin.
3. Using a spatula, mix the butter and sugar together in a bowl until well combined. Work in the red colouring, then fold in the flour to make a smooth paste that's evenly coloured. If the colour isn't strong enough, you can add more and mix again.
4. Put the paste onto a square of parchment paper, spread it out slightly and cover with another piece of parchment. Roll out between the 2 squares until about 3mm thick. Freeze until firm enough to cut out.

MAKE THE CHOUX PASTRY AND BAKE THE BASE OF THE TART

5. Make the choux pastry following the instructions on page 37. Spoon it into the prepared piping bag fitted with the 8mm nozzle. Take the puff pastry out of the fridge and pipe a thin, even line of choux around the edge. Save the rest for the choux buns.
6. Mix the egg yolk and water in a small bowl until smooth. Brush all over the choux ring. Bake for 12 minutes, then lower the temperature to 200°C/180°C fan/gas mark 6 and bake for another 8–10 minutes, until cooked through.

BAKE THE CHOUX PASTRY BALLS

7. Remove the craquelin from the freezer and peel off the top sheet of parchment. Using a 2cm cutter, stamp out 23–25 circles (this will give you some spares).
8. Pipe 23–25 hazelnut-sized balls of choux paste onto the prepared tray, spacing them well apart so they have room to expand. (You might find it easier to draw well-spaced 2cm circles on the parchment, then turn the paper over and use the outlines as a guide. It's important to pipe a few extra so you can pick the best ones to assemble the gâteau.)
9. Carefully place a circle of craquelin on top of each ball and bake for 15–18 minutes, until golden and puffed up. Remove the pastry base if it's cooked during this time, and transfer to a wire rack to cool.

MAKE THE CRÈME PÂTISSIÈRE AND FILL THE CHOUX BUNS

10. Put the gelatine into a small bowl, add the water and set aside to soak.
11. Make the crème pâtissière following the instructions on page 26, but omitting the butter. Spoon about 180g into a separate bowl, cover the surface with clingfilm and allow to cool. Whisk the soaked gelatine into the remaining warm crème pâtissière until dissolved, transfer to a medium bowl, cover the surface with clingfilm and set aside to cool.
12. Choose the best choux buns – you'll need about 19 for the gateaux. Spoon the 180g quantity of crème pâtissière into the piping bag fitted with the 5mm nozzle. Using a skewer, make a small hole in the base of each bun, then push in the nozzle and fill with the crème pâtissière.
13. Melt the chocolate in a microwave or very small bain-marie (see page 34). Dip the base of each filled bun into the chocolate, scrape off any excess against the side of the bowl, and gently press it onto the choux edging the puff pastry base. Allow to set.

MAKE THE CRÈME CHIBOUST AND MASCARPONE CREAM

14. Put 50g of the caster sugar in a heavy-based pan with the water. Heat gently to dissolve the sugar, then increase the heat until the temperature reaches 121°C (this makes a stronger meringue).
15. Meanwhile, whisk the egg whites in the stand mixer until stiff peaks form. Add the remaining 10g sugar and whisk again.
16. With the motor running at a slow speed, pour the sugar syrup down the side of the egg white bowl, making sure it doesn't hit the beaters, and continue whisking until the meringue is thick, smooth, glossy and cool. Fold into the cooled crème pâtissière until smooth.
17. Spoon the chiboust into the puff pastry base, first pressing the pastry down gently if it has risen slightly. Spread the cream around until it's touching the inside of the choux ring. Transfer to the fridge while you make the mascarpone cream.
18. Scrape the vanilla seeds into a large bowl. Add the mascarpone and sugar and whisk with an electric hand whisk until soft and smooth.
19. Gradually add the whipping cream, mixing slowly at first, then increasing the speed a little until the mixture is smooth and firm. Take care not to overwhip or the mixture will split and it won't be smooth enough to pipe. If this happens, add a couple more tablespoons of the cream and very slowly mix again.
20. Spoon into the piping bag fitted with the St Honoré nozzle and pipe curved sweeps over the chiboust filling, working from the outside edge to the centre. Finish by piping a zigzag in the middle and place 1 more choux bun in the centre. Dust with icing sugar and serve.

PETITS GÂTEAUX

RUM BABAS

PEACH ÉCLAIRS

CRAQUELINS
RÉLIGIEUSES

PARIS — BREST

MACARONS
RÉLIGIEUSES

VANILLA
AND STRAWBERRY PYRAMIDS

CHOCOLATE CYLINDERS

APPLE DOMES

JASMINE, MANGO
AND YUZU SPHERES

PETITS GÂTEAUX

The name of this patisserie section translates literally as 'small cakes', and it's where patisserie chefs can let their creative talent run riot.

These are the *pièces de résistance* of patisserie, as they combine all the skills and more that have been learnt in the pastry kitchen. For example, both chocolate and baking skills are needed for the Chocolate Cylinders on page 187, which are filled with silky fruit custard and light-as-air mousse and sit on a coconut dacquoise. By contrast, the Jasmine and Mango Spheres on page 197 involve inserting a ball of ganache inside a mousse, which are set together in a spherical silicone mould. The sphere is coated with a passion fruit glaze, served on a crisp round of chocolate sablé and finished with an exquisite edible flower.

Petits gâteaux are made and constructed individually, and may be served as desserts, as well as for afternoon tea. Although they sometimes call for more time and patience than other recipes in this book, you'll be amply rewarded by the stunning appearance of the finished pieces.

RUM BABAS

Soft, golden dough buns drenched in sweet rum syrup

The light, almost cake-like consistency of a rum baba is achieved by enriching a bread dough with milk, sugar, eggs and butter. It's known in the patisserie world as a savarin dough and, in its raw state, is so soft and sticky that it can't be touched by hand – instead it is piped or spooned into moulds for baking.

As with the Butterkuchen on page 45, the key to a rum baba is the yeast, which is a living organism that needs just the right conditions to work properly – warmth, moisture and food, in this case sugar. If your mix gets too hot, if it isn't wet enough or is over- or underfed, the yeast will die, or simply won't be activated, and the baba won't rise.

The syrup has to have the right balance of sugar to water – too little sugar and it will be watery and make the spongy buns fall apart. Each bun must be baked until golden all over so that, as the syrup soaks into the soft crumb, the delicate texture of the bun isn't spoilt.

These rum babas are delicious served alone or, for a fun twist, filled with a just-set vanilla buttermilk cream (very similar to a light panna cotta mixture) and served with pipettes filled with Apricot and Honey Sauce – see *Finish it like a Pastry Chef* on page 163.

MAKES 10

TIMING

Hands-on time: *55 minutes,*
   plus about 1 hour 30 minutes proving
Cooking time: *40 minutes*

PREPARE IN ADVANCE

These babas can be wrapped in clingfilm once
   baked, but before filling, and stored in a sealed
   container in the freezer for up to 1 month.

HAVE READY

Eggs at room temperature and butter melted.
Stand mixer, if using, fitted with the dough hook.
Moulds or muffin tin lightly greased.

EQUIPMENT

stand mixer, optional
  – dough hook
8 tall baba moulds, dariole moulds
   or an 8-hole muffin tin
digital scales
sieve
small pan
microwave and microwavable bowl, optional
digital thermometer
small bowl
large bowl and wooden spoon, optional
plastic bag or damp cloth
2 piping bags
baking sheet
slotted spoon
wire rack
pastry brush

100g milk

10g dried yeast

340g strong bread flour

10g salt

30g caster sugar

150g eggs (3 medium)

165g just warm melted butter,
    plus extra to grease

FOR THE SYRUP

250g water

150g caster sugar

20g rum

TO GLAZE

3 tablespoons apricot jam, sieved

MAKE THE SAVARIN DOUGH

It is important to start this stage by mixing the milk and yeast together to make a ferment as there is a lot of fat in a savarin dough, from the butter and eggs, which can slow down the yeast. This method helps to make the best use of the yeast by getting it working from the very start.

1. Put the milk in a small pan or microwavable bowl and warm just to blood temperature (37°C).
2. Put the warm milk and the yeast in a small bowl and mix together. Set aside to allow the yeast to activate. It's ready when bubbles appear on the surface and the mixture looks frothy, at least 30 minutes.
3. Sift the flour into a large bowl or the bowl of a stand mixer. Make a well at one side and pour the yeast and milk mixture into it. Gently stir it, mixing in a little flour from the edge of the well until it forms a soft batter consistency. Take a spoonful of flour from the bowl and use it to cover the yeast mixture as if you're burying it. Set aside and wait for the surface of the flour to crack. Depending on the heat of your kitchen, this will take about 15–30 minutes.
4. Add the salt, sugar and eggs to the bowl and mix everything together on a low speed or with a wooden spoon to form a dough. Continue to work the mixture for about 10 minutes until smooth and shiny.
5. Pour the melted butter over the top of the dough without mixing it in – this is to stop a skin from forming on top of the dough. Cover and set aside for 40 minutes to 1½ hours to allow the mixture to rise until it has doubled in size.
6. Once the dough has doubled, mix it again to incorporate the butter.

BAKE THE BABAS

The key to filling the moulds is to pipe directly into the centre of the base, keeping the bag vertical until the dough has filled halfway. Don't pipe in a spiral or you'll have uneven babas.

The second bake of the babas is really important for depth of colour and enough structure to support the sponge once it's soaked in the syrup.

7. Spoon the mixture into a piping bag and snip about 2cm from the end. Pipe directly into the base of the prepared moulds to about half full. Alternatively, spoon the mixture into the moulds. Cover and set aside in a warm place to prove until doubled in size, about 1 hour.
8. Preheat the oven to 180°C/160°C fan/gas mark 4.
9. Once proved, transfer to the oven and bake for 15–20 minutes until golden on top. Carefully turn the babas out of the moulds, then transfer them to a baking sheet, pale sides facing up, and continue to bake for another 10 minutes until a rich golden colour all over. Set aside to cool on the sheet.

TO MAKE THE SYRUP AND DIP THE BABAS

10. Put the water into a small pan over a low heat and add the sugar. Heat gently until the sugar is dissolved, then bring to the boil and immediately take the pan off the heat.

11. Dip the babas one at a time into the hot syrup. Use a slotted spoon to gently toss them around – they should feel completely saturated in the syrup. Transfer to a wire rack over a tray to drain off any excess.

12. Sprinkle the rum evenly over the top of the babas then brush them with the sieved apricot jam to glaze.

THE SECRETS OF SUCCESS

———◆———

If the soaking syrup is too thick… You've overboiled it and it won't soak all the way through the buns. Add more water to thin it down.

FINISH IT LIKE A PASTRY CHEF

Serve the babas filled with Buttermilk Cream and with pipettes filled with Apricot and Honey Sauce (see below).

To make the cream, soak 5g gelatine in 25g cold water. Spoon 200g buttermilk into a pan and add 45g sugar and the seeds from ¼ vanilla pod. Heat gently to warm through, then stir in the gelatine. Fold in 200g double cream, then pass the mixture through a sieve into a bowl. Cover the surface with clingfilm to stop a skin from forming and allow to cool.

To make the sauce, purée *125g tinned apricots* and press through a sieve. Place in a small pan over a medium-high heat with *50g honey, 25g water* and *5g lemon juice* and stir together. Bring to the boil and simmer for 3–4 minutes until the mixture has thickened slightly. Strain again, then use to fill the pipettes.

Use a sharp bread knife to cut about three-quarters of the way through each baba. Whisk the cooled buttermilk cream to loosen, then spoon into a piping bag, snip off the tip and pipe it into the splits to fill the babas. Put each filled baba into a shallow bowl and poke each one with a pipette so that the apricot and honey sauce can be squeezed into the buns at the table.

Additional equipment: *2 small bowls, medium pan, blender, 8 pipettes 3–5mm in diameter, bread knife, piping bag, 8 shallow bowls.*

———◆ ◆ ◆———

PEACH ÉCLAIRS

Delightfully light open éclairs piped with fruit cream and
decorated with fresh peaches and mint leaves

These classic long buns are made by piping choux pastry into finger-length strips and baking them until crisp and golden. Traditionally, they're filled with cream and crème pâtissière and decorated with a slick of thick icing.

Pastry chefs pride themselves on rows of identically piped and filled éclairs. The current fashion is for buns filled with unusual flavours and iced in garish colours. This one features a delightful twist on the traditional offerings. After baking, the éclairs are split open like little canoes and piped with peach *crémeux*, a silky, butter-rich cream set with gelatine and flavoured with the fruit. To finish, it's garnished with pieces of fresh peach and mint leaves for a light and refreshing dessert slice.

Look out for special éclair piping nozzles, which have tiny little teeth that produce a very effective ridged outer crust.

SERVES 8–10

TIMING

Hands-on time: *1 hour 15 minutes*
Cooking time: *25–35 minutes*

PREPARE IN ADVANCE

The choux fingers can be made ahead
and frozen, uncut, in an airtight
container for up to 1 month.
If you're decorating the éclairs with
vanilla shortbread dice (see *Finish it
like a Pastry Chef*, page 167), they can
be made up to 5 days ahead and
stored in an airtight container.

HAVE READY

Stand mixer, if using, fitted with the
paddle attachment.
Baking sheets lined with parchment paper
or silicone mats.
Piping bags fitted with the nozzles.
Oven preheated to 200°C/180°C fan/
gas mark 6.

EQUIPMENT

stand mixer, optional
  – paddle attachment
  – whisk attachment
2 large baking sheets
parchment paper or 2 x silicone mats
2 large piping bags
  – 16mm star éclair nozzle
  – 5mm round nozzle
digital scales
sharp knife
chopping board
sieve
medium heavy-based pan

wooden spoon
large bowl, optional
ruler
pastry brush
sharp serrated knife
small bowl
medium pan
digital thermometer
balloon whisk
stick blender
medium bowl
clingfilm

FOR THE CHOUX PASTRY

125g cold water

65g butter, chopped

7g caster sugar

1.5g table salt

125g strong bread flour, sifted

125g beaten eggs (2½ medium)

25g beaten egg (½ medium), for
egg wash

FOR THE PEACH CRÉMEUX

5g powdered gelatine

25g cold water

160g peach (from about 1 whole),
strained

60g egg yolks (3 medium)

50g eggs (1 medium), beaten

100g caster sugar

120g butter, at room temperature
and chopped

FOR THE ASSEMBLY

1 peach, cut into small triangles

small fresh mint leaves, to decorate

edible gold lustre

MAKE THE CHOUX FINGERS

To make sure you pipe even shapes, draw 12 well-spaced lines each 12cm long on the parchment paper lining the baking sheet. Flip the paper over and put it back on the baking sheet. You should be able to see the lines through the paper so you can pipe directly onto them.

Before baking, the éclairs are brushed with an egg wash glaze to give them a shine and to prevent them from cracking. Be careful not to brush over too much egg or your éclairs will look like they've been baked with omelettes on top.

1. Make the choux pastry using the method on page 37.
2. Spoon the paste into the piping bag fitted with the star éclair nozzle and carefully pipe it onto the prepared baking sheets in lengths measuring 2cm wide and 12cm long, leaving about 5–6cm between each one as they will expand and double in size during baking.
3. Brush the remaining 25g beaten egg very lightly over each bun, taking care not to flood the top with beaten egg. Bake for 20–30 minutes until the éclairs are completely dried out. Remove from the oven and allow to cool on the baking sheets.
4. Once the pastries are completely cool, use a sharp serrated knife to cut a long rectangle out of each one so that the pastry shells look like canoes. This means removing about a quarter of each éclair.

MAKE THE PEACH CRÉMEUX

Take care not to overheat the mixture, otherwise you'll end up with a pan of peach-flavoured scrambled eggs.

5. Make the peach crémeux following the instructions on page 27.
6. Transfer the mixture to a bowl, cover the surface with clingfilm and chill for 2–3 hours.

FILL AND ASSEMBLE EACH ÉCLAIR

7. Whisk the chilled *crémeux* until smooth and spoon it into the piping bag fitted with the 5mm nozzle. Carefully pipe neat domes along the length of the éclairs.
8. Place the peach triangles between the *crémeux* domes and brush the peach lightly with the apricot glaze. Decorate with the small mint leaves brushed with a little gold lustre and serve.

FINISH IT LIKE A PASTRY CHEF

Tiny sugared Vanilla Shortbread Dice add a little crunch to these soft, *crémeux*-filled éclairs. This recipe makes double what you'll need, but the remainder can be cut into biscuits to serve with tea.

Put *75g butter, at room temperature*, into a medium bowl and beat in *35g caster sugar*. Scrape the *seeds from ½ vanilla pod* and add them to the bowl. Beat again to distribute the seeds and give additional flavour to the butter and sugar mixture. Sift *110g plain flour* over the mixture and work it again to make a soft dough. Bring it together with your hands and knead it lightly, as if making pastry. Roll out the dough on a lightly floured work surface to 5mm thick. Chill for 30 minutes – this will make it easier to cut. Preheat the oven to 200°C/180°C fan/gas mark 6. Cut half the mixture into 5mm dice and the remaining dough into fingers for biscuits. Spread them out on a lined baking sheet and bake the dice for about 8–10 minutes until golden, giving a little longer to the shortbread biscuits. Allow to cool, then roll the dice in *icing sugar*. Store in an airtight container and enjoy within 5 days.
Additional equipment: *rolling pin.*

You could also add a luxurious flourish to your éclairs by garnishing them with *gold leaf*. Use a fine brush to lift the delicate leaves and dot pieces over the top of the éclairs.
Additional equipment: *fine brush.*

CRAQUELINS RÉLIGIEUSES

*Choux buns filled and decorated with two types of
cream and topped with a crunchy golden crown*

These classic French pastries are named after nuns because of their shape. Two dainty choux buns, one larger and one smaller, are filled with crème pâtissière and stacked on top of each other, then buttercream is piped around the join to create what looks like an ecclesiastical collar, making them look like miniature nuns.

Pastry chefs bake choux until it is dark golden, firm, crisp and holds its shape. This is to ensure that it doesn't collapse when taken out of the oven and that it doesn't become soft when filled with a creamy filling, such as a crème pâtissière. The larger choux bun here needs to be firm enough to support the smaller bun on top. Make sure you poke a hole in the bottom of the buns when they come out of the oven to allow steam to escape, otherwise you may find that the inside of the buns are raw choux paste.

In place of the classic fondant coating, this recipe features an oh-so-modern craquelin topping. It's a simple butter, demerara sugar and flour mix, which is rolled out thinly, well-then cut into circles and baked on the choux. If you want to flavour the filling with fruit, colour the craquelin accordingly.

SERVES 8

TIMING

Hands-on time: *1 hour 50 minutes*
Cooking time: *50 minutes*

PREPARE IN ADVANCE

The *craquelin* can be made and
  frozen up to 1 month ahead.
The vanilla crème pâtissière can
  be made up to 3 days ahead.
The buttercream can be made
  up to 4–5 days ahead.

HAVE READY

Stand mixer, if using, fitted with
  the whisk attachment.
Baking sheet and trays lined with
  parchment paper or silicone mats.
Piping bags fitted with the nozzles.

EQUIPMENT

stand mixer, optional
  – paddle attachment
  – whisk attachment
2 large baking sheets
3 baking trays
parchment paper or silicone mats
2 piping bags
  – 8–10mm plain round nozzle
  – 3mm star nozzle
digital scales
sieve
food-processor or blender
medium heatproof bowl
wooden spoon

rolling pin
mini cutters
  – 2cm
  – 4cm
2 x medium heavy-based
  stainless steel pans
electric or balloon whisk
clingfilm
large bowl
digital thermometer
large metal spoon

50g butter, at room temperature

60g demerara sugar

60g plain flour

FOR THE VANILLA
CRÈME PÂTISSIÈRE

40g egg yolks (2 medium)

30g caster sugar

2g (½ teaspoon) vanilla extract

16g cornflour

200g milk

½ vanilla pod, split lengthways

40g butter, at room temperature, cubed

150g whipping cream, whipped
    and chilled

FOR THE CHOUX PASTRY

125g cold water

65g butter, chopped

7g caster sugar

1.5g table salt

125g strong bread flour, sifted

125g beaten eggs (2½ medium)

25g beaten egg (½ medium), for
    egg wash

FOR THE ITALIAN
MERINGUE BUTTERCREAM

60g egg whites (2 medium)

120g caster sugar

50g water

250g butter

½ vanilla pod, split lengthways

100g blueberries, blended and
    strained through a sieve

15g aniseed or blueberry liqueur

FOR THE DECORATION

edible gold flakes

MAKE THE CRAQUELIN TOPPING

This is made simply with a creamed butter and sugar mixture. The crystals in the demerara sugar create the crackle effect during baking.

1. Put the butter and sugar into a medium bowl and use a wooden spoon to cream until soft and smooth. The sugar won't completely dissolve as the demerara has a bigger crystal than caster, but it just needs to be incorporated evenly with the butter. Beat in the flour.
2. Spoon the mixture onto the lined baking sheet. Lay a piece of parchment paper on top and roll out the mixture to 2mm thick. Transfer to the freezer for 1 hour, until hard.
3. Take the *craquelin* out of the freezer and use the mini cutters to cut out eight 4cm rounds, and eight 2cm rounds. Set aside while you prepare the rest of the ingredients.

MAKE THE VANILLA CRÈME PÂTISSIÈRE FILLING

This is used to fill the buns.

4. Make the pastry cream following the method on page 26. You won't need to add the whipping cream at this stage.

MAKE THE CHOUX BUNS

To make sure you're piping even balls of pastry, take the parchment paper from the remaining baking sheet and use the mini cutters to draw eight well-spaced circles of each size onto the parchment paper lining the baking sheet. Flip the paper over and put it back on the baking sheet. You should be able to see the circles through the paper and use them as a guide when piping the dough.

As the buns bake, the craquelin will cook and expand with them to form the crunchy topping.

5. Preheat the oven to 200°C/180°C fan/gas mark 6.
6. Make the choux pastry following the method on page 37.
7. Spoon the paste into a piping bag fitted with the plain round nozzle. Pipe eight 4cm balls onto one of the prepared baking trays, leaving a space between the balls for them to double in size during baking. Pipe eight 2cm balls onto the second baking tray, spaced well apart.
8. Lay the *craquelin* circles on top of the choux buns and bake for 20–30 minutes. Check the smaller buns after 20 minutes and take them out of the oven if they're ready.

9. Allow the cooked buns to cool slightly so that you can handle them. Use a plain piping nozzle to make a small hole in the top of each of the bigger choux buns and the bottom of the small buns. Leave them to cool on their trays until completely dried out, quite crisp and not at all soft, particularly the larger buns.

MAKE THE ITALIAN MERINGUE BUTTERCREAM

This is used to stick the smaller buns on top of the large ones, and for piping the buttercream collars.

10. Make the buttercream using the method on page 146. Whisk in the vanilla seeds, blueberries and liqueur. Spoon into a piping bag fitted with the star nozzle.

FILL THE BUNS WITH THE LIGHT CRÈME PÂTISSIÈRE

11. Put the chilled crème pâtissière into a large bowl and whisk until smooth. Add a spoonful of the whipped cream to loosen the mixture, then fold in the rest. Spoon the mixture into a piping bag fitted with an 8–10mm nozzle and use it to fill the choux buns.

ASSEMBLE THE RÉLIGIEUSES

12. Take one large choux bun and pipe a small blob of buttercream on top. Position a smaller choux bun on top and press down lightly to secure. Repeat with the remaining buns.
13. Pipe the buttercream around the joins where the two buns meet to create buttercream collars. Sprinkle gold flakes over each of the little nun-shaped buns and serve.

PARIS–BREST

A ring of crunchy vanilla choux encasing a hazelnut
praline mousse and garnished with caramelised nuts

These sweet choux buns, shaped like bicycle wheels, were originally created in 1910 by French pastry chef Louis Durand to celebrate the Paris–Brest cycle race. They were very popular with the cyclists as their calorific value gave much-needed energy. There are many filling and topping variations of this classic patisserie, but this recipe features a crunchy topping on the choux and a nut mousse filling.

SERVES 12

TIMING

Hands-on time: *2 hours 45 minutes, plus cooling,*
   freezing and chilling
Cooking time: *15–20 minutes*

PREPARE IN ADVANCE

The almond praline mousse can be made
   up to 3 days in advance.

HAVE READY

Baking sheets lined with parchment paper.
Piping bags fitted with the nozzles.
Oven preheated to 220°C/200°C fan/
   gas mark 7.

EQUIPMENT

2 baking sheets
parchment paper
2 piping bags
   – 1.5cm plain nozzle
   – 1cm star nozzle
sieve
medium bowl
wooden spoon or whisk
board
rolling pin
7.5 and 5.5cm plain round cutters
small palette knife
medium, heavy-based pan
large bowl, optional
wide slice
skewer
wire rack
small bowl
frying pan
small, heavy-based pan
sharp knife

FOR THE VANILLA CRUNCH

50g butter, softened

50g soft light brown sugar

5g plain flour

25g ground almonds

3g sea salt

1g (a few drops) vanilla extract

FOR THE CHOUX PASTRY

40g milk

90g water

50g butter, cubed

10g caster sugar

a good pinch of salt

2g (¼ teaspoon) vanilla extract

75g strong flour, sifted

100g eggs, beaten (2 medium)

FOR THE HAZELNUT
PRALINE MOUSSE

3g powdered gelatine

15g cold water

40g milk

25g caster sugar

2g (¼ tsp) vanilla extract

250g mascarpone

300g double cream

80g ready-made hazelnut praline paste
(available online)

FOR THE CARAMELISED
ALMOND DECORATIONS

15g espresso coffee

100g icing sugar, sifted,
plus extra for dusting

25g flaked almonds

FOR THE CARAMELISED
HAZELNUT DECORATIONS

a little vegetable oil

75g caster sugar

30g whole, skinned hazelnuts, toasted

MAKE THE VANILLA CRUNCH

These circles of caramel are placed on top of the choux rings.

1. Put the butter and sugar into a bowl and beat together. Beat in the flour, ground almonds, salt and vanilla until it becomes a smooth paste.
2. Lay a sheet of parchment paper on a board. Spoon the mixture onto it, spread it out a bit and cover with another piece of parchment. Roll out to a thickness of about 2mm. The mixture is very soft, so freeze it between the parchment until it is firm enough to cut.
3. Use a 7.5cm cutter to stamp out as many circles as you can from the vanilla crunch, then stamp out the middles with a 5.5cm cutter. Keep them all on the paper and freeze again until they have firmed up a bit more. Using a small palette knife, carefully remove the centres and trimmings to leave just the rings on the paper. Work quickly as the mixture can soften. Freeze the rings on the paper until ready to use. Gather up all the trimmings and reroll on fresh parchment. Freeze as before, then stamp out more circles and refreeze them. Repeat this process until you've cut out 12 rings, which will give you a few spares in case of breakages.

MAKE THE CHOUX PASTRY

4. Once all the vanilla crunch rings are in the freezer, make the pastry, following the intructions on page 37 (but note that this version contains milk as well as water, and both should be added at the same time).
5. Spoon the mixture into the piping bag fitted with the 1.5cm nozzle and carefully pipe 12 rings 7.5cm in diameter onto a prepared baking sheet, spacing them well apart so they have room to expand. (You might find it easier to draw well-spaced 7.5cm circles on the parchment, then turn the paper over and use the outlines as a guide.)
6. Remove the vanilla crunch rings from the freezer. Using a wide slice to lift them carefully off the paper, place a crunch ring on each choux ring. Bake for 15–20 minutes until the rings are a rich golden colour and firm enough to be sliced.
7. When done, use a skewer to puncture a hole in the side of each ring. Leave to cool on a wire rack.

MAKE THE HAZELNUT PRALINE MOUSSE

This mousse is used as the filling for the buns.

8. Put the gelatine into a small bowl, add the water and set aside to soak.
9. Meanwhile, put the milk, sugar and vanilla into a saucepan and bring just to the boil. Take the pan off the heat and stir in the gelatine until it dissolves. Set aside to cool a little.
10. Mix the mascarpone and cream together in a bowl just until smooth. Add the cool milk mixture, then fold in the hazelnut praline paste.

MAKE THE CARAMELISED ALMOND DECORATIONS

When you're ready to serve, make the caramelised decorations – they set very quickly – and assemble the choux buns.

11. Place a frying pan over a medium heat. When hot, add the espresso, icing sugar and flaked almonds and toss together, heating until the sugar has caramelised. Pour onto a prepared baking sheet and allow to cool. Break into small pieces each containing an almond.

MAKE THE CARAMELISED HAZELNUT DECORATIONS

12. Reline a baking sheet with fresh parchment and brush with the oil. Heat the caster sugar in a small, heavy-based pan until it becomes a golden caramel. Lower the heat as much as possible, then dip each hazelnut in the caramel and place on the prepared sheet to set.

FILL AND ASSEMBLE THE BUNS

13. Carefully cut each choux ring in half horizontally. Spoon the hazelnut mousse into the piping bag fitted with the star nozzle and pipe a ring of it on the bottom half of each bun.
14. Replace the top half of each bun and dust with icing sugar. Pipe 6 small, evenly spaced blobs of mousse on each bun and push a caramelised hazelnut into 3 of them, and a caramelised almond in the others. Serve straight away.

THE SECRETS OF SUCCESS

The choux mixture is too soft to pipe… This means that you've either not cooked the panade enough in the pan, or you've added too much egg. Sadly, there's nothing that can be done to rescue the mixture, so it's necessary to start again.

MACARONS RÉLIGIEUSES

*Two crisp macarons filled with a nugget of jelly and swirl of creamy
caramel chocolate filling, set in the classic style of a réligieuse*

This combination of macarons arranged in the shape of a *réligieuse* (nun) is a delightful way
to show off your baking skills. The centre of each macaron holds a square of apple jelly and
is matched with a sweet milk chocolate and caramel cream.

It's important to grind the almonds and icing sugar together in a food processor before
using them in the recipe so that the almonds are as fine as they can be. This ensures that the
finished macaron has a pleasing, smooth finish, but with a melt-in-the-mouth texture inside.

It will make life easier if you have four baking sheets, but if you have only two, pipe the
macarons onto flat sheets of parchment paper and bake in batches, sliding one lot off and
another lot on. The dough will sit happily at room temperature once piped.

If you have any leftover ganache, use a teaspoon to roll it into balls, then dust in cocoa
powder or icing sugar for an after-dinner treat.

MAKES 32

TIMING

Hands-on time: *1 hour 30 minutes*
Cooking time: *12–15 minutes*

PREPARE IN ADVANCE

The fillings can all be made up to
  1 day ahead. Allow the ganache
  to come to room temperature
  so that it's soft enough to pipe
  before using.

HAVE READY

Stand mixer, if using, fitted with
the whisk attachment.
Parchment paper marked with the
  macaron templates (see step 1)
  and laid on the baking sheets,
  drawn side down.
Piping bags fitted with the nozzles.
Ice-cube tray well oiled.
Oven preheated to 150°C/
  130°C fan/gas mark 2.

EQUIPMENT

stand mixer, optional
 – whisk attachment
parchment paper
4 baking sheets
2 piping bags
 – 1cm nozzle
 – 0.5cm nozzle
ice-cube tray
digital scales
sharp knife
chopping board
mini food processor
sieve
large bowl
spatula
skewer or cocktail stick
large bowl, optional
electric hand whisk, optional
2 small pans

digital thermometer
large metal spoon
2 medium bowls
wooden spoon
medium pan
small bowl
small clean paintbrush

FOR THE MACARONS

150g ground almonds

150g icing sugar

2.5g ground cinnamon

110g egg whites (about 4 medium)

edible green colouring

150g caster sugar

40g water

iridescent green edible lustre

FOR THE CARAMEL CHOCOLATE FILLING

125g milk chocolate (about 36–40% cocoa solids), very finely chopped

85g caster sugar

3g lemon juice

170g double cream

20g butter

FOR THE APPLE AND WHITE CHOCOLATE GANACHE

50g apple juice

75g white chocolate, very finely chopped

32g double cream

FOR THE APPLE JELLY

1g citric acid

3g fruit pectin powder

125g caster sugar

100g apple juice

25g apple purée

17g liquid glucose

a little sunflower oil, for greasing

PREPARE THE TEMPLATES FOR YOUR MACARONS

1. Draw sixty-four 5cm circles on two sheets of parchment paper and sixty-four 2cm circles (the size of a one pence piece) on two more. Line the baking sheets with the paper, drawn-side down.

MAKE THE MACARONS

The macarons are made by folding an Italian meringue mixture into an almond paste. Process the almonds and sugar finely before using, as any large pieces will ruin the smooth texture of the finished macarons.

Use the colouring sparingly, but remember that the shade will soften slightly once the paste is folded together with the meringue, so you might want it to look slightly darker than your desired shade at this stage.

Once baked, a well-made macaron should have a smooth rounded top with a ridge around the base, known as the foot, which should be in line with the macaron and not spread out.

2. Put the almonds and icing sugar into a mini food-processor and whizz until very fine. Pass through a sieve into a large bowl, pressing it through with a spatula and discarding any large bits that remain in the sieve. Weigh again to ensure you have the correct quantity and continue to blitz the almonds if necessary.

3. Add the cinnamon to the bowl along with 55g of the egg whites. Bind together to make a stiff paste. Colour the batter by dipping a skewer or cocktail stick into the colour and folding it into the mixture. Set aside.

4. Put the remaining egg whites into the bowl of a stand mixer. You can also use a large bowl and an electric hand whisk.

5. Meanwhile, put the caster sugar and water into a small pan and heat gently to dissolve the sugar. Bring up to a simmer.

6. When the temperature of the syrup reaches about 110°C, slowly start to whisk the egg whites until they're stiff with a strong peak, but not dry.

7. As soon as the syrup reaches 118°C, take it off the heat and pour it over the egg whites. Continue to whisk until cool.

8. Fold a large spoonful of meringue into the almond mixture to loosen it, then fold in the remainder until all the ingredients are combined. At this stage, the mixture should resemble molten lava and not be stiff like a paste. If it needs loosening, stir it with a spatula a couple more times until it leaves a ribbon-like trail when you lift the spoon, then settles again into the mixture.

9. Spoon the mixture into the piping bag fitted with the 1cm nozzle and carefully pipe rounds into the marked circles. Set aside for about 20 minutes to allow a skin to form on top, then bake the small macarons for 12 minutes and the large macarons for 15 minutes. If you have only 2 baking sheets,

bake the large macarons first, then slide them onto a flat surface to cool. Slide the parchment with the smaller macarons onto the baking sheet and bake a second batch.

MAKE THE CARAMEL CHOCOLATE FILLING

The creamy filling involves mixing a dry caramel with the chocolate. The chocolate needs to be chopped very finely so that it melts instantly when the caramel is poured on top, without any lumps remaining.

10. Place the chocolate in a medium bowl.
11. Put the sugar into a small pan over a low to medium heat. Cook until the sugar dissolves and turns golden. Stir in the lemon juice – stand back as the syrup may splutter at this stage, then stir in the cream.
12. Strain the mixture through a sieve onto the chocolate. Mix well with a wooden spoon, working from the centre outwards to make a smooth emulsion. Beat in the butter, allow to cool, then chill.

MAKE THE APPLE AND WHITE CHOCOLATE GANACHE

Again, the chocolate here should be chopped very finely so that it melts immediately when the hot cream and apple juice are added.

13. Pour the apple juice into a small pan and bring to a simmer. Continue to cook to reduce the liquid until there's about 1 tablespoon left in the pan.
14. Place the finely chopped chocolate into a medium bowl.
15. Pour the cream into a medium pan and bring to the boil, then remove from the heat and slowly pour in the chocolate and stir with a wooden spoon, again working from the centre outwards until the mixture is smooth. Stir in the reduced apple juice. Leave to set at room temperature.

MAKE THE APPLE JELLY

16. In a small bowl, mix together the citric acid, pectin and sugar.
17. Pour the apple juice into a small pan and whisk the sugar mixture into it, followed by the apple purée and liquid glucose. Place the pan over a medium heat and slowly bring to the boil. Simmer until the temperature reaches 108°C.
18. Pour the mixture into the prepared ice-cube tray and leave to cool, then chill.

Continued…

ASSEMBLE THE MACARONS

The sandwiched macarons each have a ring of ganache between them with a cube of apple jelly in the centre.

19. Spoon the caramel chocolate filling into the remaining piping bag and pipe a small ring of ganache near the edge of half the 5cm macarons, leaving a space in the middle to put the apple jelly. Do the same with the 2cm macarons.
20. Take the apple jelly cubes out of the trays and cut them into 3cm squares.
21. Take one of the 5cm macarons piped with ganache and place a jelly cube in the centre of the ring. Place a second macaron on top. Repeat with the remaining larger macarons.
22. Cut the remaining jelly cubes into quarters and repeat the process with the 2cm macarons. Transfer all the macarons to the fridge to keep them fresh until you're ready to build your réligieuses.

CONSTRUCT THE RÉLIGIEUSES

23. Brush one side only of each macaron with some edible glitter.
24. Place one of the larger macarons flat on a clean board. Spread a little of the white chocolate ganache on one edge of a smaller macaron and place it, on its edge, onto the centre of the larger one. It should stick. Repeat until you have 32 macaron réligieuses.

FINISH IT LIKE A PASTRY CHEF

Temper some white chocolate (see page 34) and spread it thinly onto a large piece of rectangular acetate. When semi-set, use a knife to score into 6 x 1.5cm rectangles. Bend the acetate, chocolate side out, around a curved object, such as a rolling pin, and allow to set. When set, peel off the acetate, drizzle the curves with more chocolate to create a textured effect and set again. Place the upper macaron of each réligeuse on a chocolate curve, as though it's sitting in a boat. Dust with *edible red lustre powder* and serve.
Additional equipment: *acetate, rolling pin.*

VANILLA AND STRAWBERRY PYRAMIDS

A vanilla and kirsch cream mousse, layers of strawberry compote,
balsamic jelly and lemon sponge on a crisp biscuit base

Making a petit gâteau – whether it's a cylinder, sphere, dome or, in this case, a pyramid –
is a wonderful creative challenge for a patisserie chef. There's a chance to combine different
flavours and textures and, of course, myriad skills, and box them into one delightful small
piece of patisserie.

   Here a pyramid mould is used to create some of the parts, so it's very important to cut
other individual pieces precisely so that they fit properly. A simple decoration of tempered
chocolate enhanced with red cocoa butter completes it.

SERVES 6

TIMING

Hands-on time: *1 hour 45 minutes,*
   plus chilling and freezing
Cooking time: *1 hour*

PREPARE IN ADVANCE

The shortbread and sponge can both
   be made up to 3 days ahead and
   stored in separate airtight containers.
The whole recipe can be made and
   assembled up to the end of step 27
   and stored in the freezer for up to
   1 day before glazing.

HAVE READY

Stand mixer, if using, fitted with the
   whisk attachment.
Baking sheet lined with
   parchment paper.
Baking tray lined with clingfilm,
   with a wire rack resting on top.
Small baking tray (about 16 x 24cm)
   lined with parchment paper.
Oven preheated to 180°C/
   160°C fan/gas mark 4.

EQUIPMENT

mini blender
6-hole pyramid mould, each hole
   measuring 71 x 40mm
small bowl
small pan
spatula
small sealable container (about 8 x
   12 cm)
chopping knife
balloon whisk
chopping board
sieve
clingfilm
stick blender
zester
stand mixer
   – whisk attachment
large metal spoon
medium bowl
small baking tray (about 16 x 24cm)
parchment paper
wire rack
baking tray
baking sheet

pastry brush
rolling pin
ruler
fork
digital thermometer
microwave and
microwavable bowl, or
   medium pan and
   heatproof bowl
acetate sheet
piping bag
small palette knife

MAKE THE STRAWBERRY COMPOTE

Mara des Bois strawberries are preferred for the compote because they are intensely aromatic and impart a luscious flavour.

1. Place the strawberries, caster sugar and lemon juice in a small blender and whizz until smooth.
2. Pour 20g of the compote into each pyramid mould and freeze for 1 hour.

MAKE THE BALSAMIC VINEGAR JELLY

A cube of zingy balsamic jelly offsets the creamy texture and flavour of the diplomat cream.

3. Put the gelatine into a small bowl, add the water and set aside to soak.
4. Place the balsamic vinegar and sugar in a small pan and bring to the boil. Take the pan off the heat and stir in the gelatine until dissolved.
5. Lightly dampen the sealable container with water, then pour the jelly into it. Transfer to the fridge for 1 hour. Once set, slide a knife around the edge to loosen the jelly and turn it out. Cut into six 4cm squares.

MAKE THE VANILLA AND KIRSCH DIPLOMAT CREAM

The diplomat cream is made from a classic crème anglaise mixture, combined with whipped cream and flavoured with vanilla and kirsch.

6. Put the gelatine into a small bowl, add the water and set aside to soak.
7. Pour the milk into a saucepan. Scrape in the vanilla seeds, add the pod and bring to the boil. Cover and set aside.
8. Whisk the caster sugar egg yolks and together in a bowl for 20 seconds. Whisk in the flours.
9. Strain the milk over the egg and flour mixture and whisk together until smooth. Pour back into the pan and gently return to the boil, stirring all the time.
10. As soon as the mixture is boiling, simmer for 1 minute, whisking well to ensure there are no lumps. Take the pan off the heat.
11. Stir the gelatine into the pan until dissolved. Pour into a bowl. Cover the surface directly with clingfilm and transfer to the fridge for 20 minutes.
12. Whip the cream and icing sugar together until soft peaks form. Whisk in the kirsch.
13. Fold a third of the whipped cream into the crème anglaise and whisk gently, then carefully fold in the remaining cream.
Continued…

FOR THE STRAWBERRY COMPOTE

75g strawberries, preferably Mara des Bois, washed and trimmed

7.5g caster sugar

3g lemon juice

FOR THE BALSAMIC VINEGAR JELLY

2g powdered gelatine

10g cold water

60g balsamic vinegar

6g caster sugar

FOR THE VANILLA AND KIRSCH DIPLOMAT CREAM

3g powdered gelatine

15g cold water

125g full-fat milk

½ vanilla pod, split lengthways

40g egg yolks (2 medium)

25g caster sugar

7g cornflour

7g plain flour

110g whipping cream

15g icing sugar

6g kirsch

FOR THE WHITE CHOCOLATE AND VANILLA GLAZE

40g whipping cream

180g full-fat milk

70g caster sugar

20g liquid glucose

½ vanilla pod, split lengthways

5g powdered gelatine

25g cold water

300g white chocolate (about 33% cocoa solids), finely chopped

Continued…

FOR THE LEMON MADELEINE SPONGE

zest and juice from 1 lemon

50g egg (1 medium)

50g caster sugar

10g milk

50g plain flour, sifted

1.5g baking powder, sifted

20g butter, melted

30g grapeseed oil

25g icing sugar

FOR THE TONKA BEAN SHORTBREAD

85g butter

40g caster sugar

2g salt

1g tonka bean, optional, finely grated or finely chopped

120g plain flour

FOR THE DECORATION

200g white chocolate

40g red cocoa butter

edible gold lustre powder

6 fresh strawberries

MAKE THE WHITE CHOCOLATE AND VANILLA GLAZE

This provides the ultimate finish to the petits gâteaux and has just enough gelatine to set over the top of the diplomat cream.

14. Place the cream, milk, sugar and glucose in a saucepan. Scrape in the vanilla seeds and add the pod too. Heat gently to dissolve the sugar, then bring to the boil. Take the pan off the heat, cover and set aside to infuse.
15. Put the gelatine into a small bowl, add the water and set aside to soak for about 5 minutes. Stir into the cream mixture until dissolved.
16. Put the white chocolate into a bowl and pour the cream mixture over it. Mix with a stick blender until smooth, then strain into a clean bowl.

MAKE THE LEMON MADELEINE SPONGE

Brushing syrup over the sponge ensures it stays moist inside the cream.

17. Put the lemon zest, egg and caster sugar into a stand mixer and whisk on full speed until the mixture is thick and mousse-like. You can also do this in a bowl with an electric hand whisk. Lower the speed and quickly whisk in the milk.
18. Add the flour and baking powder to the bowl and fold in with the spatula, taking care not to knock out too much air. Gently fold in the butter and oil until combined. Spread onto the parchment-lined tray in a rectangle measuring 12 x 24cm and bake for 10–12 minutes.
19. Meanwhile, mix together the lemon juice and icing sugar. Slide the sponge onto the wire rack and, while still warm, brush the lemon syrup all over it. Lower the oven to 170°C/150°C fan/gas mark 3.

MAKE THE TONKA BEAN SHORTBREAD

All the ingredients for shortbread should be at room temperature so that they can be easily blended and made into a paste before baking.

20. Using a spatula, beat the butter in a bowl to soften it, then work in the caster sugar, salt and tonka bean (if using).
21. Continue to beat well until the mixture looks light and fluffy. Add the flour and mix just until a dough forms. Take care not to overwork it or the finished biscuit will be tough.
22. Put the dough between 2 sheets of parchment paper and roll into a rectangle roughly 25 x 17cm and 3mm thick. It should be perfectly smooth. Freeze for 10 minutes to chill quickly.
23. Peel off the top layer of paper and trim the dough into a 24 x 16cm rectangle, discarding the offcuts. Cut the dough into six 8cm squares. Transfer them to the prepared sheet and bake for 20–22 minutes.

MAKE THE DECORATION

Follow the tempering instructions carefully to create the stunning red triangles to decorate each side of the pyramid.

24. Temper the white chocolate following the method on page 34, and melt the red cocoa butter. Neither should get hotter than 45°C. Stir the cocoa butter into the white chocolate, then allow the temperature to drop until it's tempered. Spread into a 38 x 12cm rectangle on a sheet of acetate and mark out 24 triangles, each with a base of 3cm and height of 5cm. Allow to set.

ASSEMBLE THE PYRAMIDS

25. Turn the strawberry pyramids out of the mould and put on a tray. Return to the freezer to ensure they stay frozen. Wash the mould and dry well.

26. Spoon the vanilla cream into a piping bag and cut about 1cm off the tip. Pipe it into the moulds until they are half-filled, then use the palette knife to spread it evenly around the sides. Carefully return the strawberry pyramids to the cream-lined moulds and spread a little cream on top. Add the balsamic jelly and cover with a little more cream.

27. Cut the lemon madeleine sponge into 6 squares measuring 6 x 6cm and place a piece on the base of each pyramid. Freeze for 2 hours.

28. Turn out the pyramids again – they should pop out easily – and sit each one on its base on the prepared rack.

29. Heat the white chocolate glaze until it reaches 35°C, then spoon it over each pyramid. If the glaze runs off the sides, scoop it up and spoon over again as a second coat. Allow to set, then lift each one up with a palette knife and place on a square of shortbread.

30. Carefully lean a chocolate triangle against each side of the pyramids and sprinkle with a little gold lustre powder. Serve with a strawberry.

CHOCOLATE CYLINDERS
WITH MANGO AND PASSION FRUIT

Crisp chocolate collars, base-lined with a disc of coconut dacquoise, filled with a soft tropical fruit custard and light-as-air caramel chocolate mousse, topped with fresh mango and lime

Petits gâteaux are individual little cakes that allow patisserie chefs to go to town with their creativity. They can be served as part of a traditional afternoon tea or after a meal, and consist of multiple elements – a biscuit or sponge base, a mousse, a glaze and a twirl of decoration. For this recipe, the skill lies first in tempering the chocolate so that it snaps crisply when the fork breaks into it, and second in perfectly baking the dacquoise so it's neither squidgy and wet, nor dry and crunchy, all of which would make it difficult to cut neatly. The mango custard provides a balance between these two elements, and the caramel chocolate mousse in turn must not overpower the other ingredients. In short, the recipe is an exercise in balance and creativity.

SERVES 6

TIMING
Hands-on time: about *3 hours,*
  plus cooling and chilling
Cooking time: *10–12 minutes*

PREPARE IN ADVANCE
This recipe can be made up to the
  end of step 8 several hours before
  needed. Keep the custard in a
  separate bowl, covered with
  clingfilm, next to the moulds
  containing the chocolate collars
  and the dacquoise bases.
If you prefer, the petits gâteaux can
  be made and assembled up to the
  end of step 13 a day ahead. Keep
  chilled, then decorate with the
  mango and lime before serving,
  leaving them out for about 30
  minutes to come to room
  temperature.

HAVE READY
Stand mixer, if using, fitted with
  the whisk attachment
Board lined with parchment paper
  taped in place; this is to cover the
  acetate strips, but you'll need to
  reline and tape it again after each
  strip is covered with chocolate so
  each piece remains clean.
Both baking trays lined with
  parchment paper.
Oven preheated to 190°C/
  170°C fan/ gas mark 5.

EQUIPMENT
2 medium bowls
digital thermometer
microwave and microwavable
  bowl, or medium pan and
  heatproof bowl
board

parchment paper
sticky tape
8 acetate strips, 19 x 4.5cm
palette knife
6 x 6cm ring moulds
2 baking trays
stand mixer
  – whisk attachment
large metal spoon
5.5cm round cutter
medium pan
balloon whisk
electric hand whisk, optional
spatula
disposable piping bag
2 ramekins
pastry brush
chopping knife
zester

FOR THE CHOCOLATE COLLARS

200g dark chocolate (about 64% cocoa solids)

15g yellow cocoa butter

15g white cocoa butter

FOR THE DACQUOISE

75g egg white (almost 3 medium)

25g caster sugar

55g desiccated coconut

70g icing sugar, sifted

FOR THE PASSION FRUIT AND MANGO CUSTARD

70g egg yolks (3½ medium)

70g caster sugar

50g passion fruit purée (about 4–5 fruits)

40g mango purée (about ½ large mango; use the remaining mango for the salsa)

a drop of vanilla extract

20g whipping cream

FOR THE CARAMEL CHOCOLATE MOUSSE

140g dark chocolate (about 64% cocoa solids), broken into pieces

60g egg yolks (about 3–4 medium)

a pinch of salt

40g caster sugar

50g + 330g whipping cream (weighed separately)

FOR THE MANGO SALSA

about ½ ripe mango, peeled, stone removed and flesh diced (see above)

finely grated zest of 1 lime

MAKE THE CHOCOLATE COLLARS

These are easy to make using a strip of acetate and a ring mould in which to set them.

1. Temper the dark chocolate, following the instructions on page 34. Place an acetate strip on the lined board and pour over a little of the chocolate. Use a palette knife to spread it evenly and quite thinly over the strip, then lift it up and curve it into a circle, chocolate side out. Lower into one of the ring moulds. Don't worry if the chocolate goes slightly over the edge of the acetate: if it is at the correct temperature, the acetate lifts easily off the board and the chocolate won't drip off the strip. Place the lined mould on a prepared baking tray and put aside to set.
2. Repeat step 1 five more times, so all the moulds are lined and resting on the same baking tray.

MAKE THE COCONUT DACQUOISE

3. Put the egg whites in a stand mixer and whisk until soft peaks form. Whisk in the caster sugar, one-third at a time, until the mixture becomes a smooth, glossy meringue.
4. Fold in the coconut and icing sugar with a large metal spoon and mix until combined. Spread out thinly and evenly on the second lined baking tray to a thickness of about 4mm. Bake in the oven for 10–12 minutes until golden.
5. Set aside to cool, then peel off the paper. Put on a board and stamp out six circles using the cutter. Turn them over so they are smooth baked side down and place one in the bottom of each lined ring mould, gently pressing to make a tight fit. Any leftover pieces of dacquoise can be stored in an airtight container for up to 5 days and enjoyed with a cup of tea.

MAKE THE FRUIT CUSTARD

The usual method of making custard applies here, although fruit purée is used rather than milk.

6. Mix the egg yolks and sugar together in a medium bowl.
7. Put the purées into a medium pan with the vanilla and bring to the boil. Pour into the egg yolk mixture and stir well.
8. Return the mixture to the pan and cook until it reaches 84–86°C and has thickened, simmering if needed. Transfer to a bowl to cool, stirring every now and then. Stir the cream into the mixture, then allow to cool completely.
9. Spoon equally between the chocolate-lined moulds and chill.

PREPARE THE MOUSSE AND PIPE INTO THE MOULDS

10. Melt the chocolate in a microwave or bain-marie (see page 34). Set aside to cool.

11. Put the sugar into a small, heavy-based pan and heat gently, shaking occasionally but not stirring, until the sugar dissolves and becomes a light golden caramel. Watch carefully that it doesn't turn dark golden – at this stage it's too thick to pour. At the same time, heat the 50g quantity of whipping cream in a small pan or a bowl in the microwave. Add to the caramel, then stir in the yolks and salt. Whisk until the mixture is cool and slightly thickened. It should leave a thin trail when the whisk is lifted.

12. Once cool, fold in the melted chocolate. Whip the 330g cream in a separate bowl until thick and mousse-like, then fold it into the chocolate mixture. Spoon into a piping bag and snip 1.5cm off the tip.

13. Take the ring moulds out of the fridge and pipe in the chocolate mixture until each is completely full. Level the top with a palette knife. Chill for at least 30 minutes, until set. Chill any leftover mousse.

DECORATE THE CHOCOLATE COLLAR

14. Melt the cocoa butters in separate ramekins in the microwave.

15. Line a work surface and the wall behind it with paper to protect from splashing in the next step. Lift the rings off the petits gâteaux and carefully peel off the acetate strips.

16. Use a brush to flick first the white cocoa butter, then the yellow cocoa butter all around the chocolate collars to cover.

17. Spoon the mango salsa evenly in a small, neat pile on top of each petit gâteau, sprinkle with a little lime zest and serve.

FINISH IT LIKE A PASTRY CHEF

Temper *300g white chocolate* following the instructions on page 34. Spoon it onto the acetate and spread it from one end to the other in a rough rectangle about 8cm wide. Sprinkle with *50g toasted desiccated coconut*. Using a thin sharp knife, mark out 6 thin oval shapes about 6cm long. Bend the acetate into a circle, chocolate side out, and tape the ends together. Allow to set. Carefully remove the acetate and cut out the shapes. Place a white chocolate curl slightly off-centre on each dessert, spoon the mango beside it and serve.

Additional equipment: *A4 acetate sheet, knife, sticky tape.*

APPLE DOMES

Demispheres of fragrant apple mousse encasing sweet apple compote and crisp vanilla almond biscuit

These apple-green petits gâteaux look incredibly professional, but are, in fact, simple in their execution, cleverly hinting at the delicious flavours within.

As with other moulded cakes, the skill here is in casting and moulding various mixtures, and in being creative with a variety of textures and flavours. The *glaçage* (glaze) must be smooth and shiny, the textured edge of crushed sablé biscuit must be applied evenly around the base and the chocolate needs to be tempered so that it is shiny and has the perfect snap.

SERVES 10

TIMING

Hands-on time: *1 hour 40 minutes*
Cooking time: *1 hour 10 minutes*

PREPARE AHEAD

The sablé base can be made up to 3 days
   ahead, stored in an airtight container
   at room temperature.
The gâteaux can be made up to the end
   of step 11 and stored in the freezer
   for up to 1 day.
The chocolate curl decorations can be
   made up to 5 days ahead, stored in an
   airtight container at room temperature.

HAVE READY

Stand mixer, if using, fitted with the
   paddle attachment.
Chopping board lined with
   parchment paper.
Both baking sheets lined with
   parchment paper.
Cartouche prepared (see *Make
   the Tatin Inserts*, overleaf).
Baking tray lined with clingfilm,
   with a wire rack rested on top.
Oven preheated to 180°C/
   160°C fan/gas 4.

EQUIPMENT

stand mixer, optional
   – paddle attachment
chopping board
parchment paper
baking tray
clingfilm
wire rack
digital scales
large bowl and wooden spoon,
   optional
rolling pin
5cm plain round cutter
2 baking sheets
peeler
small sharp knife
medium pan with a lid
balloon whisk

small bowl
melon baller
stick blender
sieve
disposable piping bag
5cm-hole demisphere
   silicone mould
microwave and
microwavable bowl, or
   medium pan and
   heatproof bowl
digital thermometer
A4 acetate sheet
curved mould
comb scraper
small pan

FOR THE SABLÉ BASE

125g unsalted butter,
    at room temperature
40g icing sugar
a pinch of salt
100g plain flour, sifted,
    plus extra for sprinkling

FOR THE TATIN INSERT

150g Cox or Braeburn apples
40g + 10g caster sugar
15g warm water
10g butter
3g powdered fruit pectin

FOR THE APPLE PURÉE

400g (about 2½) apples, peeled
    and chopped
30g caster sugar
30g water

FOR THE APPLE MOUSSE

4g powdered gelatine
20g cold water
50g eggs (1 medium)
60g egg yolks (3 medium)
60g caster sugar
80g unsalted butter
200g apple purée, above

FOR THE CHOCOLATE
CURLS

100g dark chocolate

FOR THE WHITE
CHOCOLATE GLAÇAGE

1.5g powdered gelatine
7.5g cold water
185g white chocolate (minimum
    33% cocoa solids)
150g apricot glaze
110g whipping cream
a few drops of apple green colouring
    (suitable for chocolate use)

FOR THE DECORATION

small sprigs of fresh mint leaves

MAKE THE SABLÉ BASES

This is a sticky dough, so use plenty of parchment paper to make it easier to handle.

1. Put the softened butter, icing sugar and salt into a large bowl or the bowl of a stand mixer and beat together until pale and fluffy. Add the flour and beat again until the mixture just comes together and forms a dough.
2. Tip the mixture onto the prepared chopping board and lay a second sheet of parchment over the top. Roll it out to 3mm thick, then transfer to the freezer for 10 minutes to firm up.
3. Remove the dough from the freezer and peel away the top layer of parchment. Lightly flour the dough, then turn it over, back onto the parchment paper, and peel off the top layer. Lightly flour again. Stamp out 10 circles 5cm in diameter, rerolling the dough as necessary, then prick each circle all over. Place the sheet of circles onto a prepared baking sheet.
4. Cut any final trimmings into misshapen pieces and place on the second prepared baking sheet. Bake both lots of sablés for 12–15 minutes, then transfer to a wire rack to cool. Reline the baking sheet with fresh parchment paper.

MAKE THE TATIN INSERTS

A cartouche is a folded circular sheet of parchment paper cut to fit your pan and laid inside it to cover the contents. The cartouche helps to create steam and prevents the liquid in the pan from evaporating. To make one, use the pan you'll be cooking with as a template to draw a circle onto parchment paper. Cut about 2cm outside the outline as it must be slightly bigger than the pan, and your cartouche is ready.

5. Peel and core the apples, then cut them into 5mm cubes.
6. Make a dry caramel by putting 40g caster sugar in a medium pan over a medium heat. Cook until the sugar dissolves and is a rich golden brown, then whisk in the water and butter.
7. Add the apples to the pan. Fold the cartouche in half, then in half again, repeating until the original circle of parchment becomes a thin wedge. Open it out again and put it over the apples like a roof so that it will trap the steam, and cover the pan with a lid. Cook over a medium heat for 15–20 minutes, stirring every now and then, until soft.
8. Stir the pectin and the remaining 10g caster sugar together in a small bowl, then stir into the apples. Cover and set aside for 10 minutes to allow the apples to soak into the syrup.
9. Use a melon baller to scoop up demispheres of the apple mixture and transfer them to the baking sheet lined with parchment paper. Transfer to the freezer for about 1 hour, until frozen.

MAKE THE APPLE PURÉE

10. Put the apples in a medium pan over a medium heat with the sugar and water. Cover and bring to the boil. Simmer for 5–10 minutes until soft, then blend until smooth.

MAKE THE APPLE MOUSSE

11. Put the gelatine into a small bowl with the water and set aside to soak.
12. Add the eggs, egg yolks, caster sugar and butter to pan with the apple purée and cook over a low heat for 2–3 minutes, making sure the mixture heats through but doesn't boil. Take the pan off the heat and stir in the gelatine. Mix well, then blend together. Pass the mixture through a fine sieve, then spoon it into the piping bag.

MAKE THE DOMES

13. Snip 2cm off the tip of the bag and pipe the mousse into the demisphere moulds. Take the frozen tatin inserts, unmould them and push one into the centre of each demisphere, level with the top of the apple mousse.
14. Carefully insert a sablé disc on top of each mousse and freeze for 2–3 hours, until set.

MAKE THE CHOCOLATE STALKS

The apple stalks are made from tempered chocolate curls, which are snapped into short pieces. For an alternative you could pipe tempered chocolate into stalk shapes on a sheet of acetate and leave them to set.

15. Temper the dark chocolate and make chocolate curls using the method on page 151. Leave to set.

GLAZE THE DOMES WITH THE WHITE CHOCOLATE GLAÇAGE

16. Carefully remove the frozen domes from the moulds – they should pop out easily. Sit them on the prepared wire rack set over clingfilm.
17. Put the gelatine into a small bowl with the water and set aside to soak.
18. Heat the chocolate using the instructions on page 34 until half-melted.
Continued…

19. Put the apricot glaze into a small pan and melt over a gentle heat. Stir in the cream. Take the pan off the heat and stir in the gelatine, then pour over the chocolate and stir well from the centre outwards to make a smooth emulsion. Stir in the food colouring.

20. Check the temperature of the glaze – it should be about 35–40°C – and spoon it over each dome to coat the outside completely.

DECORATE WITH THE CHOCOLATE STALKS

21. Crush 15–20g of the sablé trimmings into crumbs and carefully press them around the edge of each dome to decorate the bottoms.

22. Snap the chocolate curls into smaller lengths and push a chocolate 'stalk' and a sprig of mint leaves into each dome to decorate.

FINISH IT LIKE A PASTRY CHEF

For extra sparkle, add a few drops of *sparkly green colouring* to the white chocolate glaçage.

◆ ◆ ◆

JASMINE, MANGO AND YUZU SPHERES

Milk chocolate and jasmine tea ganache combines with mango and yuzu-flavoured mousse and glaze on a crisp chocolate biscuit base

Petit gâteau spheres can be made with any flavour and texture, so they offer a great chance for patisserie chefs to be creative. The challenge, of course, is to create a perfect sphere of ganache and mousse with a smooth coating of glaze all over it. In this recipe the sphere has a milk chocolate centre – nothing too dark or powerful in flavour – so that it complements the tropical fruit flavours used in both the mousse and the glaze.

The spheres are finished with a simple decoration of an edible flower and sit on a crunchy base made from a chocoate sablé biscuit.

SERVES 8

TIMING

Hands-on time: *about 2 hours, plus chilling and freezing time*
Cooking time: *30 minutes*

HAVE READY

Baking sheet lined with parchment paper.
Tray lined with clingfilm.
Oven preheated to 200°C/180°C fan/ gas mark 6.

EQUIPMENT

2 small bowls
small pan
tea strainer
spatula
digital scales
chopping knife
chopping board
electric hand whisk
disposable piping bags
digital thermometer
microwave and microwavable bowl, or medium pan and heatproof bowl
parchment paper
baking sheet
eight 6cm spherical silicone ice-ball moulds
clingfilm
board
rolling pin
4cm round cutters
wide, deep jug or beaker of similar size
skewer
tray

1g powdered gelatine

10g cold water

50g full-fat milk

5g jasmine-scented green tea

5g liquid glucose

90g milk chocolate, finely chopped

100g whipping cream, lightly whipped

FOR THE MANGO YUZU
MOUSSE

4g powdered gelatine

20g cold water

110g mango purée

60g whipping cream

60g mascarpone

100g caster sugar

20g water

40g egg yolks (2 medium)

25g yuzu or passion fruit purée

FOR THE CHOCOLATE
SABLÉ BISCUIT BASES

90g milk chocolate, finely chopped

90g butter, at room temperature

100g demerara sugar

100g flour, sifted

1.5g baking powder, sifted

3g sea salt

18g cocoa powder, sifted

FOR THE MANGO GLAZE
AND DECORATION

300g mango purée

40g yuzu or passion fruit purée

160g water

40g + 65g caster sugar (weighed
separately)

80g liquid glucose

15g yellow pectin

8 edible flowers

MAKE THE JASMINE GANACHE

These small balls of ganache sit inside the centre of each mousse sphere.

1. Put the gelatine into a small bowl, add half the water and set aside
to soak. Heat the milk and tea in a small pan, then set aside to infuse
for 10 minutes. Put the glucose, milk chocolate and remaining 5g water
into a small bowl.
2. Strain the tea, then return the milk to the pan and bring back to
the boil. Pour into the bowl with the chocolate and stir well to form
a smooth emulsion.
3. Fold in the cream, set the bowl over an ice bath and whisk until the
mixture looks thick enough to pipe. Spoon into a piping bag, snip off
the tip and pipe 8 balls, each 18–20g, on the prepared baking sheet.
Transfer to the freezer.

MAKE THE MANGO YUZU MOUSSE

The spherical mould for this mousse has two halves. The lower one is
filled, then the upper half is replaced and filled through a hole in the top.

4. Put the gelatine into a small bowl, add the water and set aside to soak.
5. Heat half the mango purée in a saucepan, then take off the heat and
stir in the gelatine until dissolved. Set aside.
6. Put the cream and mascarpone in a bowl and beat together lightly
until smooth. Transfer to the fridge to chill.
7. Put the sugar and water into a small saucepan and heat to 118°C,
then pour over the egg yolks. Whisk with an electric hand whisk until
thick and mousse-like.
8. Allow to cool, then fold into the cream mixture along with the gelatine
mixture, remaining mango purée and yuzu purée.
9. Spoon the mousse into a piping bag and snip about 3mm off the tip. Fill
the lower half of each mould, allowing space for the ganache ball. Freeze
for 15 minutes, then place a ganache ball in each one and cover with the
other half of the mould. Pipe the remaining mousse through the hole in
the top to fill the mould, then freeze for 2–3 hours until completely frozen.

MAKE THE CHOCOLATE SABLÉ BASES

These crisp biscuit rounds provide a base for the sphere to sit on.

10. Put the chocolate in a bowl and melt on low in a microwave or over
a pan of simmering water. Set aside.
11. Put the butter and sugar into a large bowl and beat together with a
spatula until the mixture looks smooth. Add the flour, baking powder,
salt and cocoa and mix again until the dough just comes together.

12. Add the melted chocolate and mix briefly to combine. Bring the mixture together with your hands, then shape into a disc and wrap in clingfilm. Chill for 30 minutes.

13. Unwrap the chilled dough and put on a board. Roll out to a thickness of about 3mm. Stamp out eight 4cm rounds. (You can stamp the leftover dough into whatever shapes you like and bake along with the other biscuits.) Transfer to the prepared baking sheet and bake for 8–10 minutes.

MAKE THE MANGO GLAZE

Using pectin in the glaze helps it to set. You need to work quickly while coating the spheres so that the glaze is warm from first to last.

14. Pour the purées into a pan and add the water, 40g sugar and liquid glucose. Heat gently until it reaches 45°C. Add the pectin and remaining 65g sugar and stir together. Bring to the boil and simmer for 2–3 minutes.

15. Transfer the glaze to a jug or beaker (it must be wide so the balls can be coated easily). Allow to cool to 35°C.

16. Meanwhile, take the moulds out of the freezer and carefully turn out the mousse balls. Push a skewer into the middle of a ball and dip into the glaze. Transfer to the prepared tray and return to the fridge to set while you cover the remaining spheres.

17. Put a sablé base on each plate. Carefully lift the balls on to the base and decorate each sphere with an edible flower.

FINISH IT LIKE A PASTRY CHEF

Temper *300g white chocolate* (see page 34). Spoon half of it over a 40 x 5cm acetate strip and spread out thinly. Run a knife along it 3 times at 5mm intervals to make 4 thin strips. Bend the acetate into a 12cm circle and fasten it with sticky tape. Stand it upright until the chocolate has set. Repeat this step with the remaining chocolate and acetate strip. (Allow any leftover chocolate to set and save it for future use.) Unfasten the acetate, then carefully cut between each chocolate strip to release them. After putting a sablé biscuit on to each plate, put a white chocolate strip on each (securing it with a dab of melted chocolate) and carefully place the balls on top. Garnish with the flower, as above, and serve.

Additional equipment: 2 acetate strips – each 40 x 5cm, ruler, palette knife, chopping knife, sticky tape.

TARTS

BLACKBERRY, APPLE
YOGURT AND WALNUT TART

GRAPEFRUIT
MIRLITON

CHOCOLATE TART

PEANUT BUTTER AND WHITE
CHOCOLATE TART

CHERRY AND ALMOND
DACQUOISE TART

BRETON TARTE AUX FRUITS

FIG TART

PITHIVIER

TARTS

Served whole or in individual slices, tarts are always crowd-pleasing confections, and a wonderful introduction to the world of patisserie. Those included in this chapter present exciting challenges and draw on a range of skills. For example, a sweet shortcrust pastry forms the base of the Cherry Dacquoise Tart on page 221, in which the dacquoise is built up over the pastry inside a round tin to provide structure to the finished bake. It's then filled with a quick-to-make jam to contrast with the texture of the pastry and sponge.

Making the celebratory Pithivier (see page 237) provides a chance to hone puff pastry skills. The lacy layers are created by rolling and folding a block of butter into the base dough, then the heat of the oven helps to create steam that puffs up the pastry and makes it crisp. Although just half the quantity of pastry is used in this recipe, it's worth making a whole batch as it freezes well. The leftovers can be used for the glamorous Gâteau St Honoré on page 153 in the Patisserie chapter, or for the classic Fig Tart (see page 233), which is layered with vanilla-rich crème pâtissière and port-glazed figs.

Whether you're planning on making a whole tart to share with friends and family, or crafting individual Breton Tartes with melt-in-the-mouth sablé pastry and orange-scented summer fruit (see page 227), this chapter offers something tempting for would-be patissiers at every level of experience.

BLACKBERRY, APPLE YOGURT AND WALNUT TART

A deep, crisp pastry shell filled with creamy, fruit-flavoured yogurt and topped with a spiced crumble and fresh blackberries

The yogurt filling to this delicious autumnal tart sets to a creamy layer and is flavoured with chopped apples and blackberries. Use seasonal apples, such as Cox's Pippins, which have plenty of flavour and a little bit of acidity to balance the richness. Dust with icing sugar to serve.

Pâte sucrée is a favourite of pastry chefs as it has the strength of a normal shortcrust, but additional sugar brings sweetness and lightness to the structure of the dough. Neither the pastry base nor the crumble topping should be overworked or they will be heavy rather than crisp and crumbly.

SERVES 8–10

TIMING
Hands-on time: *35 minutes, plus chilling*
Cooking time: *1 hour*

PREPARE IN ADVANCE
The pastry can be made and chilled up
   to 4 days ahead. Remove from the fridge
   about half an hour before rolling so that
   it has a chance to soften.
It can also be frozen for up to 1 month.

HAVE READY
Stand mixer, if using, fitted with the
   paddle attachment
Tart tin greased and base-lined with
parchment paper.

EQUIPMENT
stand mixer, optional
   – paddle attachment
   – whisk attachment
22–24cm x 2.5cm fluted round loose-
   bottomed tart tin or ring (you'll need
   a baking sheet lined with parchment
   paper if you're using a ring)
parchment paper
2 large bowls
wooden spoon
sieve
clingfilm
baking sheet
rolling pin
small sharp serrated knife
baking beans
medium bowl
balloon whisk
large metal spoon
small bowl
electric hand whisk, optional
18–20cm round teaplate or base of
   a cake tin

FOR THE PÂTE SUCRÉE

100g butter, softened

100g caster sugar

40g beaten egg (about ¾ medium)

200g plain flour, plus extra for dusting

FOR THE APPLE
YOGURT FILLING

350g full-fat natural yogurt

40g caster sugar

100g plain flour

100g eggs (2 medium)

1.5g (½ teaspoon) vanilla extract

1g (¼ teaspoon) fine sea salt

400g Cox Pippin apples (about
   2 medium whole apples), peeled
   and cut into 1cm cubes

200g fresh blackberries

FOR THE CRUMBLE
TOPPING

80g plain flour

50g caster sugar

50g light muscovado sugar

2.5g (½ teaspoon) ground cinnamon

0.5g (⅛ teaspoon) salt

55g walnuts, chopped

55g butter, melted

icing sugar, to dust

FOR THE MASCARPONE
CREAM

250g mascarpone

50g icing sugar

seeds from ½ vanilla pod

250g double cream

TO SERVE

a few fresh blackberries

fresh mint leaves

icing sugar, to dust

MAKE THE PASTRY CASE

Pâte sucrée is a sweet shortcrust pastry and all the usual pastry rules apply – keep the ingredients and your hands cool so that the butter doesn't melt, and try not to overhandle the dough or the result will be tough.

1. Make the *pâte sucrée* and bake the case following the instructions on pages 35–6.
2. Keep the oven at 180°C/160°C fan/gas mark 4.

PREPARE THE FILLING

3. Put the yogurt, sugar, flour, eggs, vanilla extract and salt into a large bowl and whisk together using a balloon whisk until the mixture looks like a thick batter. Set aside.

MAKE THE CRUMBLE TOPPING

A light touch is required here so that the topping doesn't become heavy and cloying and has a light crumbly texture.

4. Put the flour, both types of sugar, cinnamon, salt and walnuts into a large bowl and mix together with your hands or a wooden spoon to combine. Make a well in the middle and pour the melted butter into it. Stir everything together until just mixed. You can do this in a freestanding mixer with the paddle attachment if you find it quicker, but take care not to overprocess the ingredients – you're looking for a rough crumble, not a dough.
5. Put your hands into the bowl and break up the mixture into lumps. Don't worry if it seems wet – it will dry out and crisp up in the oven.

ASSEMBLE AND BAKE THE TART

6. Add the apples and blackberries to the yogurt mixture and gently fold together, taking care not to break up the blackberries too much. Set aside. Carefully spoon the filling into the pastry case, ensuring the apple pieces and blackberries are spread evenly over the base.
7. Sprinkle the crumble over the yogurt mixture with your fingers, spreading it evenly over the top, then bake for 30–35 minutes until golden on top. Leave to cool slightly, then remove from the tin.

SERVE WITH THE MASCARPONE CREAM

8. Lay a small plate or the base of a cake tin on top of the tart. Dust icing sugar all around the edge. Place a few blackberries in the centre of the tart and add a sprig of fresh mint. Dust with icing sugar.

9. Put the mascarpone, icing sugar and vanilla seeds into a medium bowl and beat well with a wooden spoon or electric whisk until soft, then pour in 250g double cream. Beat again until thick.

10. Serve the tart warm or cold, in slices with quenelles of mascarpone cream. Make these by dipping 2 spoons into hot water and smoothing the cream between them to make perfect oval shapes.

FINISH IT LIKE A PASTRY CHEF

A swirl of Cinnamon Cream on the plate before arranging a slice of tart on top makes a lovely accompaniment and complements the apple and blackberry flavour too. First heat *100g caster sugar* in a small heavy-based pan until it dissolves and turns a light golden. Add *1 cinnamon stick*, then pour in *200g whipping cream*. Stand back at this point as the mixture may spit and sizzle. Boil for 1–2 minutes until saucy, then strain through a sieve and chill until required. The cream can be served warm, drizzled over the top of the tart, or cold, spread on the plate.

Additional equipment: *small heavy-based pan, small bowl.*

GRAPEFRUIT MIRLITON

*A moist almond tart with glazed grapefruit segments
encased in a whisked sponge on a crisp sweet pastry base*

Mirliton has several meanings in French. It can refer to a pale green, pear-shaped vegetable that we know as chayote, or to a military hat, or a cartoon cat. In the patisserie world, though, a mirliton is a sweet baked French tart from Rouen in northern France.

There are two elements to the mirliton that challenge the skills of a pastry chef. *Pâte sucrée* (sweet shortcrust pastry) forms the base and must be crisp and flaky, yet strong enough to support the filling. The filling comprises a light, whisked almond dacquoise sponge that puffs up and rises as it bakes, then, due to its delicate nature, slightly collapses after baking. Hidden beneath the cake's golden crust is a wonderfully moist interior.

The twist to this recipe is that the base is spread with grapefruit marmalade and the tart is topped with citrus-glazed grapefruit segments that cut through the sweetness of the tart and sponge.

SERVES 8

TIMING

Hands-on time: *25 minutes*

Cooking time: *45 minutes*

PREPARE IN ADVANCE

The pastry for the tart can be made
and chilled up to 2 days ahead,
or frozen for up to 1 month.

HAVE READY

Stand mixer, if using, fitted with the
paddle attachment.

Bowl lined with kitchen paper.

Tart tin greased and base-lined with
parchment paper

Piping bag fitted with the nozzle.

EQUIPMENT

stand mixer, optional
 – paddle attachment
 – whisk attachment
2 x medium bowls
kitchen paper
piping bag
 – 1cm nozzle zester
zester
sieve
large bowl and wooden
 spoon, optional
spatula
clingfilm
baking sheet
rolling pin

ruler
22cm round tart tin
parchment paper
baking beans
sharp serrated knife
chopping board
electric hand mixer, optional
balloon whisk
medium bowl
large metal spoon
pastry brush
18–20cm base of a round cake
 tin or a round cake board

FOR THE PÂTE SUCRÉE

100g butter, softened

100g caster sugar

40g beaten egg (about ¾ medium)

200g plain flour, plus extra for dusting

FOR THE FILLING

1 pink grapefruit

50g egg (1 medium)

10g egg yolk (½ medium)

zest from ½ lemon

1g vanilla extract

60g caster sugar

75g ground almonds

5g custard powder

60g grapefruit marmalade

4 tablespoons apricot jam,
   warmed and sieved

icing sugar, for dusting

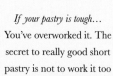

MAKE THE PÂTE SUCRÉE AND BAKE THE CASE

1. Make the pastry following the method on page 35, wrap in clingfilm and chill.
2. Roll out the rested dough on a lightly floured surface until it measures at least 28–30cm in diameter and is about 4–5mm thick. Take care not to stretch the dough or over-roll it. Carefully line the tart tin and bake the pastry case following the instructions on page 36. Set aside to cool.

MAKE THE SPONGE FILLING

Dry the grapefruit segments on kitchen paper to absorb excess juice – if they're too wet they'll make both the base and the filling soggy.

It's important to whisk the egg mixture until it's thick and mousse-like so that the structure of the filling holds once it's baked.

3. Use a sharp serrated knife to peel away the rind, pith and outer layer of skin from the grapefruit (A, B). Cut inside the skin of each segment to the centre of the fruit to release each piece (C). Lay the segments on kitchen paper to absorb any excess juice from the grapefruit (D).
4. Using the mixer with the whisk attachment, whisk together the eggs, yolk, lemon zest, vanilla and sugar for about 6 minutes, to ribbon stage – the mixture should be thick and mousse-like, and when you lift up the whisk the mixture should fall back on itself in ribbons. You can also use a handheld mixer that will take about 8 minutes to reach ribbon stage.
5. Place the almonds in a clean bowl with the custard powder and gently whisk together to remove any lumps. Gently fold into the egg mixture using a large metal spoon, taking care not to knock too much air out of it.

ASSEMBLE AND BAKE THE MIRLITON

The light sponge filling is piped into the pastry case.

6. Preheat the oven to 200°C/180°C fan/gas mark 6 and place a baking sheet inside to warm up.
7. Spread the grapefruit marmalade evenly over the base of the tart case.
8. Spoon the sponge mixture into the piping bag and pipe it in a spiral, working from the middle outwards, until you've covered the base. Arrange the grapefruit segments over the top.
9. Transfer to the preheated baking sheet and bake for about 25 minutes until light golden. It should feel just firm when pressed with a finger.
10. When the tart has completely cooled, glaze the grapefruit segments with the sieved apricot jam. To decorate the tart, lay the base of the tin or board on top of it so that you have an even ring of pastry exposed around the edges. Lightly dust with icing sugar, then carefully lift off the board before serving.

CHOCOLATE TART

A crisp shell of sweet pastry holding a sublime chocolate filling

This tart looks incredibly understated and simple, but the secret to its elegance is the combination of a sweet enriched pastry – made in the same way as a *pâte sucrée* – that melts in the mouth, filled with a butter-rich chocolate pool.

The decadent filling calls for three types of chocolate, each with a different percentage of cocoa solids to provide balance and structure to the overall taste. You could, of course, make it with just one high-cocoa chocolate – it won't have the same depth of flavour, but it will still taste amazing.

Once melted with butter, the mixture is lightened with a sabayon – a whisked mousse made with eggs and sugar. It may seem like a very short cooking time, but the quantity of fat in both the chocolate and the butter help the filling to set, resulting in a beautifully smooth texture.

An Oriental Orange Caramel Compote adds glamour, and the freshness of the fruit and sweetness of the caramel perfectly complement the rich chocolate in this magnificent tart.

SERVES 8–10

TIMING

Hands-on time: *1 hour 15 minutes*
Cooking time: *1 hour*

PREPARE IN ADVANCE

The pastry can be used
   immediately or frozen
   for up to 1 month.
Make the compote a day ahead
   and chill it overnight.

HAVE READY

Compote made and chilled
   overnight.
Eggs and butter for the filling
   at room temperature.
Stand mixer, if using, fitted with
   the paddle attachment.
Tart tin, greased and base-lined
with parchment paper.

EQUIPMENT

stand mixer, optional
   – paddle attachment
   – whisk attachment
22cm x 2.5cm tart tin
digital scales
rolling pin
parchment paper
baking beans
chopping knife
chopping board
sieve
medium bowl
small serrated knife
small pan

large metal spoon
medium pan
large bowl, optional
food processor, optional
clingfilm
microwave and microwave-proof
   bowl, or medium pan and a
   heatproof bowl
digital thermometer
balloon whisk
hand-held electric whisk, optional
spatula
pastry brush

FOR THE ORANGE CARAMEL COMPOTE

4 oranges

100g sugar

FOR THE ENRICHED SWEET PASTRY

180g butter, chilled and cut into cubes

20g caster sugar

3g salt

50g egg (1 medium), beaten

20g milk

270g plain flour, plus extra
for rolling out

FOR THE FILLING

100g dark chocolate (100% cocoa
solids), broken into pieces

100g dark chocolate (55% cocoa solids),
broken into pieces

100g milk chocolate (40% cocoa solids),
broken into pieces

200g butter, chopped

100g eggs (2 medium)

80g egg yolks (4 medium)

60g caster sugar

FOR THE GLAZE

75g dark chocolate (70–80% cocoa
solids), finely chopped

75g water

65g caster sugar

85g liquid glucose

50g condensed milk

TO SERVE

crème fraîche

MAKE THE ORANGE CARAMEL COMPOTE

This simple compote uses only two ingredients. The juice from the oranges thins a simple sugar caramel, and the orange segments are soaked in the mixture overnight.

1. Peel the rind and skin from the oranges. Using a sharp serrated knife carefully cut inside the skin of each segment to the centre of the orange to release each piece (see instructions for segmenting a grapefruit, page 210). Place in a sieve resting over a bowl to drain the juice.
2. Gently heat the sugar in a small pan over a low heat until it dissolves, liquefies, and turns the rich golden colour of dark caramel. Take the pan off the heat and carefully pour in the strained orange juice. Stand back as the mixture may spit. Shake the pan to mix everything together.
3. Spoon the orange segments into a bowl and pour over the caramel. Refrigerate overnight to allow the caramel to completely infuse into the orange segments.

MAKE THE ENRICHED SWEET PASTRY BASE

A thin pastry shell encases the rich chocolate filling, so roll out the pastry as thinly as possible.

4. Make the pastry using the method on page 35. Shape into a disc, wrap in clingfilm and chill for 1 hour to allow the dough to rest.
5. Preheat the oven to 200°C/180°C fan/gas mark 6.
6. Dust a clean work surface with a little flour and carefully roll out the pastry until it's about 2mm thick. Line the tart tin and bake using the method on page 36. Set aside to cool. Leave the oven on at 180°C/160°C fan/gas mark 4.

MAKE THE FILLING

Eggs and sugar are whisked to ribbon stage and folded with melted chocolate to create a whipped, mousse-like mixture.

7. Put all the chocolate and the butter into a microwavable bowl or the bowl of a bain-marie and melt using the instructions on page 34, making sure the temperature doesn't go any higher than 45–50°C or the fats may separate from the cocoa solids. Once melted, whisk until smooth.
8. Whisk the eggs, yolks and sugar in the mixer fitted with the whisk attachment, or in large bowl using a hand-held electric whisk, for 3–5 minutes (it may take longer with a hand-held whisk) on a medium speed until ribbon stage – the mixture will be thick and mousse-like and fold back on itself in ribbons when the whisk is lifted. Carefully fold in the chocolate and butter mixture.

BAKE AND GLAZE THE TART

Bake the tart until it's just set – the short cooking time gives a smooth and soft texture. To check it's baked enough, press the top gently with your finger – it should feel just set and not risen up and souffléd. If it's slightly underdone, it will still set thanks to the percentage of fat in the chocolate and butter, but it won't have that all-important smooth texture.

9 Pour the mixture into the tart tin and bake for 15 minutes. Take out of the oven and allow to cool completely, then lift the tart out of the tin and refrigerate so the chocolate mixture can set.

10. Put the chopped chocolate in a bowl. Put the water, sugar, liquid glucose and condensed milk into a medium pan and bring to the boil. Pour the mixture onto the chocolate and stir well with a spatula until smooth.

11. Just before serving, brush the glaze over the cake. Use any remaining sauce to spoon alongside the tart and serve with crème fraîche and the orange caramel compote.

PEANUT BUTTER AND WHITE CHOCOLATE TART

White chocolate and peanut butter ganache fills a crumbly almond pastry shell topped with fresh raspberries

Although it might sound like a Franco-American mash-up, this tart is in fact gloriously elegant, balancing the rich flavour of peanut butter and sweet taste of white chocolate.

The almond sablé pastry is so called because the dry mixture resembles sand. Traditionally pastry chefs would make it by hand, using the fingers and thumb of one hand to 'peck' the butter and icing sugar together, rather like the jerky movement of a bird eating crumbs. The pastry is short and rich because of the high fat content from the butter and almonds, the latter giving a extra hit of nuts to the overall flavour.

This pastry does expand on baking due to the addition of the baking powder. The relatively large quantity of raising agent lightens the pastry and gives it a biscuit texture that's a bit like shortbread, and perfectly offsets the moussey texture of the filling.

The ganache is set with gelatine to ensure the piped domes maintain their shape, but vegetarian setting agents are available if you prefer. Raspberries, placed carefully on top, complete this pretty tart.

SERVES 8–10

TIMING

Hands-on time: *1 hour 20 minutes, plus chilling*

Cooking time: *25 minutes*

PREPARE IN ADVANCE

Make the pastry and line the tin up to 1 day ahead. Store covered in clingfilm in the fridge.

HAVE READY

Stand mixer, if using, fitted with the paddle attachment.
Tart tin, greased and base-lined with parchment paper.
Piping bag fitted with the nozzle.

EQUIPMENT

stand mixer, optional
  – paddle attachment
piping bag
  – 2cm round nozzle
digital scales
chopping knife
chopping board
grater
food processor, optional
large bowl
wooden spoon
clingfilm

rolling pin
22cm round tart tin
parchment paper
baking beans
sharp serrated knife
small bowl
large pan
2 x heatproof bowls
balloon whisk
digital thermometer
small pan
pastry brush

FOR THE ALMOND
SABLÉ PASTRY

200g plain flour

125g butter, cut into cubes

65g icing sugar

0.5g salt

50g ground almonds

4g baking powder

50g egg (1 medium), beaten

FOR THE GANACHE FILLING

300g double cream

2g powdered gelatine

10g cold water

20g egg yolk (1 medium)

30g caster sugar

25g orange juice

100g white chocolate, finely chopped

100g smooth peanut butter

25g dark chocolate, grated

TO ASSEMBLE THE TART

25g white chocolate, melted

100g raspberries

10g dark chocolate

icing sugar, to dust

MAKE THE ALMOND SABLÉ PASTRY

The secret to perfect, short pastry is to keep all your ingredients cool before you start. Take care not to overwork it once the dough has been mixed together, and don't overstretch it when rolling it out and lining the tin.

1. Make the pastry following the instructions on page 36. Wrap in clingfilm and chill for 20 minutes.

BAKE THE PASTRY CASE

2. Preheat the oven to 180°C/160°C fan/gas mark 4.
3. Roll out the chilled dough on a lightly floured work surface to 24–25cm in diameter and 5mm thick. Take care not to overstretch it – roll in one direction only, giving the pastry a quarter turn after each roll. Lift the pastry up and over the rolling pin and use it to transfer the pastry to the tart tin. Lay the pastry loosely over the tin, smooth the bottom, easing out any air that might be trapped and gently press the pastry into the corners of the tin, leaving a centimetre overhang. Prick the base all over, cover and chill again for 20 minutes.
4. Once the tart is chilled, line the case with parchment paper and fill it with the baking beans. Bake blind for 15 minutes until the pastry is set at the edges, then remove the paper and beans and continue to bake for 10 minutes until the pastry is golden brown. Trim the edges with a serrated knife to neaten them, then set aside to cool.

PREPARE THE GANACHE FILLING

The base of the ganache is a sabayon, which is made by whisking egg yolks, sugar and flavourings in a bain-marie. The temperature must not exceed 65°C or the mixture will start to solidify.

Also make sure the cream isn't too hot when you add the gelatine or it may overheat and lose its setting properties. Heat it just to the point where it's starting to bubble around the edges.

5. Whip 200g of the cream in a large bowl to stiff peaks. Cover and transfer to the fridge to chill.
6. Put the gelatine into a small bowl with the water. Set aside to allow the gelatine to absorb the water.
7. Prepare a bain-marie by putting 5cm water into the bottom of a large pan over a low heat. Put a heatproof bowl over the pan, making sure the base doesn't touch the water. You want the water to be hot, but not boiling. Make a sabayon by adding the egg yolk, sugar and orange juice to the bowl and whisking with a balloon whisk until the mixture is thick and foamy and reaches 65°C. Take the bowl off the heat and set aside.

8. Put the chocolate into a separate heatproof bowl. Pour the 100g cream into a small pan over a high heat and bring it just to the boil, then immediately take it off the heat. Stir in the gelatine until dissolved, then slowly pour this mixture over the chocolate, stirring all the time until the mixture is smooth and shiny. Stir in the peanut butter, then fold in the sabayon. Cover with clingfilm and chill for 10–20 minutes to thicken. Stir every now and then to check the consistency.

9. Fold in the chilled whipped cream and finally stir in the grated chocolate until just combined.

ASSEMBLE THE TART

A thin layer of white chocolate brushed over the base will help the tart stay crisp for longer.

10. Once the tart shell is cool, brush the base with the melted white chocolate.

11. Spoon the filling into the piping bag and pipe even-shaped balls, about 4cm wide, all over the base of the tart so that it's completely covered. Grate over the dark chocolate. Decorate with the fresh raspberries, each dusted with icing sugar.

THE SECRETS OF SUCCESS

If the ganache is difficult to pipe…
It's too warm. Chill the piping bag on a tray for 5 minutes, then try again.

If the ganache is light brown rather than cream-coloured speckled with chocolate…
It was too warm when the chocolate was folded in, so the chocolate melted and discoloured the mixture.

FINISH IT LIKE A PASTRY CHEF

For an exquisite professional touch, make these False Meringue Jelly Cubes, so called because their texture is more akin to marshmallow than jelly.

The day before you make the tart, make a raspberry purée by blending *100g raspberries*, then straining through a sieve to get 60g purée. Put in a pan over a high heat with *5g sugar*, bring to the boil, then cool. Put *10g gelatine* into a bowl with *50g cold water* and set aside to soak. Put *110g caster sugar* and *130g water* into a pan over a high heat and bring to the boil. Add the gelatine and allow to dissolve, then stir in *75g lemon juice* and *raspberry purée*. Return to the bowl and refrigerate overnight. Whisk the set mixture with an electric hand whisk or in a stand mixer until the texture is light and mousse-like. It will take about 15 minutes. Pour into an 18cm square mould lined with clingfilm. Freeze for 2 hours, then cut into 2cm cubes and arrange over the top of the tart and leave to defrost before serving.

Additional equipment: *blender, sieve, medium pan, electric hand whisk, optional, 18cm square mould.*

CHERRY AND ALMOND DACQUOISE TART

A pretty, almond-topped tart filled with cherry compote
and delicate meringue on a sweet pastry base

This tart is a mesmerising collection of textures and flavours. There's more skill required here – making pastry, jam and a cut-above meringue mixture in the form of the dacquoise, a classic meringue favoured by pastry chefs for its crisp outer shell containing a soft, nutty centre. Plus there's the chance to show off your piping skills. You'll be rewarded for all your hard work with a real showstopper of a tart that will delight all your guests.

A sweet enriched pastry forms the foundation on which the dacquoise meringue is built. The filling is a simple and just-sweet cherry compote. Cherries don't contain a lot of pectin, the natural gel that aids the setting of jams and jellies, so for this mixture a little additional liquid pectin is used to help it on its way. A scattering of flaked almonds, which toast to a golden hue in the oven, finishes it off beautifully.

SERVES 8–10

TIMING

Hands-on time: *1 hour*
Cooking time: *45–50 minutes*

PREPARE IN ADVANCE

The pastry and cherry filling can be
made up to 1 day ahead. Store the
pastry wrapped in clingfilm and the
cherry filling in an airtight container
in the fridge.

HAVE READY

Stand mixer, if using, fitted with the
paddle attachment.
Grease the base and sides of the
cake tin and line the base with
parchment paper.
Piping bag fitted with the nozzle.

EQUIPMENT

stand mixer
  – paddle attachment
  – whisk attachment
20 x 5.5cm deep loose-bottomed or
  springform cake tin
parchment paper
piping bag
  – 2cm plain nozzle
digital scales
chopping board
cherry pitter, optional
zester
large bwl
food processor, optional
rolling pin
clingfilm
pan

small bowl
digital thermometer
medium heavy-based pan
sieve
electric hand whisk,
optional

FOR THE ENRICHED
SWEET PASTRY

90g butter, chilled and cut into cubes

10g caster sugar

1½g salt

25g egg (½ medium)

10g milk

135g plain flour, plus extra for rolling

FOR THE CHERRY FILLING

250g fresh, frozen and thawed,
    or canned cherries, pitted and
    drained if necessary

250g caster sugar

finely grated zest and juice of 1 lemon

10g powdered fruit pectin

FOR THE ALMOND
DACQUOISE

150g egg whites (5 medium)

1g cream of tartar, or a few drops
    of lemon juice

70g caster sugar

150g ground almonds

150g icing sugar, sifted,
    plus extra to dust

25g plain flour, sifted

25g flaked almonds

MAKE THE ENRICHED SWEET PASTRY BASE

It's important to keep all the different elements – the bowl, the counter, the temperature of the kitchen – cool when you make this tricky pastry to ensure the butter doesn't melt before it's incorporated into the flour.

1. Make the enriched pastry following the method on page 35. Shape into a disc, wrap in clingfilm and chill for 1 hour. Preheat the oven to 200°C/180°C fan/gas mark 6.
2. Dust a clean work surface with a little flour and carefully roll the pastry into a circle about 4mm thick. Roll in one direction only, giving it a quarter turn after each roll. Place in the base of the tin (A, overleaf).
3. Bake for 12–15 minutes until pale golden. Remove and leave in the tin to cool. Reduce the temperature of the oven to 180°C/160°C fan/ gas mark 4.

MAKE THE CHERRY FILLING

To check if the jam is set, put a spoonful on a chilled saucer and leave for 1 minute. Push with your finger, and if it wrinkles, it's ready.

4. Put the cherries and 110g of the caster sugar in a medium heavy-based pan over a medium heat with the lemon zest and juice. Slowly bring to the boil so that the sugar dissolves.
5. Mix together the remaining 15g sugar and the pectin in a small bowl and stir into the pan. Bring to the boil and simmer until the mixture reaches 104–106°C and the consistency of the mixture looks like jam. Do the wrinkle test (see above) to test if it's set, then spoon into a bowl and allow to cool.

MAKE THE ALMOND DACQUOISE

Whisk the egg whites for the base of the meringue just until stiff peaks form. Don't overwhisk until the mixture looks dry or there won't be enough volume to support the meringue.

The cream of tartar or lemon juice helps to strengthen the protein/ albumen to give a thick mixture.

6. Whisk the egg whites with the cream of tartar or lemon juice in a spotlessly clean large bowl just until stiff peaks form. It's ready when you can hold the bowl over your head without the mixture falling out.
7. Gradually whisk in the caster sugar, one tablespoon at a time, until it's completely dissolved.
8. Remove the bowl from the machine and add the ground almonds, icing sugar and flour to the bowl and gently fold all the ingredients together.
Continued…

ASSEMBLE THE TART

The extremely light dacquoise is piped into the tin so that none of the precious air in the mixture is lost. For the same reason, use a light touch when adding the cherry filling.

9. Spoon about half the dacquoise into the piping bag and, starting from the middle of the pastry, pipe a spiral, working outwards to the edge of the tin (B). Pipe one or two more rings around the edge to build it up slightly.
10. Carefully spoon the cherry filling over the base meringue and spread it to the edges of the dacquoise (C). Spoon the rest of the dacquoise into the piping bag and pipe another spiral over the cherries until the filling is completely covered (D). Sprinkle with the flaked almonds and bake for 45–50 minutes until golden and the top feels firm when pressed. Set aside to cool in the tin.
11. Run a palette knife around the inside of the cake tin, or simply release the clip, and transfer the cake to a plate. Dust with icing sugar before serving.

FINISH IT LIKE A PASTRY CHEF

Garnish the tart with a handful of *fresh cherries* and dust them with *icing sugar*. Alternatively, dip them in a warmed and sieved *apricot jam glaze* and leave to set before arranging on top.

◆ ◆ ◆

BRETON TARTES AUX FRUITS

A buttery biscuit base topped with orange-scented
custard cream and summer fruits

These handcrafted tarts originate in Brittany and are made from a butter-rich sablé biscuit with a crisp, crumbly texture. The skill is in shaping the pastry so that each tart is alike, and in uniformly piping the rich crème pâtissière and crème diplomat.

The tarts are flat, with no edge to support the filling; therefore the crème pâtissière needs to be cooked until it is very thick because it forms the outer ring of the cream topping as well as the base of the diplomat cream, which needs to holds its shape when piped onto the tart.

In addition, it's important that the glaze is thick, cool and brushed carefully over the fruit because any that drips onto the cream will loosen it and make the fruit slide off the edge of the biscuit.

SERVES 8

TIMING

Hands-on time: *2 hours, plus chilling*
Cooking time: *45 minutes*

PREPARE IN ADVANCE

The biscuit can be baked up to 4 days
   ahead and stored in an airtight container.
The crème pâtissière can be made up to
   3 days ahead, sealed with clingfilm
   and stored in the fridge.

HAVE READY

Stand mixer, if using, fitted with the
   paddle attachment.
Baking tray lined with parchment paper.
Piping bags fitted with the nozzles.

EQUIPMENT

stand mixer, optional
   – paddle attachment
baking tray
parchment paper
2 disposable piping bags
   – 12mm nozzle
   – 5–6mm nozzle
chopping knife
chopping board
zester
large bowl
electric hand whisk, optional
clingfilm
rolling pin
blender or food-processor
fine sieve
medium pan
3 medium bowls
balloon whisk
small pan
pastry brush

FOR THE SABLÉ BISCUIT

110g chilled butter, cubed

60g caster sugar

165g plain flour

40g ground almonds

25g egg yolks (just over 1 medium)

a good pinch of salt

seeds from ½ vanilla pod

FOR THE WILD STRAWBERRY GLAZE

100g strawberries, wild if
    you can get them

2.5g powdered fruit pectin

40g caster sugar

15g liquid glucose

40g water

juice from ¼ lemon

FOR THE CRÈME PÂTISSIÈRE

80g egg yolks (4 medium)

60g caster sugar

25g plain flour

15g cornflour

zest from ¼ lemon

200ml milk

seeds from ½ vanilla pod

FOR THE CRÈME DIPLOMAT

185g crème pâtissière (from recipe
    above)

seeds from ½ vanilla pod

45g caster sugar

2.5g orange blossom water

zest from ½ orange

7g orange liqueur

250ml double cream

FOR THE ORANGE GLAZE

50g liquid glucose

30g caster sugar

80ml water

pared rind and juice from 1 orange

FOR THE DECORATION

a selection of strawberries, blueberries,
    raspberries and sprigs of redcurrants

MAKE THE SABLÉ BISCUITS

Take care not to overwork the mixture when you're mixing it to a dough as you don't want the finished biscuit to be tough. Mix it just until a dough forms. Chilling the dough gives the gluten a chance to develop so that the biscuits shrink less during baking.

1. Cream together the butter and sugar in a stand mixer, stopping it every now and then to scrape down the sides to ensure the two ingredients are combined together. You can also do this in a large bowl with an electric hand mixer.
2. When the mixture is smooth, pale and creamy, add half the flour, half the almonds and half the egg yolks and quickly combine, then add the remaining quantities, plus the salt and the vanilla seeds. As soon as the mixture starts to form a dough, tip it out onto a clean work surface.
3. Knead the dough lightly by hand and roll it into a log about 5cm thick and about 11 cm long. Wrap tightly in clingfilm and leave to rest in the fridge for at least 1 hour.

SHAPE AND BAKE THE BISCUITS

4. Weigh the chilled dough and cut it into 8 equal-sized pieces.
5. Roll each piece out on a clean work surface and carefully mould each one into a marquise shape (a rounded diamond), using a little flour if you need to to stop the dough from sticking. They should be about 5mm thick, 11cm long from point to point and about 7cm wide (A, page 231). Place on the prepared baking tray and chill for 30 minutes to firm up before baking – this will help them to keep their shape. Preheat the oven to 200°C/180°C fan /gas mark 6.
6. Bake the chilled biscuits for 12 minutes.

MAKE THE WILD STRAWBERRY GLAZE

The glaze will continue to thicken as it cools, so make sure it's not too thick when you take it off the heat. It should be like a syrup or a runny jam.

7. Whizz the strawberries to a purée in a blender or food-processor, then pass through a sieve into a pan.
8. Stir the pectin and 1 teaspoon of sugar together in a small bowl and add to the pan along with the remaining sugar, the glucose, water and lemon juice. Place over a medium heat. Bring the mixture to the boil, stirring constantly to ensure the glaze doesn't burn.
9. Reduce the heat and continue to simmer for 3–4 minutes until the mixture has thickened and looks syrupy and jam-like. When the glaze is ready, strain it into a bowl and keep warm.

MAKE THE CRÈME PÂTISSIÈRE

This mixture makes enough to provide the base for the *crème diplomat*, with a little left over for piping the biscuits.

10. Put the egg yolks and sugar into a large bowl and whisk together to combine. Add both the flours and the lemon zest. Whisk again lightly.
11. Pour the milk and vanilla seeds into a small pan over a medium heat and bring to the boil. As soon as the milk is boiling, take it off the heat and pour it over the egg yolk mixture, stirring continuously until smooth.
12. Pour the mixture back into the pan and bring it to a simmer, stirring continuously to prevent any lumps from forming. Cook for 2–3 minutes until the mixture is really thick.
13. Weigh 185g of the cream into a bowl and seal the surface with clingfilm – this is for the crème diplomat. Spoon the remainder into a separate bowl and seal with clingfilm. Set both aside to cool.

MAKE THE CRÈME DIPLOMAT

Transform simple crème pâtissière with whipped double cream and scented orange into a light and luscious filling to complement the sliced fruit.

14. Whisk the 185g of cold crème pâtissière briefly to break it down and make it smooth again. Add the vanilla seeds, sugar, orange blossom water, orange zest and liqueur.
15. Whip the double cream until firm, then fold into the mixture.
16. Spoon the crème diplomat into a piping bag fitted with the 12mm nozzle. Chill until required.

MAKE THE ORANGE GLAZE

17. Put the liquid glucose, caster sugar, water and orange rind and juice into a small pan. Heat gently to dissolve the sugar, then increase the heat and bring to the boil. Simmer for about 10 minutes – the mixture will reduce by about two-thirds and make a soft and sticky syrup. Set aside to cool.
18. Lift out and discard the orange rind, then strain the glaze through a sieve into a bowl. Cover the surface with clingfilm to seal it and set aside.
Continued…

Continued…

THE SECRETS OF SUCCESS

◆

If the tarts are soft and crumble after baking…
The dough hasn't been baked for long enough. Return it to the oven and continue to bake until golden, then transfer to a wire rack to cool.

If the glaze is too thick to use…
Reheat it gently in a pan over a very low heat until it softens.

ASSEMBLE THE TARTS

The tarts are first glazed with the wild strawberry glaze, then topped with crème pâtissière and crème diplomat and colourfully finished with the glazed fruit.

19. Warm the wild strawberry glaze and brush it over each sablé biscuit.
20. Spoon the remaining crème pâtissière into the piping bag fitted with the 5–6mm nozzle and pipe a thin line around each biscuit, leaving a little border around the edge (B). If the crème pâtissière seems thick, fold in 20ml double cream to loosen it.
21. Pipe the diplomat cream into the space in the middle of each biscuit (C). If you're not serving the tarts straightaway, you can chill them for up to half an hour at this stage.
22. Slice the strawberries and brush all the fruit with the bitter orange glaze (D). When you're ready to serve, arrange the berries artistically over the top of the cream and serve immediately.

FINISH IT LIKE A PASTRY CHEF

Garnish each tart with a little spun sugar. See page 266 for how to do this.

To finish, add an edible flower and a sprig of lime basil, if you like.

FIG TART

A crisp puff pastry tart topped with a creamy custard layer and syrupy caramelised port figs

The pastry base for this tart is made from a round of puff pastry, which is baked underneath a wire rack to ensure the layers rise evenly and aren't too high for the topping. The secret to great puff is to turn the dough after each rolling to ensure the butter is incorporated evenly throughout to create a light and flaky pastry.

Pastry chefs make large quantities of puff pastry because the lamination process of rolling and folding is highly skilled and labour-intensive, so it's worth making in bulk. The same applies at home – puff can be successfully frozen without losing any of its qualities – so this recipe makes twice the amount you need. Keep the rest for next time, storing it in a sealable bag in the freezer.

When choosing and buying the figs for this dessert, make sure they feel heavy for their size and are smooth, without any blemishes. They should be just ripe so that they keep their shape after being caramelised. If you have any leftover glaze, store it in the fridge for up to five days and serve over ice cream or stir into Greek yogurt.

SERVES 8–10

TIMING

Hands-on time: *2 hours 15 minutes,*
 plus chilling
Cooking time: *25 minutes*

PREPARE IN ADVANCE

The pastry, crème pâtissière and syrup for
 the glaze can all be made separately up to
 1 day ahead. Keep the pastry wrapped well
 in clingfilm and store the filling and syrups
 in separate airtight containers in the fridge.

HAVE READY

Stand mixer, if using, fitted with the paddle
 attachment.
Baking tray lined with clingfilm.
Large baking sheet lined with parchment
 paper or a silicone mat.

EQUIPMENT

stand mixer, optional
 – paddle attachment
baking tray
clingfilm
baking sheet
parchment paper or a silicone mat
digital scales
sharp serrated knife
chopping board
large bowl
wooden spoon, optional
rolling pin

26cm round plate or tin
 (for a template)
medium pan with a lid
sieve
3 medium heatproof
 bowls
balloon whisk
wire rack
large heavy-based
 frying pan
spatula
pastry brush

FOR THE PUFF PASTRY BASE DOUGH

350g strong bread flour,
   plus extra to dust
9g salt
a few drops of lemon juice
180–195g iced water
40g butter, softened

FOR THE BUTTER INCLUSION (BEURRAGE)

375g cold butter, cut into cubes
70g plain flour

FOR THE CARAMELISED FIGS

250g ruby port
50g crème de cassis
40g caster sugar, plus 1 tablespoon
5g cinnamon sticks
½ vanilla pod, halved lengthways
pared rind and juice from 1 orange
pared rind and juice from 1 lemon
8 whole fresh firm figs, cut horizontally
   into 5mm rounds

FOR THE CRÈME PÂTISSIÈRE

40g egg yolks (2 medium)
30g caster sugar
2g (½ teaspoon) vanilla extract
16g cornflour
200g milk
½ vanilla pod, split lengthways
40g butter, at room temperature, cubed

TO SERVE

300g crème fraîche

MAKE THE PUFF PASTRY BASE DOUGH

When doing the prep for pastry, it's important that the ingredients, kitchen, counter and equipment are kept cool to ensure that the dough doesn't become warm, and that the butter is incorporated evenly.

1. The day before you want to bake, make the puff pastry following the method on page 38 up to the end of step 4. The following day complete the recipe.
2. Roll out the pastry on a lightly floured work surface to 4mm thick. Use a 26cm round plate or base of a tin as a template to cut out a 26cm perfect round with a small sharp knife, then prick all over with a fork.

MAKE THE BASE FOR THE GLAZE

While the pastry is chilling, make the glaze. Steeping the ingredients for a couple of hours gives them time to meld together for a richer flavour.

3. Pour the port and cassis into a medium pan over a high heat. Add the 40g sugar and the cinnamon sticks. Scrape the seeds from the vanilla pod and add to the pan with the pod, then add the orange and lemon rind and juice and bring to the boil, then reduce the heat slightly and simmer for 10 minutes. Remove from the heat, cover with a lid and let steep for 2 hours. Strain into a pan and set aside.

MAKE THE CRÈME PÂTISSIÈRE

4. Make the crème pâtissière using the method on page 26. Spread it out on the baking tray lined with clingfilm and cover the top with more clingfilm to prevent a skin from forming. Set aside to cool.

BAKE THE PUFF PASTRY BASE

It's important to bake the pastry until it's cooked all the way through, otherwise it will become soggy once filled.

5. Preheat the oven to 200°C/180°C fan/gas mark 6.
6. Transfer the pastry to the prepared baking sheet. Cover with a piece of parchment paper and lay a wire rack on top to make sure it stays flat in the oven. Bake for 18–20 minutes until golden and crisp, then reduce the temperature to 180°C/160°C fan/gas mark 4 and continue to bake for 10 minutes until cooked all the way through. Lift off the rack and paper and lay on the rack to cool.

CARAMELISE THE FIGS

7. Sprinkle 1 tablespoon caster sugar into a large heavy-based frying pan and place over a medium heat for about 1 minute. In batches, place the sliced figs into the pan and cook quickly just until they caramelise – it will only take 1–2 minutes on each side for the sugar to gently bubble and caramelise around them, so make sure the heat isn't too high and you don't leave them in the pan for too long, otherwise they may burn. Transfer to a large tray lined with parchment paper.

8. Put the base of the glaze into a medium pan over a medium heat. Bring to the boil, then simmer fast for about 10–12 minutes to reduce the mixture to a syrup. It will thicken on cooling, so make sure it's not too thick at this stage. Pour into a clean bowl and leave to cool. It should be thick, but brushable.

ASSEMBLE THE TART

9. Place the pastry base on a large flat serving plate.

10. Unwrap the crème pâtissière and put it into a bowl. Use a balloon whisk to gently beat until smooth, then spread all over the base of the pastry and smooth with a spatula.

11. Arrange the warm fig slices in the centre of the tart, leaving a border of cream exposed. Brush the figs with the glaze.

12. Serve the tart cold in slices with crème fraîche or warm it in a 180°C/160°C fan/ gas mark 4 oven for 5 minutes. Brush the figs with any remaining glaze and serve with crème fraîche on the side.

THE SECRETS OF SUCCESS

◆

If the crème pâtissière is too thick to beat with a whisk… It has been boiled for too long. Take a wooden spoon and gently break the thick custard down until it's malleable enough to get a whisk in there. Add 2 tablespoons of milk or cream to help loosen it. It should be thick enough to stay on the tart without running off the sides.

PITHIVIER

A magnificent pie made with puff pastry encasing a rich,
creamy filling flavoured with almond and vanilla

This French puff pastry tart – pronounced 'pit-i-vee-ay' – is also known as a Galette des Rois (King's Cake) in France, as it's traditionally served every year on 6 January, the date in the Christian calendar when it's thought the three wise men arrived in Bethlehem to visit the baby Jesus. It is often baked with a figurine enclosed, to be discovered by one of the guests.

The tart requires several skills. It has a puff pastry base over which a whipped almond cream is piped. A puff lid is laid carefully over the filling and the edges are gently sealed and decorated to completely enclose it. The top of the tart must be smooth and even, and the air in the filling must be maintained so that the baked tart isn't heavy and dense. It is then decorated with neat scallops and intricate spirals.

The pithivier cooks at two heats – the first, higher temperature gives a quick blast that helps the pastry to rise, then the second, slightly lower temperature helps to cook the pie all the way through. If you're left with pastry trimmings, bake them until golden and crisp and dust with icing sugar and cinnamon for a simple petit four.

SERVES 8–10

TIMING

Hands-on time: *1 hour 50 minutes, plus resting*
Cooking time: *35–45 minutes*

PREPARE IN ADVANCE

The pastry and filling can each be made up to
   1 day ahead. Keep the pastry wrapped well in
   clingfilm and the filling in an airtight container,
   both stored in the fridge.

HAVE READY

Stand mixer, if using, fitted with the paddle
   attachment.
Baking sheet lined with parchment paper.
Chopping board lined with clingfilm.

EQUIPMENT

stand mixer, optional
   – paddle attachment
baking sheet
parchment paper
chopping board
clingfilm
digital scales
sieve
wooden spoon
rolling pin
large bowl, optional
electric whisk, optional
disposable piping bag
ruler
20cm, 24cm and 26cm round plates
   or lids (for templates)
sharp serrated knife
spatula
small bowl
pastry brush

FOR THE PUFF PASTRY BASE DOUGH

350g strong bread flour,
   plus extra to dust

9g salt

a few drops of lemon juice

180–195g iced water

40g butter, softened

FOR THE BUTTER INCLUSION (BEURRAGE)

375g cold butter, cut into cubes

70g plain flour

FOR THE ALMOND CREAM

85g butter

85g caster sugar

50g egg (1 medium)

65g ground almonds

30g plain flour

a few drops of almond extract

a few drops of vanilla extract

FOR FINISHING

4 tablespoons apricot jam, sieved

20g egg yolk (1 medium)

a pinch of salt

icing sugar, to dust

MAKE THE PUFF PASTRY BASE DOUGH

Keep the kitchen cool and chill the dough between each round of folding and rolling so that the butter doesn't start to soften and ooze out.

1. Make the pastry using the method on page 38. Wrap and chill until you're ready to assemble the pithivier.

MAKE THE FILLING

The filling must be beaten until soft and airy for a light end result.

2. Beat together the butter and sugar in a mixer with the paddle attachment, or in a large bowl with an electric whisk, until creamy. Gradually beat in the eggs, followed by the ground almonds, flour and almond and vanilla extracts until thoroughly combined. Spoon into the piping bag and set aside.

ASSEMBLE THE PITHIVIER

The pastry is split into two pieces. The smaller piece is rolled out to make the base of the tart, while the larger piece forms the lid.

3. Cut off about one third of the pastry so that you have two pieces. Roll out the smaller piece on a lightly floured work surface to 24cm round and 2–3mm thick. Use a template to cut a neat circle, if necessary. Slide on to the prepared baking sheet.

4. Carefully score a smaller, 20cm circle in the centre of the pastry and spread a thin layer of apricot jam in the central circle, making sure you don't brush it into the border.

5. Snip about 1cm from the end of the piping bag and pipe the almond cream into the round, on top of the apricot jam, again making sure it doesn't go into the border.

6. In a small bowl, beat the egg yolk with the salt and 2 teaspoons water to make an egg wash. Brush this all over the border of the base.

7. Roll out the remaining pastry on a lightly dusted work surface to 26cm round and about 6mm thick. Trim using a template to neaten, if necessary.

8. Using the rolling pin to help you, lift the pastry lid over the base and filling. Carefully smooth it over the filling, starting from the centre of the pie and making sure there are no air bubbles trapped inside. Press firmly around the edges to seal well. Transfer to the fridge for 30–40 minutes to chill.

FINISH THE PITHIVIER

A dusting of icing sugar added three-quarters of the way through baking gives the pie a super-shiny glaze.

9. Preheat the oven to 200°C/180°C fan/gas mark 6.

10. Use a sharp knife to cut scallop shapes all around the rim of the tart and score each scallop in a cross-hatch pattern. Brush the egg wash all over the top. Lightly score the top of the pithivier with neat spiralling curves from the centre to the edge, about 5mm apart.

11. Bake for about 15 minutes, then reduce the temperature to 180°C/160°C fan/gas mark 4 and continue to bake for 15 minutes. Take the pie out of the oven and dust it with a fine layer of icing sugar, then return it to the oven to cook for a further 15 minutes, or until golden.

CLASSIC PUDDINGS
AND DESSERTS

APPLE CRUMBLE
AND CUSTARD POTS

TROPICAL MERINGUE
ROULADE

BLACK FOREST VERRINES

LEMON MERINGUE PIE

STICKY TOFFEE PUDDING

TRIFLE

CHOCOLATE
CHEESECAKE

CLASSIC PUDDINGS AND DESSERTS

Think of this chapter as the wild card! It's the classics… but not as you know them or have ever seen them before. We've taken all our favourite recipes – from homely treats such as cheesecake and crumble, to the 1970s' classic Black Forest Gâteau – and deconstructed each of their elements. They've all been reinvented with new flavours and ingredients, thus giving you a collection of brand-new, jaw-dropping centrepieces.

The elegant make-over of Sticky Toffee Pudding on page 263, for example, features curves of crisp tempered chocolate and golden threads of spun sugar, both sitting on top of a light sponge ring. It can be served hot or cold, along with any extra warm glaze spooned generously on top. Old-school trifle, featuring layers of soft custard, sponge fingers and cream, has been transformed into a pretty-as-a-picture cake, displaying eye-catching rounds of fruit jelly set in vanilla bavarois and sandwiched between a homemade savoiardi sponge.

Pastry chefs are always on the lookout for new ways to present a pudding, flavour or ingredient, and for fresh recipe ideas. There is plenty of imagination in this chapter, and we hope it will inspire you to create your own classics.

APPLE CRUMBLE AND CUSTARD POTS

Caramelised apples, soft apple purée, crumble, lemon sponge and more combine in this delightful pudding

Here's a new spin on the humble apple crumble. All the elements have been deconstructed and put back together – with a couple of added extras – to create an exquisite patisserie recipe from a classic pudding. This can be made either in individual serving dishes or layered up inside lidded jars so that underneath the lid is a delicious surprise.

When choosing the apples for the purée, select a variety with a rosy skin, which will colour it a pleasing pink rather than a less attractive sludgy green. The squares of almond *pain de Gênes* sponge are flavoured with lemon and add a textural contrast to the soft fruit purée and piped domes of mousse-like crème diplomat (crème pâtissière enriched with butter and whipped cream). The crumble mixture requires a firm touch to create rubble-like pieces, which are dusted in edible gold lustre and used to decorate the vanilla cream at the end.

SERVES 4–6

TIMING:

Hands-on time: *1 hour*
Cooking time: *25 minutes*

PREPARE IN ADVANCE

The lemon sponge and crumble
   can be made up to 4 days ahead.
   Wrap the sponge well in clingfilm
   and store the crumble in an airtight
   container at room temperature.
The apple purée can be made up
   to 2 days ahead, stored in an
   airtight container in the fridge.

HAVE READY

Baking sheet lined with parchment.
   paper
Piping bags fitted with the nozzles.
Oven preheated to 220°C/
   200°C fan/gas mark 7.

EQUIPMENT

baking sheet
parchment paper
2 x disposable piping bags
   – 2 x 1cm nozzles (or use
   a 1cm and 1.5cm nozzle)
digital scales
zester
small bowl
large bowl
balloon or electric hand whisk
large metal spoon, optional
spatula
pastry brush
chopping board
small sharp knife
peeler
Parisienne scoop or melon baller
medium pan with a lid
stick blender

small pan
sieve
clingfilm
medium bowl
4–6 glass serving dishes
dessertspoon
jug

20g butter, melted and cooled

60g eggs (just over 1 medium)

60g mandelmassa almond paste,
  warmed (see page 131)

5g lemon juice

20g plain flour

1g baking powder

zest from 1 lemon

1 tablespoon lemon liqueur

FOR THE ALMOND
STREUSEL

35g plain flour

30g ground almonds

30g caster sugar

a few drops of vanilla extract

a good pinch of sea salt

30g butter

edible gold dust

FOR THE CARAMELISED
APPLES

3 Cox's apples

100g caster sugar

20g butter

FOR THE APPLE PURÉE

apple peelings from the caramelised
  apples, above

400g Cox's apples (about 4), cored and
  diced

juice from ½ lemon

100g water

50g caster sugar

MAKE THE LEMON PAIN DE GÊNES

This is a French almond sponge, not to be confused with a genoise sponge. A little of the whisked egg mixture is added to the butter first, before the butter is folded in. This is to stop it splitting.

1. Put the melted butter into a small bowl. In a large bowl, whisk together the eggs and almond paste until light and fluffy. Stir a little of the mixture into the melted butter, then fold the butter mixture back into the batter, along with the lemon juice.

2. Fold in the flour, baking powder and lemon zest, then spoon the mixture onto the prepared baking sheet and spread out with a spatula to a 10cm square that's about 1cm thick. Bake for 6–8 minutes until golden.

3. Remove the sponge from the oven and brush the lemon liqueur over the top. Allow to cool. Reduce the oven to 180°C/160°C fan/gas mark 4.

4. Transfer the cold sponge to a board and cut it into 1.5cm squares. Reline the tray with parchment paper.

MAKE THE ALMOND STREUSEL

This is a simple crumble mixture that's squeezed together to get bigger 'nuggets' of crumble that will be dusted with edible gold lustre.

5. Put the flour, ground almonds, sugar, vanilla extract and salt into a large bowl. Rub the butter into the dry ingredients until a crumble forms, then squeeze the mixture together roughly with your hands until it forms chunky pieces.

6. Spread the streusel out on the prepared sheeet and bake for 20 minutes until dry and crisp. Set aside to cool, still on the tray.

CARAMELISE THE APPLES

The apples appear as delicate balls of caramelised fruit. If you don't have a scoop, you can shape the apples with a small sharp knife.

7. Peel the apples, saving the apple peelings for the apple purée, below. Use a Parisienne scoop or melon baller to scoop balls about 2cm wide from the apples.

8. Heat the sugar in a medium pan over a medium heat. Cook until the sugar has become liquid and golden. Stir in the butter, then add the apple balls and toss them in the caramel. Cook for 3–4 minutes until just tender. Allow to cool.

MAKE THE APPLE PURÉE

9. Put the apple peelings, diced apple, lemon juice and water into a pan over a medium heat. Cover with a lid and bring to the boil, then reduce the heat slightly and simmer for 2 minutes until the apples have completely softened.

10. Take the lid off the pan. Stir in the sugar then continue to cook without the lid for 2–3 minutes more to reduce the liquid.

11. Allow the mixture to cool a little, then liquidise until smooth. If the mixture seems a little watery at this stage, return it to the clean pan and bring it back to the boil for a short time to thicken. Allow to cool, then spoon into one of the prepared piping bags.

MAKE THE CRÈME DIPLOMAT

This is simply a vanilla crème pâtissière whisked with whipping cream.

12. Put the egg yolks into a large bowl and whisk in the caster sugar until combined. Whisk in the cornflour.

13. Pour the milk into a small pan over a medium heat. Scrape down the length of the vanilla pod and add the seeds to the milk, along with the pod. Bring to the boil.

14. Strain the milk mixture onto the egg yolk mixture, stirring well. Return to the pan and bring to a simmer. Cook for 1–2 minutes until the mixture thickens. Stir in the vanilla extract and butter.

15. Line a tray with clingfilm and spread the cream onto it thinly; cover the surface with clingfilm to completely seal it and set aside to cool.

16. Spoon the cold crème pâtissière into a bowl and beat it until smooth. In a separate bowl, whisk the whipping cream until thick and moussey. Fold the cream into the crème pâtissière and beat until smooth.

17. Spoon the crème diplomat into the prepared piping bag and chill.

MAKE THE MASCARPONE VANILLA CREAM

18. Beat the mascarpone in a bowl to soften it. Add the vanilla seeds and sugar and whisk well, then gently stir in the cream using a spatula (the mixture thickens very quickly so don't be tempted to whisk it). Chill in the fridge until ready to use.

Continued…

FOR THE CRÈME DIPLOMAT

40g egg yolks (2 medium)

30g caster sugar

15g cornflour

200g milk

½ vanilla pod, split lengthways

2g vanilla extract

40g butter, cubed

125g whipping cream

FOR THE MASCARPONE VANILLA CREAM

65g mascarpone

seeds from ¼ vanilla pod

15g caster sugar

65g double cream

FOR THE DECORATION

boiling water

fine chocolate curls (see page 151 for instructions)

ASSEMBLE THE DESSERT

The individual components are layered up in the serving dishes and topped with quenelles of mascarpone vanilla cream, golden streusel nuggets and chocolate curls. The quenelles are made using a hot dry dessert spoon, which shapes the cream into a smooth oval.

19. Divide the lemon pain de Gênes and the caramelised apple balls among the serving dishes. Set aside about 12 chunks of streusel.

20. Pipe 1cm domes of crème diplomat into the dishes followed by domes of apple purée to fill in any gaps. Scatter over a little of the streusel, then add another layer of crème diplomat and apple purée domes. Continue until all the mixtures are used up.

21. Dip a dessert spoon into a jug of boiling water and dry the spoon. Scrape it across the mascarpone vanilla cream and allow the cream to fold over itself to make a small oval or quenelle shape. If you find this tricky, take a scoop of the cream in one spoon and roll another spoon of the same size around the scoop from back to front so the cream slides into the second spoon. Pass the cream between the spoons a few more times to mould it into a nice smooth quenelle shape. Place it on top of one of the dishes, then make more quenelles in the same way.

22. Toss the remaining streusel chunks in some edible gold dust so that they look like little gold nuggets and carefully place them on top of the cream quenelles. Push a chocolate curl into the top of each one and serve.

TROPICAL MERINGUE ROULADE

A soft roll of meringue encasing a sweet crème patissière flavoured with four flower fruits

This roulade uses a simple French meringue in which egg whites whisked to soft peaks are combined with sugar. All the usual principles for making meringues apply – the bowl must be spotlessly clean and free of any grease or dirt, otherwise the eggs won't whip up and they'll lose volume. They are then whisked with sugar until they're smooth and glossy and stabilised by cornflour to give the meringue a soft texture similar to that of marshmallow, which makes it easy to roll.

The crème pâtissière is flavoured with four flower fruits – orange, pineapple, banana and lemon – which add flavour and texture. They need to be puréed first so that they're very smooth when you fold them into the crème pâtissière. To finish, the leaves from the pineapple are used to add a splash of colour, along with fine slices of caramelised pineapple and segments of orange, plus a generous dusting of icing sugar.

SERVES: 10–12

TIMING

Hands-on time: *1 hour, plus chilling*
Cooking time: *8 minutes*

PREPARE IN ADVANCE

The roulade can be made up to
 1 month ahead and frozen in its
 tray, wrapped well in clingfilm.
 Thaw completely for a couple of
 hours before filling and serving.

HAVE READY

Stand mixer, if using, fitted with the
 whisk attachment.
Baking sheet lined with
 parchment paper.
Baking tray lined with clingfilm.
Large chopping board lined with
 parchment paper.
Piping bag fitted with the nozzle.
Oven preheated to 230°C/
 210°C fan/gas mark 8.

EQUIPMENT

stand mixer, optional
 – whisk attachment
large baking sheet,
 about 45 x 30cm
parchment paper
baking tray
clingfilm
large chopping board
disposable piping bag
 – 1.5cm plain nozzle
digital scales
sharp knife
electric hand whisk, optional
sieve

large metal spoon
spatula
stick blender or food-processor
small bowl
medium bowl
small heavy-based pan
2 large bowls
clingfilm
kitchen paper
flameproof baking sheet, optional
blowtorch, optional
scissors
pastry brush

200g egg whites (about 7 medium)

200g caster sugar

50g cornflour

40g flaked almonds

FOR THE FOUR-FLOWER CRÈME DIPLOMAT

135g pineapple, chopped

55g freshly squeezed orange juice (about ¾ orange)

25g lemon juice (about ½ lemon)

40g banana (about ¼ medium)

4g powdered gelatine

20g cold water

60g egg yolks (3 medium)

20g plain flour

50g caster sugar

seeds from ¼ vanilla pod

150g double cream, lightly whipped

FOR THE CHANTILLY CREAM

200g double cream

20g caster sugar

a few drops of vanilla extract

FOR THE DECORATION

2 thin slices of pineapple, plus a few leaves

1 orange, cut into segments (see page 210)

2 tablespoons apricot glaze (see page 74), warmed slightly

MAKE THE MERINGUE

Take care not to overwhisk the eggs or they'll get dry, then you won't be able to whisk in the sugar easily and your meringue won't have volume.

1. Put the egg whites in the bowl of a stand mixer and whisk to soft peaks. You can also do this in a large bowl using an electric hand whisk.
2. Add the sugar, a heaped tablespoon at a time, and continue to whisk the mixture until it is stiff and glossy. Sift over the cornflour and gently fold in with a large metal spoon until it is fully incorporated.
3. Slide the paper off the baking sheet and dot each corner with a blob of meringue. Flip the paper over and lay it back on the baking sheet, pressing each corner to stick it to the sheet.
4. Spread the meringue evenly over the square. Sprinkle the flaked almonds evenly over the top and bake for about 8 minutes. Leave the meringue in the tin and set aside to cool. It will flatten as it cools.

MAKE THE FOUR-FLOWER DIPLOMAT CREAM

Whipped cream is added to crème pâtissière to make it a crème diplomat, then it is flavoured with blended fruit purées.

5. Blend the pineapple, orange juice, lemon juice and banana with a hand blender or food-processor until very smooth. Weigh the purée and make sure you have about 250g.
6. Put the gelatine into a small bowl with the water. Set aside to allow the gelatine to absorb the water.
7. Put the egg yolks into a medium bowl and add the flour and 25g of the sugar. Whisk together until smooth.
8. Put the purée into a small, heavy-based pan over a medium heat with the remaining 25g sugar and the vanilla seeds. Bring to the boil then immediately pour into the bowl with the egg mixture, stirring continuously.
9. Scrape the mixture back into the pan and bring back to the boil, stirring constantly to make a smooth custard. When it comes to the boil, cook for about 2 more minutes to allow the mixture to thicken, stirring all the time. Take the pan off the heat and whisk in the gelatine to dissolve it, whisking well until smooth.
10. Spoon the mixture onto the lined tray and spread it out with a spatula, then put another piece of clingfilm on top and smooth it down to prevent a skin from forming. Cool and chill.

MAKE THE CHANTILLY CREAM

11. Make the Chantilly cream using the recipe on page 26. Cover the bowl and chill.

PREPARE THE DECORATION

The roulade is topped with delicate caramelised pineapple and orange pieces. Only the edges of the fruit should be scorched, so be careful not to burn them too much with the blowtorch.

12. Slice the pineapple rounds into thin neat wedges and lay them on kitchen paper to drain.
13. Slice the segmented orange pieces in half so that they're about the same size as the pineapple wedges. Set them aside on the kitchen paper to drain.
14. Once the fruit is dry, put it on a flameproof baking sheet and use a blowtorch to scorch just the very edges of each piece of fruit. Take care not to burn all of it. If you don't have a blowtorch you can grill the fruit, but it won't produce quite the same effect as it will caramelise the whole piece. Brush the fruit pieces with a little apricot glaze to give them a shine.
15. Pull about 5 leaves from the top of the pineapple and wash them to remove any dust. Trim with scissors and carefully cut each into a neat triangle.

ASSEMBLE THE ROULADE

16. Carefully turn the meringue out onto the parchment-lined board and peel away the top layer of paper. Position the meringue widthways, with the longest edge nearest you.
17. Spoon the fruit crème pâtissière into a bowl and whisk to loosen it. Fold in the whipped cream. Carefully spread the mixture over the meringue, leaving a 1cm border all around the edge.
18. Spoon the Chantilly cream into the prepared piping bag and pipe a line of cream along the edge closest to you.
19. Use the parchment paper to help you carefully roll up the meringue tightly. Finish with the seam underneath the roll. Transfer to a flat serving dish.
20. Pipe balls of Chantilly cream along the length of the roll and dust with icing sugar. Arrange the small pieces of orange, pineapple and leaves on top and dust with a little more icing sugar. Serve in slices with a little extra Chantilly cream. This dessert is best eaten on the day it is made.

BLACK FOREST VERRINES

Rich chocolate and Chantilly creams topped with light-as-air espuma sponge, crisp chocolate orange soil and brandy-soaked sour cherries

Schwarzwälder Kirschtorte is the rather romantic-sounding German translation for the classic dessert on which this pudding is based. In this totally modern makeover the elements of the cake are layered in individual serving glasses and garnished with cherry jelly cubes and delicate thyme leaves. Pastry chefs prefer to use high-quality Griottines® cherries, which are Morello cherries from eastern France that have been macerated in eau de vie or kirsch, but if you can't find them, you can use any cherries in kirsch. When combining all the different parts of this dish, arrange them evenly around the inside so that each spoonful will have a little bit of each.

The light whipped sponge contains very little fat. It's known in the trade as *espuma* (meaning sponge or foam). In professional kitchens the sponge mixture is poured into a cream whipper and charged with air as it is extruded into cups. It is then cooked in a microwave for speed, but a more traditional method is outlined overleaf.

SERVES 8

TIMING

Hands-on time: *1 hour 30 minutes*
Cooking time: *1 hour*

PREPARE IN ADVANCE

You can make the chocolate soil up to 1 week
   ahead, stored in a cool, dry place.
The chocolate *crémeux* must be made the day
   before.

HAVE READY

Stand mixer, if using, fitted with
   the whisk attachment.
Baking sheet lined with parchment
   paper.
Ramekins or brownie tin, if using,
   base-lined with parchment paper.
Poke a hole in the base of each
   paper cup, if using, with a skewer.
Piping bag fitted with the nozzles.
Oven preheated to 180°C/160°C
   fan/gas mark 4.

EQUIPMENT

stand mixer, optional
  – whisk attachment
heavy-based baking sheet
parchment paper or silicone mat
4 x 250ml ramekins, or a 20 x 10cm
   brownie tin, or 4 disposable
   paper cups and a skewer
2 x disposable piping bags
  – 1.5cm nozzle
sharp knife
chopping board
zester
2 large bowls
balloon whisk
medium heavy-based pan

spatula
digital thermometer
fine sieve
stick blender, optional
clingfilm
2 airtight containers
small bowl
small pan
silicone ice-cube tray
microwave, optional
electric hand whisk,
   optional
cream whipper, optional
  – 2 gas cartridges
8 small serving glasses

FOR THE CHOCOLATE CRÉMEUX

200g dark chocolate (70% cocoa solids),
    finely chopped
80g egg yolks (from 2–4 medium)
40g caster sugar
200g full-fat milk
200g whipping cream (35% fat)

FOR THE CHOCOLATE SOIL

50g dark brown muscovado sugar
65g ground almonds
35g strong bread flour
25g cocoa powder
0.5g table salt
0.5g instant coffee powder
35g butter, melted
zest from 1 orange

FOR THE JELLY CUBES

3g gelatine powder
15g cold water
125g cherry purée, frozen and thawed,
    or fresh (see page 25)
0.7g agar agar powder

FOR THE ESPUMA CHOCOLATE SPONGE

220g eggs (about 5 medium)
80g caster sugar
1 teaspoon strawberry red
    edible food colour
30g cocoa powder
25g plain flour
kirsch syrup, from the jar of cherries

FOR THE CHERRY COMPOTE

100g fresh sour cherries, halved
    and pitted (or use sweet cherries
    if sour aren't available)
20g caster sugar
20g cold water, plus 1 tablespoon
2–3 sprigs lemon thyme
8g fresh lemon juice
1/2 teaspoon cornflour
about 2 tablespoons kirsch

TO MAKE THE CHOCOLATE CRÉMEUX

The *crémeux* is simply a crème anglaise whipped with cream and an added flavour, in this case chocolate.

1. Make the chocolate *crémeux* a day ahead using the method on page 27 and chill it in the fridge overnight.

MAKE THE CHOCOLATE ORANGE SOIL

Don't add the orange zest before baking the soil or it will burn. Residual heat in the cooked mixture will be enough to bring out the zest flavour.

2. Put the sugar, ground almonds, flour, cocoa, salt and coffee into a large bowl. Pour the melted butter into the bowl and stir everything together, then break it up into lumps with your fingers.
3. Spread the mixture out on the silicone mat or parchment paper and bake for 8–10 minutes. Remove from the oven and sprinkle the orange zest over the top, then mix it in.
4. Cool on the mat and store in an airtight container in a cool dry place.

PREPARE THE JELLY CUBES

If you don't have an ice-cube tray, pour the jelly into a small flexible plastic container, chill until set, then cut into squares.

5. Put the gelatine and water into a small bowl and set aside to soak.
6. Place the cherry purée and the agar agar powder in a small pan and heat gently. Stir constantly until the mixture reaches 92°C. Take the pan off the heat and add the gelatine, stirring until it dissolves. Strain the mixture through a fine sieve into a bowl. Carefully spoon the mixture into the ice-cube tray. Refrigerate until set.

MAKE THE ESPUMA CHOCOLATE SPONGE

This is a super-quick sponge made in professional kitchens using a cream whipper and microwave, although it can also be made in a conventional oven.

7. *Microwave method:* Put the eggs and sugar into the bowl of the mixer and whisk at a medium speed until the mixture is thick, mousse-like and leaves a ribbon-like trail when the whisk is lifted. Alternatively use an electric hand whisk for about 8–10 minutes. Whisk in the food colour. Sift the cocoa and flour over the top of the mixture and carefully fold in,

then spoon it into the prepared ramekins and cook, one at a time, in the microwave for 45 seconds on high.

Oven method: Preheat the oven to 180°C/160°C fan/gas mark 4 and line a 20 x 10cm brownie tin with parchment paper. Mix up the batter as for the microwave method above and spoon into the brownie tin. Bake for 10–12 minutes.

Cream whipper method: Mix the cocoa, eggs, sugar, flour and colouring in a bowl using a hand blender. Pour into a cream whipper and charge it with two gas cartridges, then refrigerate the whipper for 2 hours. Shake the cream whipper well and use the contents to half-fill each prepared paper cup (if using). Microwave each cup for 45 seconds on high. Cool, then run a knife around the inside of each to release the sponge.

8. Drizzle the sponges with a little kirsch syrup from the pot of cherries.

MAKE THE CHERRY COMPOTE

It's important to dissolve the cornflour for the compote in cold water before using, otherwise it won't dissolve into the hot mixture thoroughly.

9. Put the cherries into a small pan over a low heat with the sugar and 20g water, sprigs of lemon thyme and lemon juice. Heat gently for about 5–10 minutes, until the cherries have cooked down and softened.

10. Put the cornflour in a small bowl and stir in the 1 tablespoon water – just enough to dissolve it – then stir into the cherry mixture and continue to cook for a few more minutes until thickened.

11. Take the pan off the heat and stir in the kirsch, adding more if you prefer a stronger flavour. Set aside until you're ready to assemble the dessert.

MAKE THE CHANTILLY CREAM

12. Whisk up the Chantilly cream using the method on page 26. It should be a good piping consistency.

ASSEMBLE THE VERRINES

13. Spoon the *crémeux* into the piping bag fitted with the nozzle and pipe a little crémeux onto the base of each dish. Spoon the Chantilly cream into the second bag and pipe Chantilly cream over the top. Spoon over some cherry compote, followed by more *crémeux*.

14. Sprinkle chocolate soil over the top of the *crémeux*. Roughly tear the sponges and place one or two pieces on top. Finish with the Griottine® cherries, jelly cubes and sprigs of lemon thyme arranged artfully on top.

FOR THE CHANTILLY CREAM

200g whipping cream

10g caster sugar

seeds from ½ vanilla pod,
    or 1 teaspoon extract

FOR FINISHING

125g Griottines® or other cherries in
    kirsch syrup

a few sprigs of lemon thyme

THE SECRETS OF SUCCESS

—◆—

If the crémeux is too soft…
The crème anglaise hasn't cooked enough and formed a perfect emulsion. Don't throw it away, though – just fold in some whipped cream to help stabilise it. The end result will have more of a mousse-like texture, but will be no less delicious for that.

LEMON MERINGUE PIE

An exquisite bar of lemon sablé biscuit, lemon curd and almond and lemon sponge, topped with a strawberry meringue ribbon and curls of candied citrus peel

Here's a bar that's sure to delight and surprise everyone. You'll be familiar with all the elements – melt-in-the-mouth buttery biscuit, a light sponge, lemon curd and meringue, but it's put together to create a totally modern interpretation of the classic pudding.

All the textures need to work together, so take care when baking or preparing each one. The base needs to be cooked until just golden so that it's crisp but not overdone. The sponge holds the lemon curd, so again needs to be baked thoroughly in order to carry the weight. These simple layers are finished with a light strawberry meringue, just scorched with a blowtorch to give a wonderful toasted caramel flavour.

SERVES 12

TIMING

Hands-on time: *1 hour 20 minutes*
Cooking time: *30 minutes*

HAVE READY

Stand mixer, if using, fitted with
the paddle attachment
Baking sheets lined with
parchment paper.
Piping bag fitted with the St Honoré
nozzle.
Oven preheated to 190°C/170°C fan/
gas mark 5.

EQUIPMENT

stand mixer, optional
 – paddle attachment
 – whisk attachments
2 baking sheets
parchment paper
digital scales
sieve
board
clingfilm
rolling pin
fork
zester
food processor or blender
large bowl, optional
wooden spoon, optional
wire rack
2 medium bowls
spatula

28 x 18cm stainless steel
frame
pastry brush
small and medium
saucepans
digital thermometer
palette knife
sharp knife
small bowl
small plastic container
chopping knife
disposable piping bag
 – 16mm St Honoré
nozzle
ruler
blowtorch
kitchen paper

125g plain flour

100g butter, chopped

50g icing sugar

1g salt

20g egg yolk (1 medium)

zest from ½ lemon

1g vanilla extract

10–20g caster sugar, for sprinkling

FOR THE LEMON PAIN DE GÊNES

120g eggs (about 2½ medium)

120g mandelmassa almond paste,
   warmed (see page 131)

40g butter, melted and cooled

10g lemon juice

25g plain flour

1.5g baking powder

zest from 2 lemons

2 tablespoons lemon liqueur

FOR THE LEMON CURD

4g gelatine

20g cold water

200g lemon juice
   (about 8 medium fruits)

150g caster sugar

80g whole egg (about 1½ medium)

60g egg yolks (3 medium)

110g chilled butter, diced

FOR THE CANDIED LEMON AND ORANGE PEEL

pared rind of ½ lemon

pared rind of ½ orange

100g caster sugar

30g liquid glucose

30g water

MAKE THE SABLÉ BISCUIT BASE

1. Put the flour into a stand mixer, add the butter and beat on a low to medium speed until the mixture resembles fine grains. Alternatively, beat in a bowl using a wooden spoon.

2. Stir in the icing sugar, salt, egg yolk, lemon zest and vanilla and continue to mix until a dough forms. Bring together with your hands and shape into a rough rectangle. Wrap in clingfilm and chill for 20 minutes.

3. Roll out the dough until it measures 32 x 21cm and is about 3–4mm thick. Prick all over with a fork and bake on a lined baking sheet for 15–20 minutes. Sprinkle with caster sugar and cool on a wire rack. Increase the oven temperature to 200°C/180°C fan/gas mark 6.

MAKE THE LEMON PAIN DE GÊNES

4. Whisk the eggs and almond paste together in a bowl until light and fluffy. Stir a little of the mixture into the melted butter, then fold the butter mixture back into the batter, along with the lemon juice.

5. Fold in the flour, baking powder and lemon zest, then spread onto a lined baking sheet in a 28 x 19cm rectangle. Bake for 6–8 minutes until golden.

6. Brush the lemon liqueur over the top and allow to cool on a wire rack. Use the frame to mark a rectangle on the sponge, then cut out the shape. Put the frame on a board or tray covered with a fresh parchment paper and put the sponge inside.

MAKE THE LEMON CURD

7. Put the gelatine into a small bowl, add the water and set aside to soak.

8. Pour the lemon juice and caster sugar into a pan. Put the whole egg and egg yolks in a bowl and mix together.

9. Bring the pan of lemon juice and sugar to the boil, then pour over the egg mixture, stirring all the time. Return the mixture to the pan, stirring well to prevent it from splitting and making sure it doesn't get any hotter than 90°C.

10. Take the pan off the heat and stir in the gelatine until dissolved. Strain through a sieve into a bowl and slowly stir in the butter. Allow to cool, then spoon it over the sponge, spreading evenly with a palette knife. Chill for 1–2 hours until set.

MAKE THE CANDIED CITRUS PEEL

11. Put the pared lemon and orange rind into a small saucepan and cover with water. Bring to the boil and cook for 1 minute. Strain, then hold under running cold water to refresh the strips and stop them from cooking any further.
12. Return the strips to the pan and add the sugar, glucose and water. Bring to the boil and simmer until the mixture reaches 106°C (thick thread). Spoon into a sealable container and allow to cool in the syrup before chilling.

MAKE THE MERINGUE DECORATION AND ASSEMBLE THE BARS

13. Trim the sides of the sablé biscuit, then cut into 12 bars, each measuring 10 x 4.5cm. These form the base of the dessert and are slightly larger than the layers that sit on top of them.
14. Slide a knife around the sides of the cake frame and lift it off. Trim the sides of the sponge, then cut into 12 or 14 bars measuring about 9 x 4cm. Carefully lift each curd-topped bar onto a sablé base.
15. Put the strawberry purée into the stand mixer, add the egg white powder and whisk until the powder has dissolved. Add the sugar a tablespoon at a time, continuing to whisk, until the mixture forms a meringue.
16. Spoon into the prepared piping bag and pipe in a zigzag fashion along each bar to cover the top of the jellied curd. Use a blowtorch to lightly toast the meringue.
17. Drain the orange segments and strawberries on kitchen paper. Put the orange onto a metal baking sheet and use the blowtorch to caramelise the edges on each side.
18. Arrange a halved strawberry on the top of each bar. Finely slice the candied citrus peel and place a few strips on top. Add a small piece of orange and a mint leaf and serve.

FOR THE STRAWBERRY MERINGUE AND DECORATION

125g strawberries, puréed
11g dried egg white powder
200g caster sugar
1 orange, segmented
6 small strawberries, halved
small fresh mint leaves

STICKY TOFFEE PUDDING

A delicate sponge bathed in glossy caramel sauce and crowned with waves of dark chocolate and gossamer spun sugar threads

Here are all the elements of a traditional sticky toffee pudding as you've never seen them before. The fruit sponge is steamed in a savarin tin to give it a light texture. Sweetness comes from a shiny caramel glaze, then dark chocolate is drizzled all over.

The decoration that transforms this sponge into a spectacular centrepiece is where the patisserie skills really come to the fore. Tempered chocolate is set on curved acetate to produce dramatic spikes and a mound of spun sugar erupts from the centre to bring drama and sparkle to the finished cake. A chef's trick for making very fine threads of spun sugar is to cut the prongs of a balloon whisk into spikes that, when dipped into hot sugar syrup, pull out very thin strands.

SERVES 10–12

TIMING

Hands on time: *1 hour, plus cooling*
Cooking time: *1 hour 20 minutes*

PREPARE IN ADVANCE

The chocolate spikes can be made
   up to 2 weeks ahead, stored in an
   airtight box at room temperature.
The spun sugar can be stored for up
   to 1 week in a sealed airtight
   container with food-safe silica
   gel in the base, covered with
   parchment paper or kitchen towel.

HAVE READY

Stand mixer, if using, fitted with
   the whisk attachment.
Savarin mould greased and
   dusted with flour.
Card or plastic prepared into a
   curved mould (see step 12).
Tea towel folded into a square.
Baking tray lined with clingfilm
   and a wire rack resting over it.
Oven preheated to 190°C/
   170°C fan/gas mark 5.

EQUIPMENT

stand mixer, optional
   – whisk attachment
20cm savarin mould
A4 sheet of flexible card or plastic
sticky tape
tea towel
digital scales
chopping knife
chopping board
large bowl, optional
wooden spoon, optional
parchment paper
ruler
medium bowl
electric hand whisk, optional
sieve
spatula or large metal spoon
clingfilm
foil
roasting tin

skewer
palette knife
wire rack
small bowl
2 medium pans
digital thermometer
balloon whisk
baking tray
microwave and microwavable
   bowl, or medium pan and
   heatproof bowl
small disposable piping bag
small sharp knife or scalpel
long-handled wooden spoon
pastry brush
balloon whisk with the prongs
   trimmed (see tip above, and
   photo F, overleaf) or a fork

170g dried dates, pitted

55g butter, plus extra for greasing

85g caster sugar

85g soft dark brown sugar

100g eggs (2 medium)

4g coffee extract

3g vanilla extract

170g plain flour, plus extra for dusting

10g baking powder

FOR THE CHOCOLATE SPIKES

200g dark chocolate

FOR THE SALT CARAMEL CRÉMEUX GLAZE

4g gelatine powder

20g cold water

100g liquid glucose

160g caster sugar

340g double cream

seeds from 1 vanilla pod

2.5g (½ teaspoon) sea salt

100g butter, chilled and chopped

FOR THE CHOCOLATE PIPING

50g dark chocolate

FOR THE SPUN SUGAR

300g caster sugar

70g liquid glucose

100g water

a little vegetable oil, for greasing

MAKE THE STICKY TOFFEE PUDDING

The sponge is steamed in a hot water bath in the oven. The cake tin is wrapped in layers of clingfilm and foil to trap the moisture, then placed in a roasting tin that is itself covered in foil.

1. Set the dates aside for 20 minutes in a bowl of boiling water. Drain well then chop roughly.
2. Put the butter and both types of sugar into a stand mixer and cream together until the mixture looks pale and soft. Slowly add the eggs, a little at a time, then beat in the coffee and vanilla. You can also do this in a large bowl with a wooden spoon or electric hand whisk.
3. Sift over the flour and baking powder and carefully fold in, followed by the chopped dates, until combined. Spoon the mixture into the prepared tin and level the surface.
4. Wrap the whole savarin tin in clingfilm, then in foil so that it's completely sealed. Put it in a roasting tin and pour boiling water halfway up the sides of the savarin tin. Cover the roasting tin with foil and transfer it to the oven to steam for 50 minutes. Take the tin out of the oven and carefully remove the foil. Test if the cake is done by pushing a skewer through the clingfilm into the sponge – it should come out clean. If it's still a little wet, replace the foil and return to the oven, checking every 5 minutes.
5. Once the cake is cooked, remove the foil and clingfilm and carefully loosen the edges with a palette knife, then turn out onto a wire rack. Leave to cool, then chill while you make the glaze.

MAKE THE CURVED CHOCOLATE SPIKES

The tempering must be perfect here or the chocolate won't shine and the spikes will lose their shape. The natural contraction of the chocolate as it dries means it will set in the mould and come away easily once it's dry.

If you don't use all the chocolate, spoon the remainder into a cone of parchment paper, seal and cool for future use.

6. Make a mould by curling up the long sides of the card or plastic slightly and taping across the top so that you have a curved gutter shape.
7. Temper the chocolate following the instructions on page 34.
8. For this step, see the photographs on page 265. Pour the tempered chocolate onto a 24 x 15cm acetate sheet sitting on a piece of parchment paper. Use a palette knife to spread it out to a fine layer about 1–2mm thick and roughly 25 x 16cm (A). While the chocolate is still pliable, cut into 8 even rectangles each one 3cm wide (B).Carefully lift them off the acetate, transfer to a fresh sheet of parchment paper and cut in half lengthways (C).
9. Cut diagonally across the rectangles to make 16 triangles (D).
10. Place the parchment sheet of chocolate triangles inside the curved card (E). Set aside to dry.

Continued…

MAKE THE SALT CARAMEL CRÉMEUX GLAZE

Hot flavoured cream is poured over caramel to make this glaze, which contains gelatine to help it set over the sponge.

11. Put the gelatine in a small bowl, add the water and leave to soak.
12. Put the liquid glucose and caster sugar into a medium pan and heat gently, shaking the pan every now and then to mix the two ingredients. Cook until the sugars have dissolved, then turn the heat up slightly and allow it to cook until it turns into a medium golden brown caramel.
13. Meanwhile, pour the cream into a separate medium pan with the vanilla seeds and salt. Bring to the boil, then take the pan off the heat.
14. Once the sugar has turned into a caramel, take both pans off the heat and pour the hot cream into the caramel. Stir well, then leave to cool to 60°C. Stir in the gelatine, then whisk in the butter. Set aside to thicken slightly and cool to 40°C.
15. Place the cake on the rack over the prepared tray and pour the glaze all over it. Spoon up the drips and use to fill any gaps. Keep any remainder for sauce.

MAKE THE DARK CHOCOLATE PIPING

You might find it easier to practise this decorating technique on a piece of parchment paper before you decorate the cake.

16. Melt the chocolate in a bowl using the instructions on page 34 and spoon it into a small piping bag. Snip about 2mm off the tip and pipe fine zigzags of chocolate all around the ring of sponge.

MAKE THE SPUN SUGAR

Patisserie chefs will spin beautifully golden sugar that is fine and completely even. First timers will probably find a few blobs of caramel in their sugar nest, but the overall effect will be the same.
    Safety is important here, so prepare your work area well and never flick hot sugar towards yourself or anyone else in the kitchen.

17. First clear a large work area and line the surface completely with parchment paper. Stick down the edges if necessary. Wedge or tape the wooden spoon to a tall, sturdy container as shown opposite so that the handle is pointing away from you and at least 25–30cm above the work surface. Lightly oil both the parchment and the wooden handle and fill the sink with cold water. Place the folded tea towel and adapted whisk or fork beside the spoon. Fill the sink with cold water.

18. Pour the caster sugar into a small pan over a low heat. Add the liquid glucose and water and cook gently to dissolve the sugar. Bring to the boil, then cook until the mixture reaches 152°C.

19. Quickly dip the base of the pan into the sink of cold water to stop the mixture from cooking any further. Place it on the folded tea towel and leave to thicken and cool for a few minutes

20. Dip the cut-off balloon whisk or fork into the sugar and pull it up so that you have several threads of sugar hanging from the prongs (F). You may need to dip a couple of times to get good streams of sugar. Quickly flick the sugar threads over the wooden spoon from side to side (don't flick the sugar towards you) to create long thin strands (G). Continue to do this, dipping the prongs back into the caramel as necessary, until you've built up a big enough nest to sit inside the cake ring. You may need to reheat the sugar if the threads start to get too thick.

ASSEMBLE THE DESSERT

21. Place the cake on a serving plate. Carefully remove the acetate and chocolate from the cardboard mould. Release the chocolate, which should come away easily, and snap it into individual triangles. Gently push the spikes into the sponge on the inside of the ring so that you have several spikes arching out evenly from the centre of the cake.

22. Pull the nest of sugar up from the wooden spoon and shape it so that it looks like a flame. Arrange it artfully inside the ring of cake.

23. Serve the cake in slices with any remaining piping, warmed, on the side.

TRIFLE

*Layers of light sponge, berry crème brûlée, creamy vanilla bavarois
with fun tubes of berry jelly, and topped with summer fruit*

Summer berry trifle…but not as you'd know it. This stand-alone showstopper is sliced to
serve rather than assembled in a large trifle bowl. The top and bottom layers are made from
a savoiardi mixture, but instead of being piped into fingers, it's formed into a bar of sponge.
The texture is still lovely and light, perfect for sandwiching with the other elements of the
trifle. The first of these is a crème brûlée flavoured with summer fruit. Two fun tubes of
jelly lie along the middle of the vanilla bavarois, and it's finished with another layer of sponge,
an arrangement of fresh summer fruit and a light dusting of icing sugar. As with layered
slices, it's important to set each layer at the right stage, otherwise the pudding won't display
those perfect lines required for the end result.

Remember to brush the sponge with a little sherry syrup to moisten it. For a non-alcoholic
version, replace the sherry with orange juice.

SERVES 16

TIMING

Hands-on time: *about 2 hours, plus
chilling and freezing time*
Cooking time: *35 minutes*

PREPARE IN ADVANCE

Make the savoiardi sponge and set aside
to cool. Wrap well in clingfilm and store
at room temperature for up to a day.

HAVE READY

Stand mixer, fitted with the whisk attachment
Draw a 28 x 18cm rectangle on 2 separate
pieces of parchment paper. Turn them
over and place each on the baking sheets.
Fit the nozzle into the piping bag.
Roll the acetate into 2 tubes 30cm long and
2cm in diameter. Fasten with sticky tape,
and tape one end closed.
Preheat the oven to 200°C/
180°C fan/gas mark 6.

EQUIPMENT

stand mixer
 – whisk attachment
large bowl
electric hand whisk
large metal spoon
piping bag
 – 16mm plain nozzle
parchment paper
pencil and ruler
2 baking sheets
digital scales
sieve
2 medium bowls
wire rack
board
28 x 18cm stainless steel frame

wire rack
sharp knife
pastry brush
small bowl
saucepan
wooden spoon
digital thermometer
2 acetate sheets, 30 x 4cm
sticky tape
spatula
tall, narrow container,
 30cm high
small funnel
palette knife

FOR THE SAVOIARDI
SPONGE

180g egg whites (6 medium)

150g caster sugar

120g egg yolks (6 medium)

80g plain flour, sifted

60g cornflour, sifted

15g flaked almonds

icing sugar, to dust

FOR THE SHERRY SYRUP

15g caster sugar

15g water

70g sweet sherry

FOR THE MIXED BERRY
CRÈME BRÛLÉE

3g powdered gelatine

15g cold water

40g caster sugar

60g egg yolks (3 medium)

50g frozen mixed berries, thawed,
    then puréed and sieved

250g whipping cream

FOR THE BERRY
JELLY TUBES

12g powdered gelatine

60g cold water

500g fresh or frozen mixed berries,
    puréed and strained (the berries need
    to be thawed if you're using frozen)

2.5g agar agar powder

FOR THE VANILLA
BAVAROIS

9g powdered gelatine

45g cold water

100g egg yolks (5 medium)

75g caster sugar

200g double cream

200g full-fat milk

1 vanilla pod, split open lengthways

360g whipping cream

MAKE THE SAVOIARDI SPONGE AND SHERRY SYRUP

1. Whisk the whites in a stand mixer with 100g of the caster sugar until the mixture is a smooth and glossy meringue.

2. In a separate bowl, whisk the egg yolks and remaining 50g sugar until the mixture has thickened and become mousse-like.

3. Fold the egg yolk mixture into the meringue, followed by the flours. Spoon into the prepared piping bag and pipe diagonal lines over the rectangle shapes drawn on the paper lining both baking sheets. Make sure the lines touch each other and go slightly beyond the outlines.

Sprinkle with flaked almonds and dust with a little icing sugar. Bake for 15–20 minutes.

4. Meanwhile, put all the ingredients for the sherry syrup into a bowl and stir together.

5. Take the cakes out of the oven and transfer to a wire rack to cool. Slide each cake in turn, still on the parchment, onto a board and use the stainless steel frame to mark a rectangle on each. Cut around it, saving the trimmings for future use (they can be frozen or stored in an airtight container for nibbling – chef's perk!). Mark a 22 x 5cm rectangle in the middle of one of the cakes. Cut it out and save it with the trimmings if you wish. (The fruit will eventually be placed inside the rectangular hole.) Set both sponges aside.

6. Line a clean board or tray with parchment paper and put the frame on top. Peel the paper off the complete sponge and put it inside the frame. Brush some sherry syrup over the surface.

MAKE THE MIXED BERRY CRÈME BRÛLÉE

7. Put the gelatine into a small bowl, add the water and set aside to soak. Stir the sugar, egg yolks and fruit purée together in a separate medium bowl.

8. Pour the cream into a saucepan and bring to the boil. Add to the egg yolk mixture and stir well. Return to the pan and heat until the temperature reaches 85°C. Immediately take the pan off the heat and stir in the gelatine until dissolved.

9. Strain the mixture into a bowl and cool a little until it starts to thicken. At that point, pour it over the sponge in the frame and chill for 15 minutes.

MAKE THE BERRY JELLY TUBES

10. Put the gelatine into a small bowl, add the water and set aside to soak.

11. Place the fruit purée and agar agar powder in a saucepan and heat gently, stirring constantly until it reaches 92°C. Remove the pan from the heat and stir in the gelatine until it dissolves. Leave to cool to setting point (about 21°C).

12. Stand the acetate tubes in the tall container, insert the funnel and spoon the jelly mixture into them. Chill in the fridge until set.

MAKE THE VANILLA BAVAROIS

13. Put the gelatine into a small bowl, add the water and set aside to soak. Put the egg yolks and sugar into another bowl.
14. Make a crème anglaise base. Scrape the vanilla seeds into a saucepan and add the pod too. Add the cream and milk and bring to the boil. Pour onto the egg yolk mixture, stirring well.
15. Return the mixture to the pan and simmer steadily, stirring constantly, until it reaches 85°C. Strain into a bowl and stir in the gelatine until dissolved. Cool until the mixture reaches about 40°C.
16. Whip the cream until thick and mousse-like. Add to the bowl of crème anglaise and carefully fold everything together.

FINISH ASSEMBLING THE DESSERT

17. Spoon a thin layer of bavarois into the frame and freeze for 20 minutes to chill quickly.
18. Carefully remove the jelly tubes from the acetate and place them lengthways on top of the bavarois. Cut to fit if necessary.
19. Spoon the remaining bavarois around the tubes carefully, ensuring they do not move. Level the mixture.
20. Peel the paper off the remaining sponge (with the rectangular hole) and brush the underside with some sherry syrup. Turn it over again and put it into the frame, pressing it gently on top of the bavarois. Transfer to the fridge for 2–3 hours.
21. Once the trifle has set, push a hot, dry palette knife around the edges of the frame and lift it off. Transfer the trifle to a serving plate.
22. Arrange a selection of the fruit in the cut-out section, slicing some and keeping other pieces whole to create interest and texture. Add a few mint leaves, then dust with icing sugar and serve.

TO DECORATE
200g mixed berries (raspberries, blueberries, blackberries and strawberries)
a few mint leaves
icing sugar, to dust

THE SECRETS OF SUCCESS

◆

If you want to create the perfect jelly tubes...
Make sure you use the two setting agents specified. The reason that both gelatine and agar agar are used to set the mixed berries is to give the right degree of firmness to the finished jelly. Gelatine alone would make it too firm, so the agar agar is needed to slightly soften its effect.

CHOCOLATE CHEESECAKE

*A spectacular two-tiered dessert combining a rich dark chocolate
and orange cheesecake with a layer of tiramisu cream*

The two separate cheesecake layers in this stunning dessert both call for a traditional cream cheese base, while mascarpone (the Italian equivalent) is used in the tiramisu. However, all are lightened with a sabayon and set with gelatine to make a pleasing light texture.

Spraying the tiramisu cream layer with white chocolate gives the dessert a sophisticated finish, but you could finish it more simply if you wish. Just chop a couple of chocolate biscuits, as used in step 1 with the filling removed, and scatter them over the tiramisu layer. Sit it on top of the chocolate cheesecake, lightly dust with icing sugar and finish as described in the final steps.

SERVES 16–20

TIMING

Hands-on time: *2 hours 30 minutes,*
   plus chilling and freezing
Cooking time: *30 minutes*

PREPARE IN ADVANCE

The biscuit base can be made and chilled
   up to 2 days ahead.
The chocolate garnish can be made up
   to 2 days ahead and stored in an airtight
   container at cool room temperature.

HAVE READY

Lightly buttered ring tins.
Two baking sheets lined with parchment
   paper, one with the 24cm ring tin on it
   and the other with the 18cm ring tin.
Wire rack on a tray lined with clingfilm.

EQUIPMENT

food processor
saucepan
spatula
2 baking sheets
parchment paper
24cm stainless steel ring tin
18cm stainless steel ring tin
small pan
small bowl
sharp knife
chopping board
medium pan
2 medium heatproof bowls
electric hand whisk
microwave and microwavable bowl

digital thermometer
stand mixer
   – whisk attachment
stick blender
wire rack
tray
clingfilm
2 x A4 sheets of acetate
spray gun
round cutters
   – 10cm, 1cm and 2cm
palette knife
rolling pin
cake lifter

MAKE THE BISCUIT BASE

1. Put the biscuits into a food processor and whizz until finely crushed.
2. Melt the butter in a pan over a low heat, then stir in the crushed biscuits. Spoon the mixture into the 24cm ring and press down with a spoon until tightly packed and level. Chill for 2 hours.

MAKE THE CHOCOLATE ORANGE CHEESECAKE

3. Put the gelatine into a small bowl, add the water and set aside to soak.
4. Whisk the sugar and egg yolks in a bowl set over a pan of simmering water until the temperature reaches 65–70°C and the mixture is a thick and frothy sabayon.
5. Using a stand mixer or an electric hand mixer, whisk the cream cheese to break it down. Add the sabayon and whisk together.
6. Heat the liqueur, lemon juice and vanilla extract in a small pan. As soon as it is boiling, take off the heat and stir in the gelatine until dissolved. Fold into the cream cheese mixture.
7. Melt the chocolate in a microwave, making sure the temperature doesn't go any higher than 45°C. Fold into the cream cheese mixture, along with the whipping cream. Spoon onto the biscuit base and chill.

MAKE THE SECOND LAYER – THE TIRAMISU CREAM

8. Put the gelatine into a small bowl, add the water and set aside to soak.
9. Whisk the sugar and egg yolks in a bowl set over a pan of simmering water until the temperature reaches 65–70°C and the mixture is thick and frothy. Take the bowl off the heat, stir in the gelatine until dissolved, then add the coffee liqueur (if using).
10. Beat the mascarpone in a bowl to break it down, then fold in the egg mixture. Whisk until thick, then fold in the whipped cream. Spoon into the 18cm ring and freeze.

MAKE THE CHOCOLATE GLAZE

11. Put the gelatine into a small bowl, add the 100g water and set aside to soak.
12. Put the 150g water into a pan with the sugar and glucose and bring to the boil. Stir in the condensed milk, take the pan off the heat and stir in the gelatine until dissolved.
13. Put the chocolate into a bowl and pour the condensed milk mixture over it, stirring slowly from the centre, as with a ganache, until the mixture forms a smooth emulsion.
14. Use a stick blender to ensure the mixture is smooth. Cover and to cool to 30°C.

15. Slide a palette knife around the side of the cheesecake ring, then carefully lift it off. Put the cheesecake on the wire rack over the prepared tray and carefully pour the glaze all over it. Transfer to a serving plate and chill.

MAKE THE WHITE CHOCOLATE SPRAY

16. Melt the white chocolate and the cocoa butter in 2 separate bowls in a microwave or bain-marie, making sure the temperature goes no higher than 40°C.
17. Mix the two ingredients together, stir in the white colouring, then spoon the mixture into the spray gun.
18. Rest the tiramisu cream ring at room temperature for 5 minutes, then slide a palette all around the edge and carefully lift off the ring. Using the spray gun, spray the white chocolate mixture all over the tiramisu layer, then place it on top of the chocolate-glazed layer.

MAKE THE CHOCOLATE CIRCLES

19. Temper the chocolate, following the instructions on page 34. Pour about 75g onto a sheet of acetate, then put the other acetate sheet on top. Use a rolling pin to smooth it out to a thickness of 2–3mm.
20. Take a 10cm cutter (or use the base of a small cake tin) and press down once on the chocolate. Use the small cutters to press random circles in the rest of the chocolate and leave to set.
21. Peel away the acetate and carefully pop the circles out of the chocolate.

ASSEMBLE THE CHEESECAKE

22. Place the tiramisu cream on top of the cheesecake. Arrange the chocolate pearls all around the base of the cheesecake and cream layer.
23. Place the large chocolate circle on top and arrange the small chocolate circles around it. Scatter with flakes of gold leaf and serve.

FOR THE WHITE
CHOCOLATE SPRAY

350g white chocolate

150 cocoa butter

5g E171 white food colouring powder,
    also called titanium dioxide (optional)

TO DECORATE

200g dark chocolate (for circles)

100g chocolate pearls

edible gold leaf

PETITS FOURS
AND BISCUITS

DARK CHOCOLATE
TRUFFLES

SESAME TUILES

CALISSONS

VANILLA, PASSION FRUIT
AND RASPBERRY MARSHMALLOWS

CHOCOLATE ORANGE
CARAMEL LOLLIPOPS

MISÉRABLES

SHELL COOKIES

RUM AND GINGER MARBLED
CHOCOLATE TRUFFLES

SQUARE SABLÉS
HOLLANDAISE

BLUEBERRY MACARONS

PETITS FOURS AND BISCUITS

Also known as *gourmandises* (small, sweet titbits) and *mignardises* (graceful, pretty and delicate bites), petits fours offer as much of a challenge as the other creations in this book, and demand similar care and imagination. These small delicacies are traditionally served after lunch or dinner, and who can resist them? While small savoury delicacies are often offered as *amuse-bouches* at the beginning of a meal to tantalise the tastebuds, the role of the petit four is to provide a subtle sweet ending.

Novices can start with the simple ganache truffle, which is tossed in tempered chocolate to create a thin, crisp shell, then rolled in cocoa. Sprinkle the finished article with edible gold glitter, and your guests can't fail to be impressed. More demanding are Calissons, the oval-shaped almond and dried fruit treats on page 287. They look beautifully simple, but involve making a paste similar to marzipan and will test your icing skill. For a crisp, nutty ending to a meal, try the Sesame Tuiles on page 285 – they're light and crisp, and the basic mixture can be made and chilled several days before it's needed.

Whichever recipe you choose to make from this treasure trove, follow the same rule as a patisserie chef and make sure the flavours and textures of the petit four course are balanced and don't overpower those in the rest of the meal.

DARK CHOCOLATE TRUFFLES

*Rich, creamy dark chocolate drops dusted with
bitter cocoa, sweet sugar and gold dust*

A basic truffle is a ganache that is made by combining equal quantities of hot whipping or double cream with rich dark chocolate to form a smooth emulsion, which is then shaped into balls and tossed in a coating of cocoa powder or icing sugar. The cream softens the chocolate to a point that is firm yet yielding when the mixture sets.

Liquid glucose is used in this recipe to prevent crystallisation, which would give a grainy texture rather than a smooth professional finish. The butter provides additional flavour and helps to soften the mixture. You could add alcohol, or essential oils such as orange or lemon (nothing water-based), either of which would help to preserve the chocolates.

Choose a quality chocolate with a high percentage of cocoa solids as it will reward you with a good depth of flavour that isn't too sweet and cloying – you can find more details about working with chocolate on pages 33–4. Finish the truffle with a coating of tempered chocolate to protect the soft-centred ganache within, then toss in cocoa powder. If you're feeling decadent, add a sliver of edible gold leaf.

MAKES ABOUT 50

TIMING

Hands-on time: *2 hours 15 minutes, plus overnight resting*

Cooking time: *5 minutes*

HAVE READY

Baking sheet lined with parchment paper.

1 baking tray with the wire rack sitting
   on top of it.

1 baking tray dusted with plenty of
   sifted cocoa powder.

Piping bag fitted with the nozzle.

EQUIPMENT

baking sheet

parchment paper

2 x baking trays

wire rack

large bowl

small pan

spatula

digital thermometer

stick blender

disposable piping bag
   – 2cm nozzle

microwave and microwavable bowl, or
   medium pan and heatproof bowl

2 forks

medium pan, optional

sieve

FOR THE GANACHE

125g dark chocolate (65–70% cocoa
  solids), very finely chopped

15g liquid glucose

125g whipping cream

20g butter, at room temperature,
  cut into cubes

FOR THE COATING

300g dark chocolate (65–70% cocoa
  solids), finely chopped

cocoa powder, to cover

edible shimmer powder, to sprinkle

edible gold leaf, optional

THE SECRETS OF SUCCESS

◆

If the ganache is too soft to pipe…
The kitchen is too hot, so
move the bowl of ganache
to a cooler place (not the
fridge) to set.

If your hands are hot, the
heat will warm the piping
bag and the ganache might
melt and run out of the end.
The quickest remedy is to
hold your hands and wrists
under a cold running tap,
and work quickly once you
start to pipe again.

MAKE THE GANACHE

It's important that the temperature cools to 60°C before the butter is added – any hotter and the mixture will curdle, any cooler and the butter may not melt into the ganache completely.

1. Put the chocolate and liquid glucose into a large bowl and set aside.
2. Put the cream into a small pan over a high heat and bring to the boil. Slowly pour it into the bowl of chocolate and stir from the middle with a spatula until the mixture forms an emulsion and becomes smooth and silky. Set aside to cool to 60°C, checking frequently with a thermometer.
3. Add the butter to the bowl and stir in, then blend with a stick blender until very smooth, keeping the blade below the surface of the mixture so that it doesn't incorporate too much air and make it into a mousse. Set aside at cool room temperature for 45–60 minutes to set to a piping consistency, stirring occasionally to check when it's thick enough.
4. Spoon the mixture into the piping bag and pipe 2cm-wide domes onto the parchment-lined baking sheet (A), smoothing down any points from lifting the nozzle. Cover loosely with another piece of parchment paper and leave overnight at room temperature to set.

COAT THE TRUFFLES

The truffles are first coated in a thin layer of tempered chocolate to encase the ganache, then dusted in cocoa powder. For a really luxurious finish, add a sliver of edible gold leaf if you wish – you'll find a pair of wooden tweezers useful for this.

5. Temper the chocolate following the method on page 34.
6. Use two forks to lower one of the truffles into the tempered chocolate to coat it (B). Lift it out and shake off any dripping chocolate, scraping the bottom of the fork on the edge of the bowl to remove excess (C).
7. Roll the truffle in the cocoa powder (D) then set aside on the wire rack to firm up. Repeat with the rest of the truffles.
8. Dust with a little edible shimmer powder before serving.

SESAME TUILES

Crisp yet chewy wafer-thin sesame and citrus-flavoured biscuits

These wafer-like biscuits were named after curved French roof tiles because they are a similar shape. They contain very little flour, so they are exceptionally light, and the high percentage of sugar gives them a delicious crisp texture.

Pastry chefs aspire to perfectly moulded, fine tuiles with the maximum snap. Shaping them is a tricky process – if you move them too quickly once they're out of the oven, they'll be too fragile to shape. Leave them for too long on the baking sheet and they'll be too firm to mould and could crack, so make sure you take extra care at this stage.

The basic biscuit dough can be adapted to whatever ingredients you have to hand. These ones are peppered with sesame seeds and infused with citrus flavours, but swap the orange juice and lemon for lime if you wish, or sprinkle flaked almonds instead of sesame seeds over the top.

The tuiles can be served either as petits fours with coffee, or used to crown balls of ice cream and sorbets for a stylish dessert.

MAKES 16

TIMING

Hands-on time: *15 minutes, plus 2 hours chilling*
Cooking time: *about 30 minutes*

PREPARE IN ADVANCE

The mixture can be made and rolled into
   balls, then kept in an airtight container in
   the fridge for up to 4–5 days before baking.

HAVE READY

Baking sheet lined with parchment paper
   or a silicone mat .
Rolling pin sitting on a board.
Palette knife lightly greased.

EQUIPMENT

baking sheet
silicone mat or parchment paper
rolling pin
chopping board
palette knife
digital scales
zester
large bowl
wooden spoon or spatula
sieve
clingfilm

FOR THE TUILES

40g softened butter

100g caster sugar

25g plain flour

25g orange juice

zest of 1 lemon

40g sesame seeds

8g black sesame seeds

THE SECRETS OF SUCCESS

◆

If the biscuits are too firm to shape…
Return the baking sheet to the oven for a few minutes to warm the biscuits so they're soft enough to mould.

MAKE THE DOUGH

1. Put the butter and sugar into a large bowl and cream together using a wooden spoon or spatula until soft and pale.
2. Sift the flour over the top, then add the orange juice and lemon zest. Gradually work the flour and other ingredients into the mixture, then stir in the sesame seeds. Cover the bowl with clingfilm and transfer to the refrigerator to rest for 1–2 hours.

SHAPE AND BAKE THE TUILES

It's important to bake the biscuits until just golden and to work quickly when shaping them.

3. Preheat the oven to 180°C/160°C fan/gas mark 4.
4. Use a spoon to measure the dough into 13g pieces, then roll into balls.
5. Place 2 or 3 of the balls at a time on the lined baking sheet, spacing well apart, and bake for 10–12 minutes until just golden.
6. As each batch is done, carefully lift each tuile using the greased palette knife and place them over the curve of the rolling pin. Leave to cool until set, then transfer to the board to cool completely.

◆ ◆ ◆

CALISSONS

Sweet, almond-shaped petits fours made from almond
paste flavoured with citrus fruits and tropical pineapple

Ground almonds and candied dried fruit form the main flavours of these petit four treats, which have a base of edible rice paper and are topped with smooth royal icing. They're originally from Aix-en-Provence in southern France, where rows of calissons in myriad pastel shades, all precisely the same size and shape, make delightful displays in patisserie shop windows.

They are made by first drying out the almonds and sugar, then binding the mixture with candied fruit. The traditional flavours are melon and orange, but the twist in this recipe is to use pineapple, orange and lemon, instead. The almond dough shouldn't be too sticky, so make sure you give it time to dry out in the bowl, covered with a clean tea towel, before baking. Once made, store in an airtight container for up to 30 days.

MAKES 40

TIMING

Hands-on time: *1 hour*
Cooking time: *20 minutes drying out*

PREPARE IN ADVANCE

The paste can be made up to
  1 day ahead and stored, covered,
  at room temperature.

HAVE READY

Oven preheated to 130°C/110°C fan/
  gas mark 1.

EQUIPMENT

digital scales
shallow roasting tin
food-processor
large bowl
chopping board
sharp knife
batons 12mm thick, optional
rolling pin
parchment paper
stainless steel 5.5cm oval calisson cutter
  or small craft knife
balloon whisk or electric hand whisk

150g ground almonds

100g icing sugar

110g candied pineapple, roughly chopped

20g candied orange, roughly chopped

10g candied lemon, roughly chopped

1½ tablespoons orange blossom water

2 x A4 sheets edible rice paper, optional

FOR THE ROYAL ICING

45g egg whites (1½ medium)

225g icing sugar

¼ teaspoon lemon juice

THE SECRETS OF SUCCESS

◆

If the dough is too sticky to cut into the shapes…
It is still too wet. Allow it to dry out for longer until the cutter or knife can be pushed into the dough easily.

MAKE THE ALMOND PASTE

The almonds and sugar are initially left to rest in a warm oven to remove any moisture so that the final mixture is less sticky.

1. Mix the ground almonds and sugar in a shallow roasting tray and spread into a thick layer. Place in the oven to dry out for 20 minutes. Remove the tray and leave to cool for 10–15 minutes.
2. Put the candied fruit into a food-processor and whizz until very finely chopped. Add the cooled almonds and sugar and the orange blossom water and pulse until the mixture forms a paste.
3. Tip the mixture into a bowl, cover with a clean tea towel and set aside for an hour to dry out.

ROLL OUT THE ALMOND PASTE AND CUT THE SHAPES

To get a really even surface, place two batons either side of the almond mixture and roll the rolling pin over them. Your paste will be the same thickness as the batons.

4. Place the rice paper smooth side up, if using, or a sheet of parchment paper, on a chopping board and put the almond paste on top. Place batons, if using, either side and roll out the paste to a thin, even layer about 12mm thick. Set aside for 1 hour to dry out slightly.
5. Turn the dough over onto a fresh sheet of parchment, if using.
6. Cut out almond shapes using an oval cutter or a very sharp craft knife. Each should measure about 4cm from point to point. Set aside, turned onto the paper so that the rice paper is on the bottom.

ICE THE CALISSONS

7. Make the royal icing. Whisk the egg whites until frothy, then slowly add the sugar and continue to whisk. Finally add the lemon juice. The finished mixture should be the consistency of double cream.
8. Carefully dip the top of each calisson into the icing to cover, wiping the sides of the sweets if necessary to neaten them. Leave to set.

FINISH IT LIKE A PASTRY CHEF

To finish your calissons with a flourish, paint or pipe a flower decoration in a *contrasting colour* on top of the royal icing.
Additional equipment: fine brush or disposable piping bag

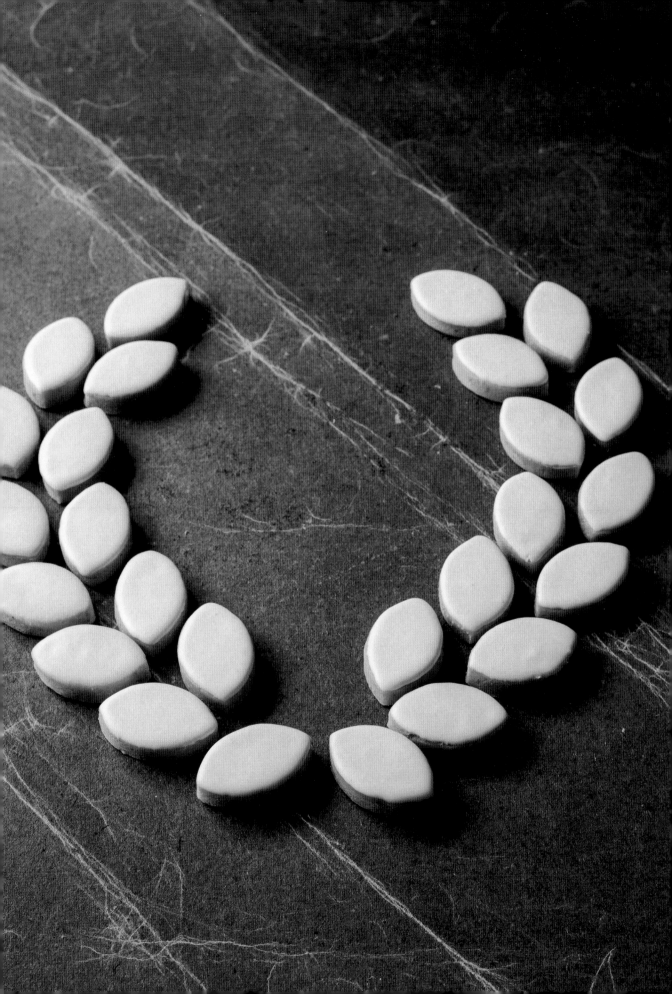

VANILLA, PASSION FRUIT AND RASPBERRY MARSHMALLOWS

A pastel-hued traffic light marshmallow,
delicately flavoured with fruit

This egg-free marshmallow recipe works by whisking together gelatine and glucose with a hot syrup until it becomes smooth and glossy. The advantage of not including any egg white in the mixture is that the squares will keep for longer, provided they are stored in an airtight container in a cool place.

There are three different layers in the cubes of soft, squidgy marshmallow – raspberry, vanilla and passion fruit – each one complementing the others. The vanilla recipe forms the basis of the fruit marshmallows, which are flavoured with simple fruit purées – this is a great recipe for experimenting with different flavours.

These light, fluffy confections are ideal for petits fours, particularly if you are serving a large number of people, as they can be made in batches ahead of time. The key to professional-looking confections is to slice the marshmallows evenly – they will always be perfectly cut and shaped in patisseries. The trick is to use a hot, dry knife and to dust the sweets with confectioner's sugar (a mixture of icing sugar and cornflour) before and after cutting to stop them sticking together.

MAKES 25–30

TIMING

Hands-on and cooking time: *1 hour 30 minutes*

PREPARE IN ADVANCE

The marshmallows can be made up to 1 month
   ahead, stored in an airtight container.

HAVE READY

Stand mixer, if using, fitted with the whisk
   attachment.
Frame lined with parchment paper, sitting
   on the baking sheet and dusted heavily
   with half the confectioner's sugar.

EQUIPMENT

small bowl
medium pan
digital thermometer
stand mixer, optional
   – whisk attachment
electric hand whisk, optional
parchment paper
baking sheet
28 x 18cm stainless steel frame
spatula
food processor or stick blender
sieve
large bowl, optional

FOR THE CONFECTIONER'S
SUGAR

125g icing sugar, sifted

125g cornflour, sifted

FOR THE VANILLA
MARSHMALLOW

8 gelatine leaves

200g liquid glucose, measured into
   2 separate bowls of 100g

300g caster sugar

125g water

2 drops vanilla extract

oil, for greasing

FOR THE PASSION FRUIT
MARSHMALLOW

8 gelatine leaves

200g liquid glucose, measured into
   2 separate bowls of 100g

300g caster sugar

125g fresh passion fruit purée (page
   25), or ready-made frozen purée

FOR THE RASPBERRY
MARSHMALLOW

8 gelatine leaves

200g liquid glucose, measured into
   2 separate bowls of 100g

300g caster sugar

150g raspberries, blended to a purée
   and strained

icing sugar, to dust

TO DECORATE

edible gold lustre

MAKE THE VANILLA MARSHMALLOWS

This forms the bottom layer of the sweet. The mixture must come to 116°C for the water to cook off so that the marshmallow can set.

1. Put the gelatine into a small bowl of cold water and soak for 10 minutes. Once the leaves have softened, squeeze out the water and put the gelatine into a large bowl or the bowl of a stand mixer with 100g of the liquid glucose.

2. Heat the sugar, the remaining 100g liquid glucose, water and vanilla gently in a medium pan. Allow the sugar to dissolve then increase the heat and simmer until the temperature reaches 116°C. Take off the heat.

3. Start to whisk together the gelatine and glucose in the mixer or with an electric hand whisk, until combined, then slowly pour the syrup into the bowl, whisking all the time. Continue to whisk, on a medium speed if using a mixer, until the mixture is thick, glossy and has cooled.

4. Spoon the mixture into the prepared tin and level with a spatula.

MAKE THE PASSION FRUIT MARSHMALLOWS

These form the middle layer of the sweet.

5. Follow the method for the vanilla marshmallow, above, but use passion fruit purée in place of the water and omit the vanilla.

6. Once the marshmallow has cooled, spread the mixture over the vanilla layer and level the surface.

MAKE THE RASPBERRY MARSHMALLOWS

These form the top layer of the sweet.

7. Follow the same method, but use raspberry purée in place of the water and omit the vanilla. Once the marshmallow has cooled, spread it over the passion fruit layer and level the top.

8. Dust the top of the marshmallow with plenty of confectioner's sugar, then leave for 2 hours to allow the marshmallow to set.

SLICE THE MARSHMALLOW SQUARES

Make sure your knife is hot and dry to get neat slices.

9. Lift the marshmallow out of the tray and remove the parchment paper. Cut it into squares using a hot and dry sharp knife and dust each square with a little more confectioner's sugar to prevent them from sticking to each other. Serve dusted with the gold lustre, or store in an airtight container for up to 3 weeks.

CHOCOLATE ORANGE CARAMEL LOLLIPOPS

Smooth milk chocolate discs subtly flavoured with warm orange and spice

There are two key skills required when making these lollipops. The first is to make a dry caramel flavoured with spices and orange zest. Once the caramel has set, it is ground into a powder and combined with the chocolate to add another flavour dimension to the finished lolly. It's essential that the set caramel is whizzed immediately to form a powder, then stored promptly in an airtight container because it is hygroscopic, which means it easily attracts moisture from the air.

The second key skill is to temper the chocolate. Choose a milk variety with a high percentage of cocoa solids (about 40%) so that it isn't over-rich once it's mixed with the caramel. There is more information about working with chocolate on pages 33–4.

When the chocolate lolly has been tempered properly and set between acetate, it becomes shiny and will have a pleasing, crisp snap when you bite into it.

MAKES 8–10

TIMING

Hands-on time: *about 45 minutes, plus setting time*
Cooking time: *about 30 minutes*

PREPARE IN ADVANCE

The caramel powder can be made
 up to 1 day ahead and stored in
 an airtight container.

HAVE READY

Baking sheet, if using, lined with parchment paper
 or a silicone mat.
The chocolate transfer sheet, cut into
 eight 6cm squares.

EQUIPMENT

baking sheet or marble slab
parchment paper or silicone mat
zester
small bowl
small pan
wooden spoon
mini food processor
2 acetate sheets
chocolate transfer sheets
microwave and microwavable bowl,
 optional, or medium pan and
 heatproof bowl
digital thermometer
disposable piping bag
8 lolly sticks
individual cellophane wrappers, and
 ribbon or paper string, optional

FOR THE FLAVOURED CARAMEL

seeds from ¼ vanilla pod

a good pinch of cinnamon

zest from ½ orange

100g caster sugar

30g butter

FOR THE LOLLIPOPS

250g milk chocolate (40% cocoa solids)

THE SECRETS OF SUCCESS

If the powder turns into a sticky mess…
There is too much humidity in the air. Unfortunately, there's nothing you can do to rescue the caramel powder at this stage, and the only thing to do is to start again.

MAKE THE FLAVOURED CARAMEL

Butter and spices are added to melted sugar to create a simple caramel, which is then ground into a powder.

1. Put the vanilla seeds, cinnamon and orange zest into a small bowl.
2. Put the sugar into a small pan over a low heat and heat gently until the sugar melts and turns to a golden brown caramel. Stir the vanilla mixture into the pan using a wooden spoon, followed by the butter. Pour over the prepared baking sheet and leave to cool and set.
3. Break up the set caramel and put the pieces into a mini food-processor. Grind to a powder and immediately put into an airtight container while you prepare the chocolate.

PREPARE THE CHOCOLATE AND MAKE THE LOLLIES

The lollipop heads are made by piping the chocolate in neat circles, then pressing them flat between acetate sheets.

4. Line the clean baking sheet or a marble slab with one of the acetate sheets.
5. Melt the chocolate using one of the methods on page 34. Stir in the powdered caramel.
6. Spoon the mixture into the piping bag and snip off the tip. Pipe 4–5cm rounds on to the acetate-lined baking sheet, spacing them about 6cm apart. Lay a stick on each one and press lightly.
7. Lay a second acetate sheet over the lollies and gently press flat. Leave to set.
8. Peel off the top sheet of acetate, then lay a square of the transfer sheet (transfer side down) over each lolly. Gently press flat, then leave to set in a cool place for 45 minutes, until the transfer can be peeled away and the chocolate is shiny.
9. Wrap the lollipops in individual cellophane wrappers and secure with ribbon or paper string.

MISÉRABLES

*A simple almond sponge sandwich filled
with a silky vanilla buttercream*

This classic Belgian patisserie is a miniature version of a layered slice and is served after dinner as a petit four. It is bite-sized – just three centimetres square – and pastry chefs love it because of the skill involved in creating the light sponge and rich buttercream.

The cakes are filled with a French buttercream that is made by whisking a hot sugar syrup into a foam of egg yolks – known as *pâte à bombe* in the trade – then whisking in butter and vanilla for flavour. It differs from other buttercreams, which are made either with butter and sugar, or butter and egg whites. The addition of the egg yolks makes a richer, smoother, more decadent buttercream.

The sponge is a classic joconde made with ground almonds, which has a firm texture to hold the buttercream, yet is light enough not to dominate the smooth filling, which is the star of this charming little cake.

SERVES 15

TIMING

Hands-on time: *1 hour, plus chilling and cooling*
Cooking time: *35 minutes*

PREPARE IN ADVANCE

The sponge and buttercream can be prepared
 up to 3 days ahead.
Store the buttercream in a sealable container
 in the fridge and the cake at room temperature,
 wrapped well in clingfilm.

HAVE READY

Line the baking sheet with parchment paper.
Grease and line the frame with parchment paper
 and place it on the lined baking sheet.
Preheat the oven to 200°C/180°C fan/gas mark 6.
Prepare a bain-marie by placing the heatproof
 bowl over a medium pan of just-simmering
 water, making sure the base doesn't touch
 the water.

EQUIPMENT

baking sheet
parchment paper
28 x 18cm stainless steel frame
heatproof bowl
medium pan
digital scales
digital thermometer
balloon whisk
spatula
large bowl
wire rack
medium bowl
electric hand whisk
small pan
long sharp knife
chopping board
ruler
sieve

FOR THE JOCONDE SPONGE

100g icing sugar, plus 25g, to dust

100g ground almonds

75g whole egg (1½ medium)

12g butter, melted

15g plain flour

50g egg whites (just over 1½ medium)

6g caster sugar

FOR THE FRENCH BUTTERCREAM

40g egg yolks (2 medium)

25g egg (½ medium)

100g caster sugar

50g water

125g butter, softened

seeds from ¼ vanilla pod

THE SECRETS OF SUCCESS

If the sponge feels dry…
Make a simple vanilla
syrup (see page 22) from
50g sugar, 50g water and a
few drops of vanilla extract.
Simmer for 1–2 minutes,
then brush over the sponge
before constructing the cake.

MAKE THE JOCONDE SPONGE

The base of the cake batter is cooked first in a bain-marie to loosen it, then whisked with a balloon whisk to give the sponge more volume.

1. Put the icing sugar, ground almonds and egg into the bowl of the bain-marie. Whisk together and allow the mixture to cook until it reaches 60°C. It will turn from a thick paste into a soft batter as it cooks.
2. Take the bowl off the heat and whisk continuously until cool. Fold in the melted butter and the flour using a spatula.
3. In a spotlessly clean bowl, whisk the egg whites and caster sugar until soft peaks form, then fold the meringue into the almond mixture.
4. Spoon the mixture into the prepared frame and spread it out evenly with the spatula. Bake for 10–12 minutes until just golden on top and the sponge feels firm when lightly pressed. Lift the sponge, still on the parchment paper, onto a wire rack and set aside to cool.

MAKE THE FRENCH BUTTERCREAM

Hot sugar syrup is poured into whisked egg yolks, then beaten until cool. The mixture must be completely cold before adding the butter.

5. Whisk the egg yolks and egg in a medium bowl using an electric hand whisk until everything has combined and the mixture looks frothy.
6. Put the sugar and water into a small pan and heat gently to dissolve the sugar. Cook until the mixture reaches soft ball stage (see page 30), about 118–120°C.
7. Beat the egg mixture with the electric whisk and, with the motor running, carefully pour in the sugar syrup. Whisk until the bottom of the bowl feels cold, then add the soft butter and whisk until the mixture is light and fluffy, then whisk in the vanilla seeds.

ASSEMBLE THE LAYERS

It is important to get the layers perfectly even so that the finished petits fours are a neat shape and uniform size. Spread the buttercream with a spatula and press the sponge firmly on top to even it out. The cake is turned over so that the neater bottom layer is on top.

8. Run a sharp knife down the edges of the sponge to loosen it from the frame and lift off the frame. Put the sponge on a clean board and carefully peel away the parchment paper.
9. Cut the sponge in half widthways to make two pieces, each measuring 18 x 14cm.

10. Spread the buttercream evenly over one half of the sponge and level the top with a spatula. Turn the second layer of sponge over and place it on top of the buttercream and gently press down so that it's firmly stuck to it.

11. Turn the whole cake over and transfer to the fridge for 1 hour to chill and set.

CUT THE SPONGE SQUARES

12. Take the cake out of the fridge. Trim the longest edges to neaten them and reduce the width of the sponge to 12cm. Using a ruler, mark the sponge into strips 3cm wide and cut them out.

13. Cut each strip into 3cm squares – you should have about 15 squares.

14. Dust each square with icing sugar and serve.

FINISH IT LIKE A PASTRY CHEF

Roll out a little *sugar paste* on a board lightly dusted with *icing sugar* and stamp out flowers. Colour them with *edible paint or lustre* and stick them on top of each petit four.

Additional equipment: *flower sugar stamp, fine brush.*

SHELL COOKIES

Meltingly buttery piped biscuits with sweet raspberry jam

These pretty petits fours are made from a simple biscuit base that is sweetened with icing sugar and either dusted in more sugar, or dipped in chocolate. The fine sugar and high quantity of flour contribute to the melt-in-the-mouth texture, while a combination of butter and double cream gives them a wonderful buttery flavour.

The dough for these biscuits doesn't require chilling and is soft, so it needs to be piped onto the baking sheet and you can, in fact, create any shape you like. Once baked, spread one half of the cookies with a slick of raspberry jam before sandwiching them together with the remaining cookies and finishing with a light dusting of icing sugar.

For pastry chefs the perfection is in achieving the crumbly, melting texture and exquisite piping.

MAKES 15

TIMING

Hands-on time: *15 minutes*
Cooking time: *15–17 minutes*

PREPARE IN ADVANCE

These biscuits can be made in advance and
   stored in an airtight container for up to 5 days.

HAVE READY

Egg yolks and double cream at room temperature.
Baking sheet lined with parchment paper or
   the silicone mat.
Piping bag fitted with the nozzle.
Oven preheated to 170°C/150°C fan/gas mark 3.

EQUIPMENT

baking sheet
silicone mat or parchment paper
large bowl
wooden spoon
sieve
piping bag
   – 1cm star nozzle
wire rack
paper cases
microwave and microwavable bowl, or
   medium pan and heatproof bowl

THE SECRETS OF SUCCESS

◆

If the butter overheats and becomes liquid…
Start again – the butter needs to be creamy and soft, but not melted. It will affect the finished texture of the biscuit if it's not the right consistency.

MAKE THE COOKIES

If the butter is too firm and difficult to beat, warm the bottom of the bowl slightly over a bowl of warm water to soften it. If using a metal bowl, you can do this with a blowtorch or heat gun. Try not to overwork the dough or it will be too tough for these light biscuits.

1. Put the butter and icing sugar into a large bowl and beat together with a wooden spoon until very soft and light. Add the egg yolk and continue to cream the mixture until the yolk has been fully incorporated, then fold in the cream.
2. Sift the flour over the top of the mixture and gently mix in, taking care not to overwork the dough.
3. Spoon the mixture into the piping bag and pipe a shell weighing about 20g onto digital scales. Use this as a templete to pipe 30 shell shapes, each the same size and weight as the first, on to the prepared baking sheet. Rest the nozzle on the parchment at a 45 degree angle and squeeze the mixture until it starts to form a shell shape. Very slowly pull the nozzle away from the mixture, then quickly pull away from the paper to break off the dough and create a point at the end.
4. Bake for 15–17 minutes until pale golden brown, then transfer to a wire rack to cool.

FILL AND SERVE

5. Spread a little raspberry jam over one shell and sandwich it together with a second shell. Repeat until all the shells are sandwiched together.
6. Dust with icing sugar and serve in pretty paper cases. Or, for a special finish, dip the narrower end in tempered chocolate, then leave to set on parchment paper.

◆ ◆ ◆

RUM AND GINGER MARBLED CHOCOLATE TRUFFLES

Dark chocolate golden demispheres encasing a white chocolate ganache flavoured with a hint of ginger and rum

The secret to these impressive chocolates is the tempering, which gives chocolate a shiny finish and satisfying snap when you bite into it. It's actually quite easy to do – you simply melt the chocolate, ensuring that the temperature reaches no more than 45°C, then cool it to between 31°C and 32°C, at which point it's ready to use. See pages 33–4 for more information on working with chocolate.

Professionals use polycarbonate moulds, which help to produce perfect shells of chocolate, although you can get silicone moulds that also do a good job. The mould is brushed first with a little edible gold lustre to create a marbled effect. The filling is made with white chocolate and cream infused with fresh root ginger, a little dark rum and just a hint of vanilla. Take care to follow the measurements exactly – a splash or two extra of the rum will make the filling too runny, which in turn will make the chocolates difficult to cap and seal.

MAKES 28

TIMING

Hands-on time: *1 hour, plus cooling time*
Cooking time: *5 minutes*

PREPARE IN ADVANCE

The chocolate mould can be lined with
chocolate up to one day ahead.

HAVE READY

Chocolate mould cleaned, dried
and polished with cotton wool.

EQUIPMENT

28-hole demisphere mould, each hole
   3cm in diameter
cotton wool
digital scales
sharp knife
chopping board
fine brush or thin plastic gloves
microwave and microwavable bowl, or
   medium pan and heatproof bowl
digital thermometer
chocolate scraper (or use a new,
   clean wallpaper scraper)
slotted spoon
sieve
disposable piping bag

FOR THE CHOCOLATE SHELL

edible gold lustre

300g dark chocolate (65% cocoa solids), broken into pieces

FOR THE GANACHE

20g double cream

15g root ginger, sliced

a good pinch of salt

¼ vanilla pod, split lengthways

100g white chocolate (34% cocoa solids), broken into pieces

35g dark rum, preferably Venezuelan

5g unsalted butter, at room temperature

THE SECRETS OF SUCCESS

If the chocolates have bloomed… This is when the chocolates don't look smooth and shiny and have a whitish tinge to them. Make sure you follow the tempering instructions on page 34 and that the temperature of the dark chocolate has dropped to between 31°C and 32°C before pouring it into the moulds.

MAKE THE CHOCOLATE SHELL

It is essential that the mould be completely clean and dry to ensure that the chocolates have a smooth shiny shell.

1. Polish the chocolate mould with cotton wool so that it's completely dry and brush it with gold lustre using a fine brush or gloved finger.
2. Put the dark chocolate pieces into a heatproof bowl and temper it following the instructions on page 34.
3. Pour or spoon the chocolate into the mould. Tap the sides to remove any air bubbles, then turn it upside down over the chocolate bowl and tap the sides to remove any excess chocolate. Sweep the top with a chocolate scraper to remove any more. You should be left with thin shells of chocolate lining each hole. Set aside in a cool place to set.

MAKE THE GANACHE FILLING

4. Combine the cream, sliced ginger and salt in a medium pan. Scrape in the vanilla seeds and add the pod too. Bring to the boil. Remove from the heat, cover the pan and let it steep for 5 minutes.
5. Lift the ginger and vanilla pod out of the cream with a slotted spoon and discard. If the ginger has broken up, strain the infused cream into a bowl through a sieve.
6. Melt the white chocolate using one of the methods on page 34.
7. Pour the infused cream into the bowl of chocolate, followed by the rum, and stir slowly and steadily to make a smooth emulsion. If the cream has cooled too much you may need to warm it up again gently before stirring it into the chocolate.
8. Fold in the butter and continue to stir until combined.
9. Spoon the ganache into a piping bag, twist the ends and leave to cool to about 30°C (push a digital thermometer into the ganache through the opening of the piping bag to test it).

FILL AND CAP THE CHOCOLATES

The ganache is piped into the moulds, and tempered chocolate is poured over the top to encase each of them.

10. Snip off about 5mm from the point of the piping bag and, holding it firmly, pipe the ganache into the centres of the dark chocolate shells, leaving a small amount of space at the top. Leave to set overnight in a cool place (not the fridge).
11. Temper the remaining dark chocolate and carefully spoon over the ganache to seal the demispheres. Allow the chocolate to set for 1 hour before turning the truffles out from the moulds. Store in an airtight container for up to 2 weeks.

SQUARE SABLÉS HOLLANDAISE

Melt-in-the-mouth vanilla and cocoa chequerboard squares

Precision and patience are two of the skills required to make these eye-catching biscuits, which are cut and shaped by hand. For pastry chefs the challenge is to create perfectly even biscuits that are exactly the same size.

Two differently flavoured and coloured doughs are rolled out and sliced into strips, which are given a slick of beaten egg white, then stacked alternately into a rectangular log that has a chequerboard pattern when seen in profile. When they come out of the oven, each square of dough should have baked uniformly.

The biscuit dough is a sablé (sandy) base, so called because when the dry ingredients are combined with the butter, the mixture resembles sand. This is what gives the biscuits their delightful crumbly texture.

MAKES 60 BISCUITS

TIMING

Hands-on time: *1 hour 15 minutes, plus chilling*
Cooking time: *10–12 minutes*

PREPARE IN ADVANCE

The doughs can be made up to 1 day ahead.
Wrap well in clingfilm and store in the fridge.

HAVE READY

Stand mixer, if using, fitted with paddle
  attachment.
Baking sheets lined with parchment paper.

EQUIPMENT

stand mixer, optional
  – paddle attachment
2 baking sheets
parchment paper
digital scales
large bowl, optional
wooden spoon, optional
clingfilm
large chopping board, optional
2 metal or wooden batons 1cm thick
rolling pin
ruler
sharp knife
pastry brush
wire rack

125g plain flour

25g ground almonds

50g icing sugar

seeds from ½ vanilla pod

50g unsalted butter, softened
  and cubed

45g salted butter, softened and cubed

25g egg yolk (1 large)

FOR THE CHOCOLATE
DOUGH

120g plain flour

20g ground almonds

50g icing sugar

15g cocoa powder

90g butter, softened

⅛ teaspoon salt

25g egg yolk (1 large)

FOR THE ASSEMBLY

plain flour, for dusting

egg white, beaten

MAKE THE VANILLA DOUGH

1. Place the flour, almonds and icing sugar into the bowl of a stand mixer and mix on a low speed to combine. Alternatively use a large bowl and a wooden spoon.

2. Add the vanilla seeds and the butters. Mix again, on a low to medium speed if using a mixer, until you have a crumble-like mixture. Add the egg yolks and continue to mix until everything has combined and the mixture looks like a dough.

3. Tip onto a clean work surface and knead briefly to ensure the dough is smooth, then wrap in clingfilm and chill for 1 hour.

MAKE THE CHOCOLATE DOUGH

4. Repeat steps 1 to 3 to make the vanilla dough, adding the cocoa in with the flour, ground almonds and icing sugar as in step 1. Wrap in clingfilm and chill as before.

ASSEMBLE THE CHEQUERBOARD DOUGH

The different doughs are cut into long strips and built up in alternate layers to create a chequerboard effect. It is essential that the strips are the same height and width so that the finished squares are an even size and shape.

5. Place the batons on a board or clean work surface, about 25cm apart. Dust a little flour over the surface between them and place the vanilla dough in-between. Roll out the dough to 1cm thick.

6. Using a ruler and a sharp knife, cut the dough into 1cm strips.

7. Repeat steps 5 and 6 with the chocolate dough to make the same number of strips.

8. Lay out a strip of vanilla dough and brush one edge with egg wash. Lay a strip of chocolate dough beside it and gently press together to seal. Repeat with a third strip of vanilla dough.

9. Brush the tops of the strips with egg white and lay another three strips over dough on top, this time starting with chocolate and laying the vanilla dough in the middle. Use the egg white to join the strips together.

10. Brush the top again and add a final layer of three strips, with the vanilla dough on the outside and the chocolate strip in the middle. You should now have a log 25cm long and 3cm square. Trim the ends to neaten them and set aside. Repeat this process to make a second log.. Transfer both logs to the fridge for 30 minutes to set.

If you wish, the unbaked logs can be wrapped tightly in clingfilm and stored in the freezer for up to 1 month, then thawed, cut and baked as required.

SLICE THE BISCUITS

Chilling the biscuit dough gives it time to rest and firm up before cutting and baking so that it doesn't spread and become misshapen in the oven.

11. Slice the chilled logs into 8mm thick slices and lay them flat onto the lined baking sheet. Transfer to the refrigerator and chill again for 30 minutes.
12. Preheat the oven to 190°C/170°C fan/gas mark 5.
13. Once the biscuits have chilled for half an hour, transfer them to the oven and bake for 10 minutes until just golden, then cool on a wire rack. If stored in an airtight container, the biscuits will keep for up to a week.

BLUEBERRY MACARONS

Smooth buttercream and candied blueberries
sandwiched between crisp almond shells

These fashionable bite-sized French fancies are a staple of patisserie kitchens, where the perfect macaron is smooth on top, with an even foot and a thin shell. The method here is simpler than that used for the Macarons Réligieuses on page 177, where a boiling sugar syrup is combined with beaten egg whites, but it gives great results. Here caster sugar and egg whites are heated over a pan of simmering water until the temperature reaches 60°C, then whisked until the mixture is stiff. There's no need to wait for a skin to form before baking with this method.

The macarons are filled with an Italian meringue buttercream, which is made by pouring hot sugar syrup onto whisked egg whites to make a smooth, shiny meringue, then incorporating softened butter to make a buttercream. As it uses only egg whites, rather than yolks or whole eggs, it has a pure white appearance and a smooth consistency that combines perfectly with the macarons. It is also less rich, so you can flavour it with whatever you want.

MAKES 40

TIMING

Hands-on time: *1 hour 50 minutes*
Cooking time: *55 minutes*

PREPARE IN ADVANCE

Make the macarons up to 5 days ahead,
   stored, unfilled, in an airtight container.
Make the buttercream up to 5 days ahead.

HAVE READY

Stand mixer, if using, fitted with the
   whisk attachment
Cut parchment paper to the size of your
   baking sheets and draw 3cm rounds onto
   them – you will need 80. Flip the paper
   over and lay it onto the baking sheets.
   These will be your templates.

EQUIPMENT

2 medium pans
stand mixer, optional
   – whisk attachment
large bowl and electric hand whisk, optional
digital thermometer
skewer or cocktail sticks
sieve
spatula
2 piping bags
   – 6mm nozzle
parchment paper
pencil
2 large baking sheets
small bowl
food processor or blender
zester
medium bowl, optional
small pan

FOR THE MACARON PASTE

120g fresh egg whites (4 medium),
   at room temperature
265g caster sugar
purple edible food colour
165g fine ground almonds

FOR THE SEMI-CANDIED BLUEBERRIES

70g caster sugar
2g powdered fruit pectin
125g blueberries, puréed
50g aniseed or blueberry liqueur
zest and juice of ½ lemon

FOR THE ITALIAN MERINGUE BUTTERCREAM

60g egg whites (2 medium)
120g caster sugar
50g water
250g butter
½ vanilla pod, split lengthways
100g blueberries, blended and
   strained through a sieve
15g aniseed or blueberry liqueur

MAKE THE MACARON PASTE

When heating the mixture, don't let it get hotter than 60°C or it may be too dry to pipe later on and you could find yourself with a mixture that looks scrambled.

For a more refined finish, make the ground almonds even finer by pulsing them in a food processor, then sifting them into the meringue, pushing them through the sieve with a spatula and binning any big bits that are left behind.

1. Quarter-fill a medium pan with water and bring to the boil.
2. Place the egg whites in the bowl of a stand mixer. Add the sugar and whisk to combine. You can also do this in a large bowl with an electric hand whisk.
3. Place the bowl over the pan of simmering water, making sure the base doesn't touch the water, and gently heat the mixture to 60°C, stirring with the whisk every minute or so to ensure that it heats evenly. Check the temperature regularly and don't let it go any higher than 60°C.
4. Remove from the heat and put the bowl back into the stand mixer, if using. Use a clean whisk attachment on a high speed to whisk until the mixture is very firm and cooled down to 30°C – it will thicken as it cools. The meringue should be very stiff and make a good beating sound when whisked.
5. Whisk in the colour, little by little, by dipping a skewer into the colour, then wiping it through the mix. Remember you can always add more, but you can never take it away, so take this stage slowly until you achieve the desired shade. Go slightly stronger than you would like as the colour will be diluted by the almonds. Whisk for 30 seconds, then sift in the ground almonds and whisk for 30 seconds more, or until the nuts are fully incorporated into the mixture.
6. Remove the bowl from the machine and use a spatula to beat it again. Make sure you scrape the sides and bottom of the bowl so that all of the mixture is turned over. It is ready when it leaves a small trail that flattens after a few seconds.

PIPE THE MACARONS

To achieve perfect rounds, hold the piping bag firmly and directly over the parchment and pipe with a gentle, controlled pressure to avoid too much mixture coming out at once.

7. Spoon the paste into the piping bag fitted with the 6mm nozzle and pipe rounds onto the prepared parchment paper, following the pencil marks on it as a guide. Set aside for 5 minutes to allow the macarons to flatten slightly.

8. Bake at 150°C/130C fan/gas mark 3 for about 12–15 minutes, until you can peel one away from the paper easily. Remove from the oven and leave to cool. Don't try to move the rest of the macarons until they've cooled down completely, at which point they'll come off cleanly.

MAKE THE SEMI-CANDIED BLUEBERRIES

9. In a small bowl, mix together 20g of the caster sugar and the powdered pectin.
10. Put the blueberry purée into a medium pan over a medium heat and add the liqueur, lemon zest and juice. Add the sugar and pectin mixture and bring gently to the boil, stirring all the time to mix everything together.
11. Stir in the remaining 50g sugar and continue to cook until the temperature reaches 103°C and the mixture becomes jam-like. Set aside to cool.

MAKE THE ITALIAN MERINGUE BUTTERCREAM

12. Put the egg whites into a stand mixer or medium bowl and start whisking on a slow speed.
13. Put the sugar and water into a small pan over a high heat and bring to the boil. Cook until the temperature reaches 121°C, or softball stage (see page 30).
14. Slowly pour the syrup over the egg whites, continuing to whisk and turn the machine up to full speed.
15. When the mixture has cooled to just warm, but not cold, slowly add small pieces of soft butter while whisking until smooth. Scrape down the length of the vanilla pod to remove the seeds and add them to the bowl, along with the strained blueberries and the liqueur. Whisk again until smooth.

ASSEMBLE THE MACARONS

16. Group the macarons in pairs, choosing equal-sized rounds to go together. Line them up in rows, one side of the pair up and the other side down.
17. Spoon the buttercream into a disposable piping bag and snip off about 5mm. Pipe a ring of buttercream around the edges of the base macarons, leaving a 1cm round in the middle of each one, then spoon the semi-candied blueberries into the centres. Place the second macaron on top and press gently to sandwich the two together over the filling. If stored in an airtight container, the macarons will keep for up to 3 days in a cool place, or up to 1 month in the freezer.

THE SECRETS OF SUCCESS

If the macarons are crispy and dry…
They're overbaked.
If you transfer them to the freezer, they'll soften up.
If they're cracked on top, the oven is too hot.

If they're flat and wrinkly…
They're underbaked. Put them back in the oven to finish cooking, but they won't look as good.

GLOSSARY

BAIN-MARIE
A bowl set over a pan of simmering water to cook the ingredients gently without direct heat. Also refers to a roasting tin filled with hot water. in which bowls of set custard stand while cooking.

BAKE BLIND
To fill and bake a pastry-lined tart tin with parchment and baking beans.

BAVAROIS
A sweet cream mixture made with cream, egg yolks and sugar, and set with gelatine.

BEURRAGE
The butter block used with a *détrempe* (see column three) to make puff pastry and layered yeasted doughs.

CARAMEL
The rich, golden brown syrup made by heating caster or granulated sugar in a pan until it dissolves. A dry caramel calls for just sugar; a wet caramel uses sugar and water.

CHIBOUST CREAM
Also known as crème chiboust, this is a pastry cream set with gelatine and folded together with Italian meringue.

CHOUX PASTRY
Known as *pâte à choux* in patisserie kitchens, this is a soft dough pastry made with a higher quantity of water than other pastries. It cannot be handled, so needs to be piped or spooned into shape before baking.

CLARIFIED BUTTER
Butter that has been heated until the milk particles and impurities separate. It imparts a rich nutty flavour, and is useful in patisserie because – unlike ordinary butter – it contains no water and can be cooked to a high temperature without burning.

CLEAR GEL
Also known as clear writing or piping gel. This is used to glaze fruit, tarts and pies, and used in the Matcha Green Tea layered slice (see page 99).

COCOA BUTTER (BEURRE DE CACAO)
This is the fat extracted from the cocoa bean, which is used to make chocolate.

COULIS
A puréed fruit sauce, sometimes sweetened with sugar, which has been strained so it is smooth and seedless.

CREAM
The thick, fatty liquid that is skimmed off milk that has been left to stand. It is also the action of beating butter and sugar together until smooth and sometimes pale and fluffy.

CRÉMEUX
A filling or accompaniment to desserts, usually flavoured with vanilla, fruit or chocolate. It falls between a cream and a mousse, and gelatine can be added to stabilise the consistency.

CRÈME CHANTILLY
Cream whipped with sugar and vanilla to serve as an accompaniment.

CRÈME DIPLOMAT
Also known as diplomat cream, this is crème patissière folded together with whipped cream.

CRÈME MOUSSELINE
Also known as mousseline cream. This is crème patissière folded together with buttercream or butter.

CRÈME PATISSIÈRE
Also known as pastry cream, this is a thick custard used on its own to fill tarts and pies, or used as a soufflé base.

DACQUOISE
A meringue-based sponge made with ground almonds, hazelnuts or coconut to give it a unique texture.

DÉTREMPE
The base dough made from flour and a little bit of fat that is used for making puff pastry and layered yeasted doughs, as in croissants. It needs the *beurrage* (see column one) to complete the recipe.

DROPPING CONSISTENCY
The way a spoonful of batter falls from a spoon when it is ready to bake. It should drop easily, but be neither runny nor too stiff.

EGG WASH
Beaten egg yolk or whole egg brushed over pastry and dough before baking to glaze.

ENTREMETS
The French term often used for desserts; it translates literally as 'between courses'.

FEUILLETINE
Finely chopped wafers, used to provide texture. Feuilletine can be mixed with praline paste and chocolate to make truffles.

FOLD
To combine one batch of ingredients with another by using a gentle lifting and turning motion with a spoon or spatula. Most often specified when making cake batters, to avoid knocking out any air.

FLAMBER
To burn off alcohol in a pudding by lighting it.

FRANGIPANE
An almond-based sponge. Can also be made by folding crème patissière together with ground almonds or crushed amaretto biscuits.

GANACHE

A chocolate and cream mixture used for topping cakes, truffles or layered slices.

GLAÇAGE

A glaze, or the process of glazing to produce a glossy surface on food. Pastry is often glazed with beaten egg, while fruit tends to be glazed with sieved and warmed apricot conserve.

INVERT SUGAR

A thick syrup made by combining sugar syrup with either citric or tartaric acid. This reduces the size of the sugar crystals and allows them to retain moisture, which helps to prevent crystallisation when used with other sugar. For this reason it is used in recipes such as ice creams and sweets. Branded invert sugars can be bought online, but liquid glucose or honey can be used instead.

JOCONDE

A moist, almond-based sponge with a dense texture; widely used in patisserie.

JULIENNE

To thinly slice or shred an ingredient, such as citrus peel.

KNEAD

To fold, push and turn bread dough until smooth. Can be done by hand or in a stand mixer fitted with a dough hook.

MACERATE

To soak an ingredient in alcohol or flavoured syrup.

MIRLITON

A pastry, fruit and almond tart that originates from Rouen in France.

PANADE

A mixture of flour and butter; also the base of choux pastry.

PÂTE BRISÉE

The French patisserie term for shortcrust pastry.

PÂTE FEUILLETÉE

The French patisserie term for puff pastry.

PÂTE SUCRÉE

The French patisserie term for sweet shortcrust pastry.

PATISSERIE

This word has two different meanings.

It can be used as an 'umbrella' term to refer to everything that is sold in a patisserie shop, from small bakes and enriched leavened breads, such as crème Parisiennes, croissants and pains au chocolat, to beautiful petits gâteaux and large celebratory cakes such as Sachertorte.

Patisserie also refers to the shop in which these wonderful cakes and pastries are sold, and in Belgium and France the title is legally controlled. A patisserie can only be called that if a licensed master pastry chef (maître pâtissier) is employed there.

PÂTE À BOMBE

A mixture of egg yolks and sugar, used as a base for mousse-like desserts. It can be made in two different ways – either by whisking the yolks and sugar in a bain-marie, or by boiling a sugar syrup and whisking that into the yolks.

PRALINE PASTE

Hazelnuts or almonds that have been whizzed or finely rolled into a paste and combined with sugar. Can be used in truffles or with other ingredients as a filling (see Paris–Brest, page 173).

PROVE

The stage of resting dough after it has risen once and been knocked back (punched to release the air). At this stage it is shaped, then left to prove (puff up) before baking.

PURÉE

To blend whole ingredients until silky smooth; most often refers to fruit in patisserie.

QUENELLE

To shape a mixture, such as a cream, sorbet or ganache, into an oval using one or two spoons. Used as decoration.

RELAX OR REST

These words refer to pastry dough when it is set aside after rolling or shaping. A period of resting allows the gluten to contract so that the pastry doesn't shrink when baked.

RIBBON STAGE

The point at which a whisked mixture falls in ribbons when the whisk is lifted. Often specified when whole eggs and sugar are whisked together.

RISE OR REST

The first stage of resting dough after kneading. This allows the yeast to work with the sugar (ferment) and improves the flavour and texture of the finished loaf.

SABAYON

A mixture made from whole eggs or egg yolks and sugar whisked over a bain-marie until thick and mousse-like.

SABLÉ

A pastry or biscuit made with ground almonds.

SOFT PEAK

The point at which whipped cream or meringue is thick enough to stand in gentle mounds when the beaters are lifted.

STIFF PEAK

The point at which whipped cream or meringue is thick enough to stand upright and unmoving when the beaters are lifted.

TEMPER

To heat chocolate, then cool it to a particular temperature (see page 34). This process stabilises the chocolate, and is required only if it is to be used for coating and decorating, or for making chocolates.

ZEST

Finely grated peel of citrus fruit.

INDEX

ACKNOWLEDGEMENTS

Hodder & Stoughton and Love Productions would like to thank the following people for their contribution to this book.

Tom Kerridge, Benoit Blin, Cherish Finden, Claire Clark, Letty Kavanagh, Rupert Frisby, Claire Emerson, Angela Nilsen, Sam Dixon, Dara Sutin, Jane Treasure, The Welbeck Estate, and The School of Artisan Food. With thanks to the Pastry Chef Captains and their teams: Corporal Liam Grime at CSCAT, Kumiko Hiwatari at Patisserie des Rêves, Felicien Christe at The Savoy, Sebastien Wind at Comptoir Gourmand Ltd, Mark Tilling at Squires Group, Sajeela Siriwardena at Hilton Park Lane, James Campbell at Marks & Spencer, Reece Collier at The Grove, Neil Rankin at Restaurant Associates, Neil Mugg at The Gleneagles Hotel, Christophe Le Tynevez at Boulangerie Jade, Julien Plumart at Julien Plumart Wholesale Ltd, Tomas Krasnan at Panoramic 34, Stephen Trigg at Lauden Chocolate, and Karl Jones-Hughes at Celtic Manor.

Also thanks to Martin Chiffers, Emma Marsden, Liz and Max Haarala Hamilton, Alexander Breeze, Kuo Kang Chen, Nathan Burton, Caroline McArthur, Patricia Burgess, Claudette Morris, Samira Kazemzadeh, Katy Gilhooly, Amanda Rogers and Katherine Mead.

Other *Great British Bake Off* books are available, including *Great British Bake Off: Celebrations*, the *Great British Bake Off: Bake It Better* titles, and *The Great British Bake Off: Step-by-Step Better Baking app*. For more information visit hodder.co.uk